Math and Science Prep for the

SAT® &
ACT®

The Princeton Review.

Math and Science Prep for the

SAT® &
ACT®

The Staff of The Princeton Review

PrincetonReview.com

Random House, Inc. New York

The Princeton Review, Inc.
111 Speen Street
Suite 550
Framingham, MA 01701
Email: editorialsupport@review.com

ISBN: 978-0-8041-2455-3

The Princeton Review is not affiliated with Princeton University.

Editor: Alyssa Wolff
Production Editor: Kiley Pulliam
Production Coordinator: Deborah A. Silvestrini

Printed in the United States of America on partially recycled paper.

10 9 8 7 6 5 4 3 2 1

First Edition

The material in this book was previously published as *Math and Science Workout for the ACT*, 2nd Edition, a trade paperback published by Random House, Inc. in 2013, and as *Math Workout for the SAT*, 3rd Edition, a trade paperback published by Random House, Inc. in 2011.

Editorial
Rob Franek, Senior VP, Publisher
Mary Beth Garrick, Director of Production
Selena Coppock, Senior Editor
Calvin Cato, Editor
Kristen O'Toole, Editor
Meave Shelton, Editor
Alyssa Wolff, Editorial Assistant

Random House Publishing Team
Tom Russell, Publisher
Nicole Benhabib, Publishing Manager
Ellen L. Reed, Production Manager
Alison Stoltzfus, Managing Editor

Acknowledgments

The Princeton Review would like to thank the following individuals for their help on this book:

Deborah Silvestrini, Kiley Pulliam, Mary Beth Garrick, Cornelia Cooke, Melissa Hendrix, and Craig Patches.

Contents

Introduction

ABOUT THIS BOOK:

Many colleges will accept either the SAT or ACT. So which should you take? The answer is: both! Since you have purchased this book, we assume that is your plan.

This book will help make that plan a successful one. First, we will give you some general information about both tests, and then we'll get right into it.

This book is designed to help you drill down and focus in on the math sections of the SAT and ACT as well as the science section on the ACT.

For more on admissions, see The Princeton Review's *The Best 378 Colleges* or visit our website, PrincetonReview.com

ABOUT THE ACT

The ACT is nothing like the math and science tests you take in school. All of the content review and strategies we teach in the following lessons are based on the specific structure and format of the ACT. Before you can beat a test, you have to know how it's built.

Structure

The ACT is made up of 4 multiple-choice tests and an optional Writing test.

The 5 tests are always given in the same order.

English	Math	Reading	Science	Writing
45 minutes	60 minutes	35 minutes	35 minutes	30 minutes
75 questions	60 questions	40 questions	40 questions	1 Essay

Scoring

See The Princeton Review's companion book, *Reading and Writing Prep for the SAT & ACT*

When students and schools talk about ACT scores, they mean the composite score, a range of 1–36. The composite is an average of the 4 multiple-choice tests, each scored on the same 1–36 scale. Neither the Writing test score nor the combined English plus Writing score affects the composite.

It's All About the Composite

Whether you look at your score online or wait to get it in the mail, the biggest number on the page is always the composite. While admissions offices will certainly see the individual scores of all 5 tests (and their subscores), schools will use the composite to evaluate your application, and that's why in the end it's the only one that matters.

The composite is an average: Let the full weight of that sink in. Do you need to bring up all 4 scores equally to raise your composite? Do you need to be a superstar in all 4 tests? Should you focus more on your weaknesses than your strengths? No, no, and absolutely not. The best way to improve your composite is to shore up your weaknesses but exploit your strengths as much as possible.

> To improve your ACT score, use your strengths to lift the composite score as high as possible.

You don't need to be a rock star on all 4 tests. Identify 2, maybe 3 tests, and focus on raising those scores as much as you can to raise your composite. Work on your weakest scores to keep them from pulling you down. With this book, focus on Math and Science. Think of it this way: If you had only one hour to devote to practice the week before the ACT, put that hour to your best subjects.

Math and Science Scores

These two subjects make a good pair. Every student is different, but many students begin with Math as one of their higher scores and Science as one of the lower. There are good reasons for this. The Math test, perhaps deceptively so, resembles school tests more than the other three. Science feels the most different, and many students are intimidated by both the content and format.

When it comes to improving scores, many students find Math scores the easiest to bring up. A strategic review of the rules and formulas coupled with rigorous practice can add several points. Science, on the other hand, can be the most difficult. The Science test is designed to test your reasoning skills using passage-based information, not tap specific outside knowledge. There are no rules or content you can review. Who knows what specific topics will appear on the next ACT? On the goods-news front, however, The Princeton Review can teach you a smart, effective approach designed to maximize your performance every time, regardless of content. It can be tough to change your ways, but dedicated practice with a strategic method can prevent the Science score from pulling down that composite.

Time

How often do you take a final exam in school that gives you *at most* a minute per question? Probably never. The ACT isn't a school test, and you can't approach it as if it is. While speed and accuracy depend on individual skills and grasp of content, almost all students struggle to finish the Math and Science tests on time. The more you treat these tests the same way you would a school final, the less likely you are to finish, much less finish with the greatest accuracy. The Princeton Review's strategies are all based on this time crunch: There's a difference between knowing *how* to do a question under the best of circumstance and getting it *right* with a ticking clock and glowering proctor in the room.

STRATEGIES

You will raise your ACT score by working smarter, not harder, and a smart test-taker is a strategic test-taker. You will target specific content to review, you will apply an effective and efficient approach, and you will employ the common sense that frequently deserts many of us when we pick up a number 2 pencil.

Each test on the ACT demands a different approach, and even the most universal strategies vary in their applications. In the chapters that follow, we'll discuss these terms in greater detail customized to Math and Science.

Personal Order of Difficulty (POOD)

If time is going to run out, would you rather it run out on the most difficult questions or on the easiest questions? Of course you want it to run out on the points you are less likely to get right. The trick is to find all of the easiest questions and get them done first.

Now

Does a question look okay? Do you know how to do it? Do it *Now*.

Later

Does a question make you go, "hmm"? If you can't find a way to get your pencil moving right away, consider leaving it and coming back *Later*. Circle the question number for easy reference to return.

> **The Best Way to Bubble In**
>
> Work a page at a time, circling your answers right on the booklet. Transfer a page's worth of answers to the Scantron at one time. It's better to stay focused on working questions rather than disrupt your concentration to find where you left off on the Scantron. You'll be more accurate at both tasks. Do not wait to the end, however, to transfer all the answers of that test on your Scantron. Go a page at a time.

Never

Test-taker, know thyself. Know the topics that are your worst and learn the signs that flash danger. Don't waste time on questions you should *Never* do. Instead, use more time to answer the Now and Later questions accurately.

Letter of the Day (LOTD)   Just because you don't *work* a questions doesn't mean you don't *answer* it. There is no penalty for wrong answers on the ACT, so you should never leave any blanks on your Scantron. When you guess on Never questions, pick your favorite two-letter combo of answers and stick with it. For example, always choose A/F or C/H. If you're consistent, you're statistically more likely to pick up more points.

Process of Elimination (POE)

In a perfect world, you'll know how to work all of your Now and Later questions, quickly and accurately, circling the correct answer among the choices. The ACT is *not* a perfect world. But even with a ticking clock and a number 2 pencil in your sweaty hand, wrong answers can be obvious. POE can be a great Plan B on Math when you're stuck, or it may be the best way to find the correct answer on Science. But even when you can't narrow the answers to only one, using POE to get rid of at least one or two wrong answers will substantially increase your odds of getting a question right.

Pacing

The ACT may be designed for you to run out of time, but you can't rush through it as quickly as possible. All you'll do is make careless errors on easy questions you should get right and spend way too much time on difficult ones you're unlikely to get right.

To hit your target score, you have to know how many raw points you need. Use the entire time allotted where it will do the most good: Go slowly enough to avoid careless errors on Now questions, but quickly enough to get to as many Later questions as you need to hit your goal.

On each test of the ACT, the number of correct answers converts to a scaled score of 1–36. ACT works hard to adjust the scale of each test at each administration as necessary to make all scaled scores comparable, smoothing out any differences in level of difficulty across test dates. Thus, there is no truth to any one test date being "easier" than the others, but you can expect to see slight variation in the scale from test to test.

This is the scale from the free test ACT makes available on its website, act.org. We're going to use it to explain how to pick a target score and pace yourself.

Math Pacing

Scale Score	Raw Score	Scale Score	Raw Score	Scale Score	Raw Score
36	60	27	45–47	18	24–25
35	59	26	42–44	17	21–23
34	58	25	40–41	16	17–20
33	56–57	24	37–39	15	14–16
32	55	23	35–36	14	11–13
31	54	22	33–34	13	9–10
30	52–53	21	31–32	12	7–8
29	50–51	20	29–30	11	6
28	48–49	19	26–28	10	5

Our advice is to add 5 questions to your targeted raw score. You have a cushion to get a few wrong—nobody's perfect—and you're likely to pick up at least a few points from your LOTDs. Track your progress on practice tests to pinpoint your target score.

Let's say your goal on Math is a 24. Find 24 under the scaled score column, and you'll see that you need 37–39 raw points. Take all 60 minutes and work 45 questions, using your Letter of the Day on 15 Never questions. With 60 minutes to work on just 45 questions, you'll raise your accuracy on the Now and Later questions. You may get a few wrong, but you're also likely to pick up a few points in your LOTDs, and you should hit your target score of 24. Spend more time to do fewer questions, and you'll raise your accuracy.

Here's another way to think about pacing. Let's say your goal is to move from a 24 to a 27. How many more raw points do you need? As few as 6. Do you think you could find 6 careless errors on your last practice test that you *should* have gotten right?

Science Pacing

Scale Score	Raw Score	Scale Score	Raw Score	Scale Score	Raw Score
36	40	27	32	18	16–17
35	39	26	30–31	17	15
34	--	25	28–29	16	14
33	38	24	26–27	15	13
32	37	23	25	14	12
31	--	22	23–24	13	11
30	36	21	21–22	12	10
29	35	20	19–20	11	9
28	33–34	19	18	10	7–8

For Science pacing is less scientific, no pun intended, than it is for Math. In the lesson that follows, we'll teach you how to pick the best passages to do first. But even the easiest passages will have some tough questions.

Our advice is to be aggressive. Spend the time needed on the easiest passages first, but keep moving to get to your targeted raw score. Use this chart below to figure out how many passages to work.

Target Score	# of Passages to Attempt
< 20	5 passages
20–23	5–6 passages
24–27	6–7 passages
> 27	7 passages

Be Ruthless

The worst mistake a test-taker can make is to throw good time after bad. You read a question and don't understand it, so you read it again. And again. If you stare at it really hard, you know you're going to just *see* it. And you can't move on, because really, after spending all that time it would be a waste not to keep at it, right? Actually, that way of thinking couldn't be more wrong.

You can't let one tough question drag you down. Instead, the best way to improve your ACT score is to follow our advice.

1. Use the techniques and strategies in the lessons to work efficiently and accurately through all your Now and Later questions.
2. Know your Never questions, and use your LOTD.
3. Know when to move on. Use POE, and guess from what's left.

Now move on to the lessons and learn the best way to approach the content.

ABOUT THE SAT

Of the eight scored multiple-choice sections on the SAT, three of them will be math. The questions will be presented in two different formats: regular multiple choice and grid-ins. We will discuss how to deal with each of these question formats.

ORDER OF DIFFICULTY

To formulate an overall test-taking strategy, the most important thing to learn is the order of difficulty of the math sections. The questions on your SAT are selected with extreme care, in the same way, every time. Knowing how the test is put together is crucial for scoring well. The chart on the next page shows you how the questions are organized on each of the math sections.

As you can see, sections are arranged in order of difficulty, with the easy questions at the beginning, medium questions in the middle, and the hard questions at the end of each section. It is crucial to know the difficulty of a question in order to know the best way to solve it. This is so important that the exercises in this book provide an easy, a medium, and a hard question for each major question type. We've kept the question numbers consistent to help you learn which questions are easy, medium, and hard.

Joe Bloggs

Joe Bloggs is our name for the average SAT tester. Joe isn't stupid—he's just average. He takes this test as he would take a math test in school, and he gets an average score. If you learn how Joe takes this test, you can learn how to take it better.

When Joe takes the SAT, he makes two important mistakes. First, he tries to finish the test. This encourages him to rush through the easy problems, which he should get right, but he makes silly mistakes because he's rushing. He rushes all the way into the hard problems, getting almost no questions right. Why? Because of Joe's second mistake: He thinks that he can solve every problem in a straightforward way. While this works on the easy problems, the hard problems are full of trap answers, which cause Joe to spend too much time on each question or pick the wrong choice.

How can you avoid being like Joe? First, learn to do the right number of problems. Second, learn some test-taking techniques that will make harder problems much easier and help you avoid the traps that the test writers have laid for you.

PACING

Almost everybody works too fast on the SAT, losing a lot of points due to careless errors. The SAT isn't your usual math situation—you don't get *partial credit* for "having the right idea." The only thing that matters is what you bubble in on your answer sheet. Slow down! If you find yourself making careless mistakes, you are throwing points out the window.

Unless you're shooting for a score of 700 or above, do not finish the math sections. Again, this isn't like math class. The test isn't designed for you to finish, and you'll hurt your score by trying to do so. If you miss a total of around five or six questions for all three sections, you're probably hitting the right pace. More mistakes than that, and you're going too quickly. If you aren't missing any questions but aren't finishing, you should guess more aggressively and try to work a bit faster.

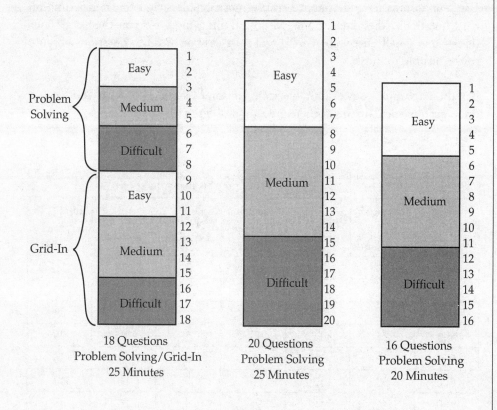

18 Questions
Problem Solving/Grid-In
25 Minutes

20 Questions
Problem Solving
25 Minutes

16 Questions
Problem Solving
20 Minutes

SCORING

If you were betting your hard-earned cash, wouldn't you want to know the odds? On the SAT, you're betting for more points, and it's important to understand how the scoring works so you'll play smart.

For each right answer, you earn one raw point. For each wrong answer, you lose one-quarter of a raw point. That's it. If you leave a question blank, nothing happens either way, except that the total number of points you can earn is reduced.

> Every right answer earns you one point, whether it's easy or hard.

That's important to understand, because most people spend too much time on hard questions. They aren't going to do anything more for you than easy questions—and you'll hurt your score if you miss easy or medium questions because you're rushing to finish.

Based on a sample conversion table, here are some examples of what you have to do to get a particular score—there are a total of 54 math questions.

To get (scaled score)	You need to earn: (raw points)	Attempt this many questions				Total # of questions to attempt
		20-question section	8-question Multiple Choice	10-question Grid-Ins	16-question section	
350	7	6	2	2	2	12
400	12	7	3	3	4	17
450	19	9	4	4	6	23
500	25	11	5	5	8	29
550	32	14	6	6	10	36
600	38	16	6	7	13	42
650	44	18	7	8	15	48
700	47	all	all	9	all	53
750	52	all	all	all	all	54
800	54	all	all	all	all	54

Amazing, isn't it? Even to get a very high score, *you don't have to finish*. Accuracy is more important than speed! (The examples are based on a sample conversion table; the table for your test may be slightly different—maybe a question or two higher or lower. We put this in just to give you an approximate idea of the score a particular number of right/wrong/blank will give you.)

GUESSING

Say you start to work on a problem and get stuck. Should you just move on? Not if you can cross out any of the wrong answer choices. Are you working on a hard problem? Then cross out any too-good-to-be-true answers and guess from what's left. Are you working on an easy question? Go with your instincts.

> If you can eliminate even one answer choice, guess.

Why? Because if you guessed randomly on five questions, without eliminating anything (let your pet monkey pick the answer), you'd have a one out of five chance of picking a right answer. That one right answer earns you (or your pet monkey) one raw point, and the four wrong answers cost you $4 \times \dfrac{1}{4}$ of a point subtracted. You break even. Eliminating one or more answer choices improves your odds considerably—so take advantage of it!

When To Guess

All of that said, we don't mean to suggest that you skip merrily through the sections guessing with abandon. There are smart places to guess and not-so-smart places to guess.

Always be aware of where you are in the section. Use the order-of-difficulty information to guide your guessing: easy questions = easy answers; hard questions = hard answers.

Good Guess
- Geometry, drawn to scale. If you can approximate the length or area or angle measurement, go for it. Applies to easy, medium, and hard questions.
- Any grid-in you've got an answer for. No penalty for wrong answers.

Bad Guess
- Too-good-to-be-true answers on hard questions
- Long, complicated word problems at the end of the section. (Spend your time on something shorter and more manageable.)
- Questions you don't have time to read.

CALCULATORS

Seems like a good deal, doesn't it? Well, maybe. It depends on the problem. Don't grab your calculator too quickly—you have to know how solve the problem first.

> Calculators can only calculate; they can't think. You need to figure out how to solve the problem before you can begin calculating.

Calculators are great for helping you avoid silly mistakes in your arithmetic, and you should use them when you can. They can help ensure that you make correct calculations, but they can't tell you which calculations are the right ones to make. So be sure you figure out how to solve the problem before you start punching numbers into your calculator.

> Think before you punch.

Tips to Calculator Happiness

- Get a calculator that follows the order of operations and has keys for x^2, y^x, and $\sqrt{\ }$.
- Use the same calculator every time you practice SAT problems.
- Check each number after you punch it in.

CARELESS MISTAKES

If you are prone to careless mistakes—and most of us are—you probably make the same kinds of careless mistakes over and over. If you take the time to analyze the questions you get wrong, you will discover which kinds are your personal favorites. Then you can compensate for them when you take the SAT.

In the world, and in math class, it's most important for you to understand concepts and ways to solve problems. On the SAT, it's most important that you bubble in the correct answer. Students typically lose anywhere from 30 to 100 points simply by making careless, preventable mistakes.

Some common mistakes to watch for:

- misreading the question
- computation error
- punching in the wrong thing on the calculator
- on a medium or hard question, stopping after one or two steps, when the question requires three or four steps
- answering a different question from the one asked

If, for example, you find you keep missing questions because you multiply wrong, then do every multiplication twice. Do every step on paper, not in your head. If you make a lot of mistakes on positive/negative, write out each step, and be extra careful on those questions. Correcting careless mistakes is an easy way to pick up more points, so make sure you analyze your mistakes so you know what to look out for.

PLUGGING IN

One of the most powerful math techniques on the SAT is called Plugging In. The idea of Plugging In is to take all of the variables—things like x, y, z—in a problem and replace them with actual numbers. This turns your algebra problems into simple arithmetic and can make even the hardest problem into an easy one.

How To Recognize a Plugging-In Question
- There are variables in the answer choices.
- The question says something like *in terms of x*.
- Your first thought is to write an equation.
- The question asks for a percentage or fractional part of something, but doesn't give you any actual amounts.

How To Solve a Plugging-In Question
- Don't write an equation.
- Pick an easy number and substitute it for the variable.
- Work the problem through and get an answer. Circle it so you don't lose track of it.
- Plug in your number—the one you chose in the beginning—to the answer choices and see which choice produces your circled answer.

Here's an example:

> Jill spent x dollars on pet toys and 12 dollars on socks. If the amount Jill spent was twice the amount she earns each week, how much does Jill earn each week in terms of x?
>
> (A) $2(x + 12)$
> (B) $2x + 24$
> (C) $\dfrac{x}{2} + 12$
> (D) $\dfrac{x+12}{2}$
> (E) $\dfrac{x-12}{2}$

Solution: Plug in 100 for x. That means Jill spent a total of 112 dollars. If that was twice her weekly salary, then she makes half of 112, or 56 dollars a week. Circle 56. Now plug 100 into the answers to see which one yields 56. (A) $2(100 + 12) = 224$. No good. (B) is 224, which is also too big. (C) $50 + 12 = 62$ (D) $\dfrac{112}{2} = 56$! Yes! (E) is $\dfrac{88}{2} = 44$. Nope. The answer is (D).

Here's a harder example:

> Karl bought x bags of red marbles for y dollars per bag, and z bags of blue marbles for $3y$ dollars per bag. If he bought twice as many bags of blue marbles as red marbles, then in terms of y, what was the average cost, in dollars, per bag of marbles?
>
> (A) $\dfrac{3y}{2}$
> (B) $\dfrac{7y}{3}$
> (C) $3y - y$
> (D) $2y$
> (E) $6y$

Solution: You don't really want to do the algebra, do you? Use simple, low numbers and plug in. How about $x = 2$ and $y = 3$? That's 2 bags of red marbles at $3 each. So he spent $6 on red marbles. (In word problems, it helps to keep track of what the numbers represent.) If he bought twice as many bags of blue marbles, then $z = 4$. So he bought 4 bags of blue marbles at $3y$ or $9 a can and spent a total of $36. Now you figure the average price by adding up the dollars spent and dividing that by the total number of bags. He spent $6 + $36 = $42 on 2 + 4 = 6 bags of marbles. So the average price per bag is $\dfrac{42}{6}$ = $7. Circle $7.

Now, plug 3 in for y in the answer choices and see which one gives you 7. (A) yields $\dfrac{9}{2}$, so eliminate it. (B) is 7, so that's the answer. The remaining choices are wrong, as well.

Here's a different kind of example:

> At his bake sale, Mr. Heftwhistle sold 30% of his pies to one friend. Mr. Heftwhistle then sold 60% of the remaining pies to another friend. What percent of his original number of pies did Mr. Heftwhistle have left?
>
> (A) 10%
> (B) 18%
> (C) 28%
> (D) 36%
> (E) 40%

Solution: If you don't plug in, you may make the sad mistake of picking (A) or of working with ugly fractions. Plugging in a number is much easier. Let's say Mr. Heftwhistle had 100 pies. 30% of 100 equals 30, so he's left with 70. 60% of 70 equals 42, so he's left with 28. Here's the great thing about plugging in 100 on percentage problems—28 (left) out of 100 (original number) is simply 28%. That's it. (C) is the answer.

Tips for Plugging In Happiness
- Pick easy numbers like 2, 4, 10, 100. The best number to choose depends on the question: Use 100 for percents.
- Avoid picking 0, 1, or any number that shows up in the answer choices.
- If the number you picked leads to ugly computations—fractions, negatives, or anything you need a calculator for—bail out and pick an easier number.
- Practice!

On the following page is a Quick Quiz, so you can practice Plugging In before you continue. The question number corresponds to the difficulty level in the 20-question multiple-choice section. Answers and explanations immediately follow every Quick Quiz.

QUICK QUIZ #1

Easy

6. If p is an odd integer, which of the following must also be an odd integer?

    (A) $p + 1$

    (B) $\dfrac{p}{2}$

    (C) $p + 2$

    (D) $2p$

    (E) $p - 1$

Medium

13. If $\dfrac{y}{3} = 6x$, then in terms of y, $x =$

    (A) $3y$

    (B) $2y$

    (C) y

    (D) $\dfrac{y}{2}$

    (E) $\dfrac{y}{18}$

Hard

18. Mary spilled $\dfrac{2}{5}$ of her peanuts, and Jessica ate $\dfrac{1}{3}$ of what was left. Jessica then gave the remaining peanuts to Max and Sam, who each ate half of what remained. What fractional part of Mary's peanuts did Sam eat?

(A) $\dfrac{1}{15}$

(B) $\dfrac{1}{10}$

(C) $\dfrac{1}{5}$

(D) $\dfrac{1}{3}$

(E) $\dfrac{4}{5}$

Answers and Explanations: Quick Quiz #1

6. **C** Because p has to be odd, make it 3. Try that in the answer choices, and cross out anything that isn't odd. (A): 3 + 1 = 4. Cross out (A). (B): $\dfrac{3}{2}$. Cross out (B). (Fractions can't be odd or even.) (C): 3 + 2 = 5, leave (C) in. (D): 2(3) = 6. Cross out (D). (E): 3 − 1 = 2. Cross out (E). Only (C) works.

13. **E** Plug in $y = 36$, which makes $x = 2$. Now plug in 36 for y in the answer choices and look for x, which is 2. (A): something huge. (B): still something huge. (C): 36. (D): $\dfrac{36}{2}$ = 18, still too big. (E): $\dfrac{36}{18}$ = 2, so (E) is correct.

18. **C** On this kind of question, there aren't variables in the answer choices, but there's an *implied* variable in the question because you don't know how many peanuts Mary started with. Let's say she had 15 peanuts, because the denominators in the fractions are both factors of 15. If she spilled $\frac{2}{5}$ of 15, she spilled 6, leaving her with 9. If Jessica ate $\frac{1}{3}$ of 9, she ate 3, leaving Mary with 6. If Max and Sam split 6, they each ate 3. The fractional part is $\frac{\text{part}}{\text{whole}}$, so Sam's fractional part is $\frac{3}{15}$ or $\frac{1}{5}$. (Whew.)

A tree diagram makes this easier to deal with:

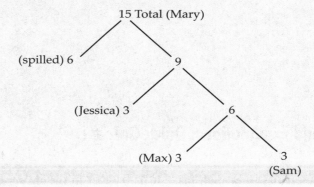

In question 13, you may have had a hard time coming up with numbers that worked evenly. That's OK—it takes practice. You can plug in any numbers you want, as long as they satisfy the conditions of the problem, so you might as well plug in numbers that are easy to work with.

In question 18, you could solve this without plugging in, but then you're dealing with fractional parts of a whole, the whole being Mary's peanuts. It's very easy to get confused doing it that way, because the numbers aren't concrete and they quickly become meaningless. The advantage of Plugging In is that you're working with actual amounts, just like real life. One more thing: We picked 15 because we expected it to work with the fractions in the problem. If we'd picked a number that didn't work well, we would have tried another number.

PLUGGING IN THE ANSWER CHOICES

Good news. Unlike the math tests you usually have in school, the SAT is primarily multiple choice. That means that on many problems, you don't have to generate your own answer to a problem. Instead, the answer will be one of the five answers sitting on the page right in front of you. All you have to figure out is *which* one of the five is the answer.

How to Recognize Questions for Plugging In the Answer Choices

- The question will be straightforward—something like "How old is Bob?" or "How many potatoes are in the bag?" or "What was the original cost of the stereo?"
- The answer choices will be actual values.

How to Plug In the Answer Choices

Don't write an equation. Instead, pick an answer and work it through the steps of the problem, one at a time, and see if it works. In essence, you're asking *what if (C) is the answer? Does that solve the problem?*

Here's an example:

If $\dfrac{3(x-1)}{2} = \dfrac{9}{x-2}$, what is the value of x ?

(A) −4
(B) −2
(C) 1
(D) 4
(E) 9

Solution: Try (C) first. (You'll soon find out why.) Plug in 1 for x and see if the equation works:

$$\frac{3(1-1)}{2} = \frac{9}{1-2}$$

$$\frac{0}{2} = \frac{9}{-1}$$

Okay, so (C) isn't the answer. Cross it out. Try (D):

$$\frac{3(4-1)}{2} = \frac{9}{4-2}$$

$$\frac{9}{2} = \frac{9}{2}$$

The equation works, so (D) is the answer. Sure, you could have done the algebra, but wasn't plugging in easier? Once again, you've seen an algebra problem turned into an arithmetic problem, and all it required was managing simple operations like 4 − 1. You're much more likely to make mistakes dealing with x than with 4 − 1. Also, when you plug in, you're taking advantage of the fact that there are only five answer choices. One of them is correct. You might as well try them and find out which one it is—and you no longer have to face the horror of working out a problem algebraically and finding that your answer isn't one of the choices.

Here's a harder example:

> Paul had twice as many potatoes as Dan, who had the same number of potatoes as Zed. If Paul were to give five potatoes to Zed, then Dan would have three times as many potatoes as Paul. How many potatoes did Dan have?
>
> (A) 10
> (B) 6
> (C) 3
> (D) 2
> (E) 1

Solution: Try (C) first. If Dan started with 3, then Zed also started with 3. Since Paul had twice as many potatoes as Dan, then Paul started with 6. If he gives 5 to Zed, Paul now has 1 and Zed has 8. Dan still has 3 potatoes, which is three times as many as Paul. So (C) is the right answer. If (C) didn't work, you could keep trying until you found the answer that did.

To keep things organized, make a chart:

	D	Z	P
Originally:	3	3	6
After exchange:	3	8	1

Tips for Happiness when Plugging In the Answer Choices

- (C) is a good answer to try first, unless it's awkward to work with.
- The answers will be in numerical order, so you will often be able to eliminate answers that are either too big or too small, based on the result you got with (C). If the answer to (C) was too small, you should try bigger answer choices. If the answer to (C) was too big, try smaller answer choices.
- Don't try to work out all the steps in advance—the nice thing about plugging in is that you do the steps one at a time.
- Plugging In questions may be long word problems or short arithmetic problems, and they can appear in the easy, medium, or difficult sections. The harder the question, the better off you'll be plugging in.
- Make a chart if you have a lot of stuff to keep track of.

QUICK QUIZ #2

Easy

6. If 4 less than the product of *b* and 6 is 44, what is the value of *b* ?

   (A) 2
   (B) 4
   (C) 6
   (D) 8
   (E) 14

Medium

13. A store reduces the price of a CD player by 20% and then reduces that price by 15%. If the final price of the CD player is $170, what was its original price?

    (A) $140
    (B) $185
    (C) $200
    (D) $250
    (E) $275

Hard

20. Triangle *ABC* has sides measuring 2, 3, and *r*. Which of the following is a possible value for *r* ?

    (A) 0.5
    (B) 1
    (C) 2
    (D) 5
    (E) 6

Answers and Explanations: Quick Quiz #2

6. **D** Try (C) first, so *b* = 6. The product of 6 and 6 is 36, and 4 less than 36 is 32. 32 isn't 44, so cross out (C). Try a higher number, (D). If *b* = 8, the product of 8 and 6 is 48, and 4 less than 48 is 44.

13. **D** Try (C) first. If the original price of the CD player was $200, then 20% of 200 is 40. That leaves us with a price of $160. Hey—the final price was $170, and you're already below that. You need a higher number. Try (D): If the original price was $250, take 20% of 250 = 50. Now the price is $200. Take another 15% ($30) off and you get 200 − 30 = 170.

20. **C** You need to know a rule here—the sum of any 2 sides of a triangle must equal more than the third side. Try (C) first. If $r = 2$, then the sides are 2, 2, 3. Add up any pair and you get a number that's higher than the remaining number. So it works. (Try some of the other answers, just for practice, and see how they *don't* work.)

Do a little analysis. See how the questions got harder as you went along? In the easy question, you had to read carefully, multiply, and subtract. In the medium question, you had to take percentages. In the hard question, you had to deal with geometry without a diagram and also know a particular rule. For all the questions, plugging in allowed you to avoid writing an equation. Less work is good.

ESTIMATING

A Rough Estimate May Be All That's Necessary

The less work the better. Maybe you'll only be able to eliminate a couple of answers. That's okay too.

For example:

> When .20202 is multiplied by 10^5 and then subtracted from 66,666, the result is
>
> (A) −46,464
> (B) 464.98
> (C) 4,646.4
> (D) 6,464.6
> (E) 46,464

Solution: First multiply .20202 by 10^5. Just move the decimal point 5 places to the right. You get 20,202. (Use your calculator if you want.) Now you're going to subtract that from 66,666—but estimate it before you continue. Looks to be around 40,000 or so, doesn't it? So pick (E) and go on.

There are two advantages to solving the problem this way. First, you avoid having to do the last step of the problem and gain yourself some time. Second, you avoid even the possibility of making a careless mistake in that last step.

We know you can subtract. That's not the issue. On a timed test, with a lot of pressure on you, the fewer steps you have to do, the better off you are.

This is a fabulous piece of news—it means that you should use your eyes to estimate distances and angles, instead of jumping immediately to formulas and equations. You aren't allowed to bring a ruler or a protractor into the test. But you can often tell if one line is longer than another, or if the shaded part of a circle is larger than the unshaded part, just by estimating. That should allow you to eliminate at least a couple of answers, maybe more.

Is this a sketchy technique? Are we telling you to take the easy way out? No and yes. ETS, the company that writes the SAT, doesn't mind if you use your common sense. Neither do we. And as for the easy way out…yes, that's exactly what you're training yourself to look for.

Estimating is not totally foreign to you. Think of geometry problems you encounter in real life—parking a car, packing a box, even shooting a basketball. We guess you don't take out a pad and pencil and start calculating to solve any of these problems. You estimate them, and see what happens.

Same deal on the SAT.

For example:

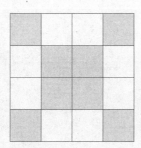

What fractional part of the square is shaded?

(A) $\dfrac{1}{4}$

(B) $\dfrac{3}{10}$

(C) $\dfrac{1}{2}$

(D) $\dfrac{7}{12}$

(E) $\dfrac{15}{16}$

Solution: Just look at it. How much looks shaded? A little? No, so cross out (A) and (B). Most of it? No, so cross out (E). That leaves you with two answer choices, which isn't bad, since you haven't done any math. If you get stuck here, guess. Or count up how many shaded squares there are, and put that over the total number of squares. So the fractional part is $\frac{8}{16}$, or $\frac{1}{2}$.

The answer is (C).

QUICK QUIZ #3

Easy

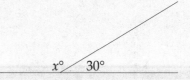

4. Which of the following is equal to $3x$?

    (A) 50
    (B) 120
    (C) 150
    (D) 360
    (E) 450

Medium

13. Dan, Laura, and Jane went grocery shopping. Dan spent three times as much as Laura and half as much as Jane. If they spent a total of $50 on groceries, how much did Jane spend?

    (A) $15
    (B) $20
    (C) $25
    (D) $30
    (E) $45

Hard

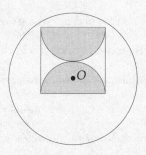

17. In the circle above with center O, the radius of the circle is equal to the length of a side of the square. If the shaded region represents two semicircles inscribed in the square, the ratio of the area of the shaded region to the area of the circle is

(A) 1:16
(B) 1:8
(C) 1:4
(D) 1:2
(E) 2:3

Answers and Explanations: Quick Quiz #3

4. **E** Angle x is pretty big, isn't it? So $3x$ is really, really big. Cross out (A), (B), and (C). Now work it out. $x + 30 = 180$, so $x = 150$. And $3x = 450$. If you fail to estimate, you might forget to multiply by 3 and pick (C). You might fall asleep for a split second and divide by 3 and pick (A). Estimating protects you against such disasters.

13. **D** You might start by asking yourself, "Who spent the most money?" Since Jane spent twice as much as Dan, and Dan spent three times as much as Laura, Jane spent the most. You can definitely eliminate (A); it's too small an amount for Jane to have spent. Now Plug In the answer choices. Begin with (C) or (D), since (A) is out. Which is the easier number to cut in half?

	J	D	L
(D)	30	15	5

$30 + $15 + $5 = $50, so (D) is your answer.

17. **C** Look at the figure. How much of it looks shaded? Less than half? Sure. Cross out (D) and (E). If you're good at estimating, maybe you can cross out (A) as well. (Try drawing more semi-circles in the big circle and see how many will fit.) Now let's figure it out, using our good friend plugging in: Let the radius = 2. So the area is 4π. If the radius = 2, the side of the square is 2. The shaded part consists of 2 semi-circles, each with a radius that's $\frac{1}{2}$ the side of the square, so the radius of the small circle is 1, and the area is π. Put the small area over the big area and you get $\frac{\pi}{4\pi} = \frac{1}{4}$, which is a ratio of 1:4.

Tips for Estimating Happiness

- With geometry, especially on hard questions, the answer choices need to be translated into numbers that you can work with.
- Translate π to a bit more than 3; $\sqrt{2}$ is 1.4; $\sqrt{3}$ is 1.7.
- Practice estimating *a lot*, even if you're going to work out the problem—and notice how your estimates improve.
- The farther apart the answer choices, the bigger the opportunity for eliminating answers by estimating.
- If the figure is NOT drawn to scale, redraw it if you can, using whatever measurements are provided. Then go ahead and estimate. If you can't redraw it, don't estimate.
- If two things look about equal, you can't assume that they're *exactly* equal.
- Trust what your eyes tell you.

How to Apply These Techniques

To study efficiently for the SAT, you must:

- Practice plugging in. Plug in whenever and wherever you can.
- Analyze your work so that you can avoid making the same mistakes over and over.
- Do the problems in this book as though you are taking the real thing—practice with the same focus and intensity you will need on the actual SAT.

Science for the ACT

For many students, the Science test is the most difficult. Whether the subject matter alone intimidates or
the time crunch stresses, the Science test can be difficult to finish. In this chapter, you'll learn how to order
the passages and apply a basic approach that makes the
most of the time you have.

FUN FACTS ABOUT THE SCIENCE TEST

The Science test consists of 7 passages and 40 questions that you must answer in 35 minutes.

This is not a test of science content, but of science reasoning. ACT describes the necessary skills required for the natural sciences as "interpretation, analysis, evaluation, reasoning, and problem solving."

Trends and Relationships

We think all those skills are best understood as identifying trends and relationships. Whether you are asked to look up a value or synthesize information, it all comes down to the patterns and connections shown by variables, figures, experiments, and scientists. Look for trends *within* a figure, and look for relationships *between* figures.

Outside Knowledge

For the topics of the passages, ACT will pull from biology, chemistry, physics, and the Earth/space sciences, such as geology, astronomy, and meteorology. Most of the questions are answered by the passages and figures provided, but you should also expect 2–3 questions on outside knowledge.

The Passages

On each ACT, the order of the passages will vary, but the distribution of passage types is always the same.

Charts and Graphs

ACT calls these "Data Representations." We call them "Charts and Graphs" because that's what they're all about. They *always* come with figures. There are 3 Charts and Graphs passages, each with 5 questions.

Experiments

ACT calls these "Research Summaries." They look a lot like the Charts and Graphs passages because they *usually* come with figures. However, they come with more reading because they include the descriptions of the experiment set up. There are 3 Experiments passages, each with 6 questions.

Fighting Scientists

ACT calls these "Conflicting Viewpoints," but admit it: Our name is way more fun. There is only one Fighting Scientists passage, featuring 7 questions, on each ACT. It is inherently different from the other 6, even if it *sometimes* comes with figures. The fundamental task of the Fighting Scientists passage is to compare and contrast opposing views of an issue.

PERSONAL ORDER OF DIFFICULTY (POOD)

There are many factors about the structure of this test that make it difficult. It's last, which doesn't help at all. But even if it were first, many would find it the most challenging. Science phobes are intimidated by the subject matter. Science geeks are thwarted by the time crunch. Pick your poison; no one benefits from following ACT's order. On every ACT, you need to work the passages in an order that makes sense for you.

Now Passages

Every time you take the ACT, for practice and for real, pick the order of the passages that makes sense for you. The best passages to do Now are those with the most transparent relationships. When you pick your Now passages, choose exclusively among the Charts and Graphs and Experiments passages. By nature the Fighting Scientists passage is different, and even superior readers find it takes longer to work than the best of the Now passages. So what makes a good Now passage? There are five signs to abide by.

1. Small Tables and Graphs

A good Now passage can have only tables, only graphs, or both. Tables should be no more than 3–4 rows or columns, and graphs should have no more than 3–4 curves.

2. Easy-to-Spot Consistent Trends

Look for graphs with all the curves heading in the same direction: all up, all down, or all flat. Look for tables with numbers in a consistent direction: up, down, or flat.

3. Numbers, not Words or Symbols

To show a consistent trend, the figure has to feature numbers, not words or symbols.

4. Short Answers

Look for as many questions as possible with short answers, specifically answers with values and short relationship words like "increase" or "decrease."

5. Your Science POOD

Don't forget to factor in your familiarity and comfort with the topic when spotting good Now passages. For example, if you've just studied DNA, a passage on DNA will strike you as easier regardless of how the figures look.

Now versus Easy

We are deliberately calling these Now passages rather than Easy passages. Even a passage with great figures will have 1–2 tough questions, but even the toughest questions are easier to crack when you get the central trends and relationships. On passages with incomprehensible figures, even the easiest questions will take you longer because you will keep asking yourself, "What is this saying again?" You'll always work good Now passages more quickly, and good time management is what the ACT is all about.

PACING

With just 35 minutes to do 7 passages and 40 questions, you have an average of 5 minutes for every passage. But should you spend 5 minutes on every passage? Of course not. If you make smart choices of good Now passages, you should be able to work them in less time, leaving yourself more time on the tougher passages. Think about the pacing chart we discussed in Chapter 1. Think about how many points you need to hit your goal.

Be Ruthless and Flexible

Need More Practice?
1,296 ACT Practice Questions provides 6 tests' worth of Science passages. That's 42 passages and 240 questions.

Every Now passage will have 1–2 tough questions, just as every Later passage will have at least 1–2 easy questions. Use Chapters 3 and 4 to practice, but even on the Now passages, know when to guess on a tough question and move onto the next passage. Don't let one tough question drag you down.

POE

The most direct Science questions will ask you to look up a value or a relationship. But the most complex will ask you to synthesize information or draw a conclusion. The more difficult the question, the less it will help to just stare at the figure waiting for divine guidance to help you magically *see* the answer. As is often the case on the ACT, spotting the wrong answers can be much easier than magically divining the right answers. In our 3-step Basic Approach, we'll discuss in greater detail how to use POE.

THE BASIC APPROACH

The most efficient way to boost your Science score is to pick your order and apply our 3-step Basic Approach to passages with figures. Follow our smart, effective strategy to earn as many points as you can.

> **Fighting Scientists**
> The Fighting Scientists passage is fundamentally different from the Charts and Graphs and Experiments passages and requires a different approach. In *Cracking the ACT 2014* we teach you how to approach the Fighting Scientists passage.

Step 1: Work the Figures

Take 10–30 seconds to review your figures. What are the variables? What are the units? In what direction do the variables move?

Graphs present trends visually. For tables, you need to make it visual. Mark the trends for each variable with an arrow. Here are three tables from a good Now passage with the trends marked.

Passage II

Table 1	
Angle between axis of first and second filters (degrees)	Intensity of emerging beam (W/m²)
0	4.00
15	3.73
30	2.99
45	2.01
60	1.00
75	0.27
90	0.00

↑   ↓

Table 2	
Angle between axis of first and second filters (degrees)	Intensity of emerging beam (W/m²)
0	8.00
15	7.46
30	6.01
45	3.99
60	2.00
75	0.54
90	0.00

↑   ↓

Table 3	
Angle between axis of first and second filters (degrees)	Intensity of emerging beam (W/m²)
0	6.01
15	5.60
30	4.49
45	2.99
60	1.50
75	0.41
90	0.00

↑   ↓

Step 2: Work the Questions

For each question, look up the value or relationship on the figures as directed. Use your POOD to leave for Later tougher questions. Read if and only when you can't answer a question from the figures.

Try an example.

12. In Experiment 1, if the angle between the axes of polarization increases by 15 , the intensity of the resulting beam:

F. halves.
G. doubles.
H. increases, but not by any constant factor.
J. decreases, but not by any constant factor.

Here's How to Crack It
Because you've already marked the trends, you know that as the angle increases, the intensity decreases. Eliminate choices (G) and (H). Look closely at the trend, and choose (J).

Both the Charts and Graphs and Experiments passages will include actual text. Read the passage intros and experiment descriptions *only* when you can't answer a question from a figure.

Try another example.

10. How does the setup of Experiment 1 differ from that of Experiment 2 ?

    F. In Experiment 1, the original beam was polarized, but in Experiment 2, it was unpolarized.

    G. In Experiment 1, the original beam was unpolarized, but in Experiment 2, it was polarized.

    H. In Experiment 1, the scientists tested a wider range of angles than they did in Experiment 2.

    J. In Experiment 1, the original beam of light was more intense than the one in Experiment 2.

Here's How to Crack It

The variables are the same in Tables 1 and 2. To answer this question, you have to read the experiment descriptions.

Experiment 1

The scientists used a laser emitting unpolarized light. The light was directed toward a polarization filter with an axis of polarization pointing straight up, and then through another whose axis of polarization varied. The scientists chose to describe the axis of the second filter by examining the angle between its axis and the axis of the first filter. The intensity of the original beam was 8 W/m² (watts per square meter). Their results are shown in Table 1.

Experiment 2

The scientists repeated the experimental setup of Experiment 1 but used a source of polarized light polarized in the same direction as the axis of the first polarization filter (straight up). The intensity of the original beam was still 8 W/m². The results are shown in Table 2.

The light in Experiment 1 was unpolarized, while the light in Experiment 2 was polarized. Choice (G) provides this information correctly.

Step 3: Work the Answers

In question 12, the central task involved looking up a relationship you've already marked. You used POE to eliminate two answers, but from the beginning you were in command of the question. On question 10, the difference between the two experiments was addressed in the first line of the experiment descriptions. However, if you didn't spot that, good POE would have eliminated choice (F), and you'd have been able to eliminate choices (H) and (J) as well.

On more difficult questions, POE will always be the best bet. You'll be asked to synthesize information from several figures, evaluate a hypothesis, or draw a conclusion, and it will always be easier to eliminate what the figures and passage disprove.

Try another example.

11. The scientists hypothesize that the color of the original beam of light will affect the intensity of the emerging beam. The frequency of a beam of light determines its color. Which of the following would be the best way to test this hypothesis?

A. Repeating the experiments using more than two polarizing filters

B. Repeating the experiments on different planets

C. Repeating the experiments using beams of both high and low frequencies

D. Repeating the experiments using different intensities for the original beam

Here's How to Crack It

Use POE. Whenever a question asks about how to test something, eliminate answers that have nothing to do with the goal. The question identifies color as an important variable on intensity and identifies frequency as the determinant of color. Eliminate any choice that doesn't address color or frequency. Only choice (C) is left standing.

Repeat

Steps 3 and 4 repeat: Make your way through the rest of the questions. Look up your answers on the figures, and read only when you can't answer a question from the figures. The less the questions involve a value or relationship, the more you should rely on POE to find the answers.

Summary

The Science test is not a test of science content but of science reasoning skills.

Pick your order of the passages.

Now passages feature small tables and graphs with easy-to-spot consistent trends made up of numbers, not words or symbols, and feature short answers.

Use the 3-step Basic Approach.

1. Work the Figures. Note the variables and mark the trends.

2. Work the Questions. Look up answers on your figures. Read if and only when you can't answer a question from a figure.

3. Work the Answers. On tougher questions, lean heavily on POE to eliminate wrong answers.

Science Passages
from the ACT

Passage I

Moth body coloration (see Figure 1) is a *hereditary* trait that can be passed from organisms to their offspring.

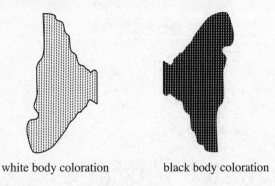

white body coloration   black body coloration

Figure 1

Scientists studied the body coloration of 2 subspecies of moths, *Biston betularia f. typica* and *Biston betularia f. carbonaria*. Both species live in City X. Only *B. betularia f. typica* lives in City Y, while only *B. betularia f. carbonaria* lives in City Z. Both subspecies live on trees found in temperate climates, such as birch. Moths with light body coloration are camouflaged from predators while living on light-colored trees, but are not hidden in heavily polluted areas where the tree bark is darkened. Moths with dark body coloration are camouflaged from predators on trees that are darkened by pollution, but not on light-colored trees.

Study 1

Scientists captured 100 *B. betularia f. typica* and 100 *B. betularia f. carbonaria* in City X. They labeled each one, recorded its color, and released it. Then they calculated the percent of birds having each of the body color intensities on a scale of 1 to 10, with 1 being completely black and 10 being completely white. The researchers followed the same methods with 100 *B. betularia f. typica* moths from City Y and 100 *B. betularia f. carbonaria* moths from City Z. The results of this study are shown in Figure 2.

Study 2

After the end of Study 1, the scientists returned to City Y over the course of 10 years, from 1983 to 1992. During each visit, they captured at least 50 *B. betularia f. typica* moths and measured their body color intensities. They then calculated the average *B. betularia f. typica* body color intensity from the 1–10 scale for each of the 10 years. The scientists noted that during the 10-period, 2 years were particularly wet, while 3 years were especially dry (see Figure 3). During wet years, pollutants tend to be washed from the surfaces of tree bark. During dry years, pollutants are more likely to concentrate on tree bark, and the tree bark itself tends to become thicker.

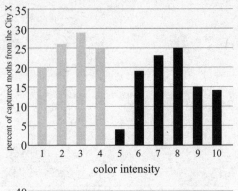

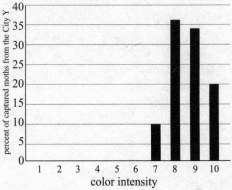

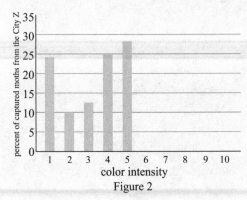

Figure 2

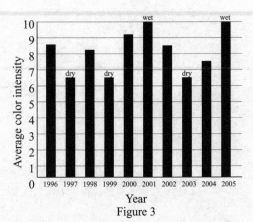

Figure 3

1. Based on the results from Study 1, the largest percentage of moths in City Y and City Z had a color intensity of:

	City Y	City Z
A.	8	1
B.	8	5
C.	9	4
D.	9	5

2. During which of the following years was birch bark most likely to be thickest in City Y?

F. 2000
G. 2001
H. 2002
J. 2003

3. How was Study 1 different from Study 2 ?

A. *B. betularia f. carbonaria* moths were captured in Study 1 but not in Study 2.
B. *B. betularia f. typica* moths were captured in Study 1 but not in Study 2.
C. The moth body coloration was measured in Study 1 but not in Study 2.
D. The moth body coloration was measured in Study 2 but not in Study 1.

4. The scientists most likely labeled the moths in Study 1 to:

F. determine how body coloration was affected by pollution in City X.
G. determine the average wingspan of each population of moths.
H. make sure that the body coloration of each moth was measured only once.
J. make sure that the body coloration of each moth was measured multiple times.

5. Based on the results from Study 2, would a moth with a body color intensity measuring 6.5 or a moth with a body color intensity measuring 9.5 have had a greater chance of surviving in 2005 ?

A. A moth with a body color intensity of 6.5, because pollutants concentrate more on tree bark during dry years.
B. A moth with a body color intensity of 6.5, because pollutants are removed from tree bark during dry years.
C. A moth with a body color intensity of 9.5, because pollutants concentrate more on tree bark during dry years.
D. A moth with a body color intensity of 9.5, because pollutants are removed from tree bark during dry years.

6. A scientist hypothesized that there would be a greater range in body coloration in the *B. betularia f. typica* moths when they are forced to coexist with another subspecies of moths. Do the results from Study 1 support this hypothesis?

F. Yes; the range of body coloration for *B. betularia f. typica* moths was greater in City X than in City Y.
G. Yes; the range of body coloration for *B. betularia f. typica* moths was greater in City Y than in City X.
H. No; the range of body coloration for *B. betularia f. typica* moths was greater in City X than in City Y.
J. No; the range of body coloration for *B. betularia f. typica* moths was greater in City Y than in City X.

Passage II

Ethylene glycol is the main ingredient in antifreeze and has the chemical structure shown below:

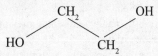

Figures 1–3 show how solutions of antifreeze vary as the concentration of ethylene glycol. Concentration is given as the percent ethylene glycol by volume in water (% EG) at atmospheric pressure (101.3 kPa). Figure 1 shows how the melting point (the temperature at which solid antifreeze would begin melting) of antifreeze varies with % EG. Figure 2 shows how the boiling point of antifreeze varies with % EG. Figure 3 shows how the density at 25°C varies with % EG.

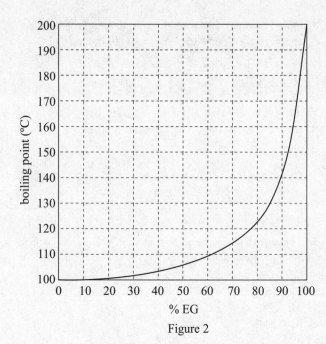

Figure 2

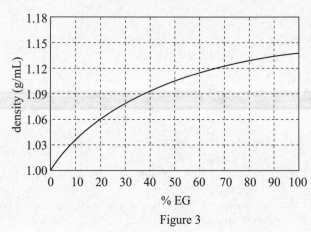

Figure 3

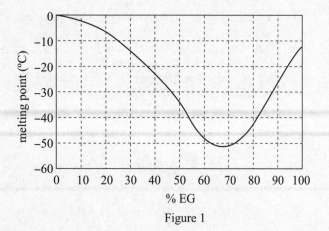

Figure 1

7. At 101.3 kPa, which of the following solutions will have the *lowest* freezing point?

   A.   100% EG
   B.   68% EG
   C.   50% EG
   D.   0% EG

8. According to Figure 1, the temperature at which solid anti-freeze begins to melt in a 60% EG solution at 101.3 kPa is closest to which of the following?

F. 0°C
G. –12°C
H. –48°C
J. –60°C

9. Based on Figure 2, which of the following solutions has a boiling point equal to pure water at 101.3 kPa?

A. 0% EG
B. 13% EG
C. 68% EG
D. 100% EG

10. At 25°C, as the % EG increases from 0% to 100%, the mass per unit volume:

F. increases only.
G. decreases only.
H. increases, then decreases.
J. decreases, then increases.

11. According to Figures 2 and 3, a solution of antifreeze that has a density of 1.09 g/mL at 25°C will have a boiling point closest to which of the following?

A. 100°C
B. 104°C
C. 111°C
D. 122°C

Passage III

A series of studies have been conducted to determine the level of harmful radiation at nuclear-waste clean-up facilities. One method of determining the level of radiation in an area is to measure the growth of certain crystals such as $Bi_4Ge_3O_{12}$ (BGO). BGO crystals come in two basic configurations that grow in environments exposed to high levels of gamma radiation. BGO(I) has a hexagonal crystalline structure and typically grows in environments that are continuously exposed to 100–200 rads of gamma radiation per day, while BGO(II) has an octagonal crystalline structure and typically grows in environments that are continuously exposed to 500–800 rads of gamma radiation per day. Scientists conducted two studies to determine which configuration of BGO crystal would be more useful in determining the amount of exposure to gamma radiation around a nuclear-waste clean-up site.

Study 1

BGO(I) and BGO(II) crystals of 4 cm³ to 8 cm³ were collected from a nuclear waste clean-up site west of Phoenix, AZ. Crystals of both types were placed into individually sealed clear-plastic containers. Ten crystals of each type were then exposed to 3 different levels of gamma radiation—150 rads per day, 450 rads per day, and 750 rads per day—for a period of 7 days. The average volume for each type of crystal and each of the 3 levels of radiation was then determined. The results are shown in Figure 1.

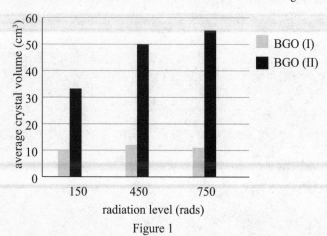

Figure 1

Study 2

The BGO (I) and BGO (II) crystals were removed from the radiation sources and weighed. The average mass of the BGO(I) was determined to be about 13 gm. The average mass of the BGO(II) crystals at each of the three levels of radiation is shown in Figure 2.

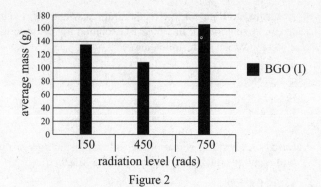

Figure 2

For each radiation level the volume and mass of the BGO(II) crystals were plotted. The best-fit curve for each is shown in Figure 3.

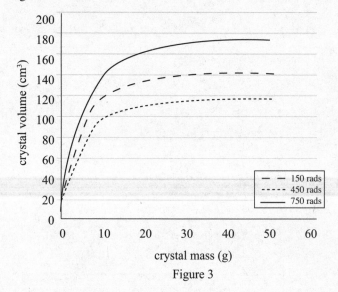

Figure 3

12. Based on Figure 3, for a radiation level of 450 rads, the size and mass of how many BGO(II) crystals were plotted?

   F. 10
   G. 12
   H. 32
   J. Cannot be determined from the given information

13. Suppose that a fourth group of BGO(II) had been exposed to radiation at a level of 300 rads. After 7 days, the average volume of each of these crystals would have been:

   A. less than 35 cm³.
   B. between 35 cm³ and 50 cm³.
   C. between 50 cm³ and 60 cm³.
   D. greater than 60 cm³.

14. At the end of Study 2, a crystal of BGO(II) was found to have a mass of 10 g and a volume of 100 cm³. Based on Figure 3, this crystal most likely had been exposed to radiations of which of the following levels?

   F. 150 rads
   G. 300 rads
   H. 450 rads
   J. 750 rads

15. Which of the following sets of data points most likely yielded the best-fit curve for BGO(II) crystals exposed to 150 rads of radiation?

A.
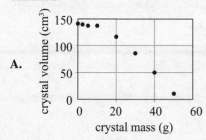

B.
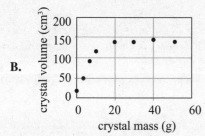

C.
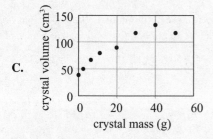

D.
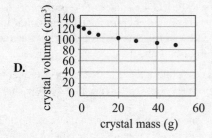

16. According to the results of Studies 1 and 2, for a given level of radiation, how did the crystals of BGO(I) compare to the crystals of BGO(II)? On average BGO(I) had:

   F. larger volume and greater mass.
   G. larger volume but lesser mass.
   H. smaller volume and lesser mass.
   J. smaller volume but greater mass.

17. Of the 10 crystals of BGO(I) that were exposed to 450 rads of radiation, 2 cracked and 8 remained whole. The total mass of all of the crystals combined can be calculated using which of the following expressions?

   A. 13 gm × 10
   B. 13 gm + 10
   C. 13 gm × 8
   D. 13 gm + 8

Passage IV

Leaf area index is a unitless measure of the percent of a rainforest floor that is covered by the leaves of tall trees. Leaf area index may increase because of an increase in *precipitation* (measured as millimeters of rainfall per km^2 per year). Table 1 shows how the leaf area index formed by the *canopy layer* (30 to 45 m above the rainforest floor) varies with precipitation in a 1000 km^2 section of the Amazon Rainforest. Figures 1–3 show the relative precipitation, RP (the percent below the rainfall measured on January 1, 1985), and the monthly average leaf area index of the *emergent layer* (45 to 55 m above the rainforest floor), *canopy layer*, and *understory layer* (0 to 30 m above the rainforest floor), respectively, over from January 1990 to January 2005.

Table 1	
Precipitation (mm/km^2/yr)	Leaf area index
1.80	5.2
1.85	5.4
1.90	5.6
1.95	5.8
2.00	6.0

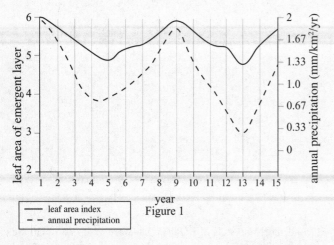

Figure 1

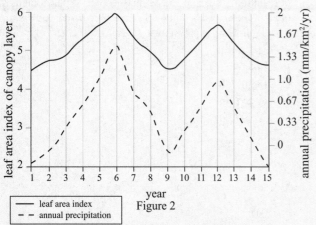

Figure 2

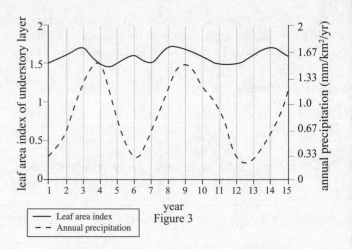

Figure 3

18. The leaf area index of the canopy layer covering the section of the rainforest in January of the 5th year studied was closest to which of the following?

F. 4.0
G. 4.5
H. 5.0
J. 5.5

19. Based on Table 1, a precipitation of 1.70 mm/km^2/yr would correspond to a leaf area index that is closest to which of the following?

A. 4.8
B. 5.5
C. 6.0
D. 6.5

20. A botanist states, "The leaf area index of the understory layer is more directly correlated with annual precipitation than is the leaf area index of the canopy layer." Is this statement consistent with Figures 1 and 3 ?

F. No, because the plot for the leaf area index of the canopy layer more closely resembles the plot for the annual precipitation.
G. No, because the plot for the leaf area index of the understory layer more closely resembles the plot for the annual precipitation.
H. Yes, because the plot for the leaf area index of the canopy layer more closely resembles the plot for the annual precipitation.
J. Yes, because the plot for the leaf area index of the understory layer more closely resembles the plot for the annual precipitation.

21. Which of the following figures best represents the leaf area index measured in the 7th year of the study?

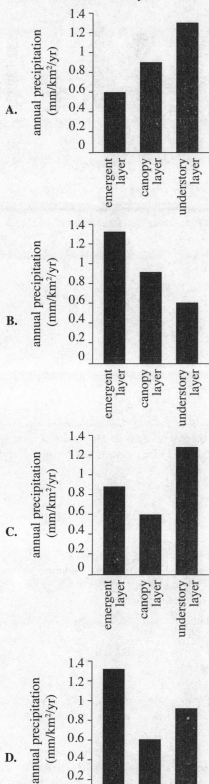

A.

B.

C.

D.

22. The emergent layer is primarily composed of small leaves that cover a wide area, while the understory layer is primarily composed of broad leaves that cover a small area. This difference is most likely because the average precipitation at heights of:

F. 0 to 30 m above the rainforest floor is above 2.00 mm/km^2/yr, whereas the average precipitation at heights of 30–45 m above the rainforest floor is below 1.80 mm/km^2/yr.

G. 0 to 30 m above the rainforest floor is above 2.00 mm/km^2/yr, whereas the average precipitation at heights of 45–55 m above the rainforest floor is below 1.80 mm/km^2/yr.

H. 0 to 30 m above the rainforest floor is below 1.80 mm/km^2/yr, whereas the average precipitation at heights of 30–45 m above the rainforest floor is above 2.00 mm/km^2/yr.

J. 0 to 30 m above the rainforest floor is below 1.80 mm/km^2/yr, whereas the average precipitation at heights of 45–55 m above the rainforest floor is above 2.00 mm/km^2/yr.

Passage V

In 1789, Mt. Mantu erupted off the coast of Brunei releasing a cloud of ash that lowered global temperatures for 15 years. When a volcano erupts, it releases a cloud of ash, dust, and debris into the atmosphere thousands of times the volume of the volcano. In addition, at the time of the eruption, the volcano produces a mud and ash flow along the sides of the volcano. The ash flow around Mt. Mantu covered an area 30 times larger than the original size of the volcano. Figure 1 shows the volume of the ash clouds released by volcanoes of differing diameters during the last 200 million years.

Figure 2 shows the average amount of time elapsed between consecutive major eruptions of various volcanoes of similar sizes, for a range of volcano sizes. Figure 3 represents the percentage of land area covered by volcanic ash flows in three different mountain ranges—the Cascades, the Appalachians, and the Himalayas—for various volcanic ash flow diameters.

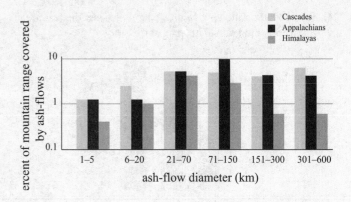

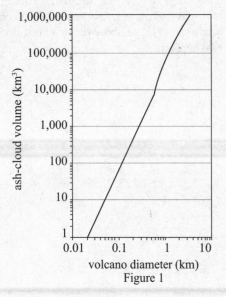

Figure 1

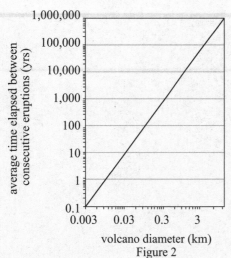

Figure 2

23. If 100 km³ of ash was released by Mt. Mantu, according to Figure 1, Mt. Mantu's diameter was most likely closest to which of the following?

   A. 0.02 km
   B. 0.01 km
   C. 0.1 km
   D. 1 km

24. According to Figure 2, for progressively larger volcanoes, the average amount of time that elapses between consecutive eruptions with the same diameter:

   F. increases only.
   G. decreases only.
   H. varies, but with no general trend.
   J. remains the same.

25. According to Figure 3, for any given range of volcanic ash flows, the percent of area covered in the Himalayas by ash flows is:

   A. less than the Cascades and the Appalachians.
   B. less than the Cascades but greater than the Appalachians.
   C. greater than the Cascades or than the Appalachians.
   D. greater than the Cascades but less than the Appalachians.

26. Suppose a volcano similar to Mt. Mantu created an ash flow that was 30 km in diameter. Based on Figure 1 and other information provided, that volcano would have released a volume of ash closest to which of the following?

F. 5,000 km^3
G. 10,000 km^3
H. 50,000 km^3
J. 100,000 km^3

27. Assume that a volcano with a diameter of 30 km erupted 500,000 years ago. Also assume that another volcano 30 km in diameter will erupt in the future. If the time that elapses between eruptions is equal to the average amount of time a given in Figure 2, a 30 km in diameter volcano should erupt approximately:

A. 250,000 years from now.
B. 500,000 years from now.
C. 1,000,000 years from now.
D. 1,500,000 years from now.

Passage VI

An astrophysics class is given the following facts about the burning out of stars.

1. The burning out of a star can be divided into 3 stages: *helium fusion*, *planetary nebula formation*, and *white dwarf development*.

2. Mid-sized stars fuse hydrogen nuclei (composed of protons) into helium nuclei at their centers, in a process known as helium fusion. These include yellow dwarves, like our Sun, and the slightly smaller orange dwarves. Helium fusion releases a significant amount of kinetic energy.

3. As kinetic energy continues to be released, a planetary nebula may form, in which colorful, ionized gas spreads out from the star's center.

4. The remaining material at the center of the planetary nebula condenses into a white dwarf, which is relatively cool and small in size.

5. Red dwarves are smaller stars that can also carry out helium fusion. These stars can develop into white dwarves sooner than yellow and orange dwarves, and do not form planetary nebulas.

Two students discuss the eventual fate of three stars in the Alpha Centauri system. Alpha Centauri A, a 1.10-solar-mass yellow dwarf star, where one *solar mass* unit is equivalent to the mass of the Sun; Alpha Centauri B, a 0.91-solar-mass orange dwarf star; and Alpha Centauri C, a 0.12-solar-mass red dwarf star. Alpha Centauri A and B comprise a binary star system that revolves around a common center of mass, while Alpha Centauri C revolves around a nearby center of mass.

Student 1

The 3 stars of the Alpha Centauri system all formed at the same time from the same collection of matter. Alpha Centauri C was initially the most massive of the three stars, and Alpha Centauri A and Alpha Centauri B had the same size. The large Alpha Centauri C had more helium fusion than the other two stars, so it quickly became the smallest of the stars. More of its matter flowed to Alpha Centauri A than to Alpha Centauri B, making Alpha Centauri A slightly larger than Alpha Centauri B.

Student 2

Alpha Centauri A and Alpha Centauri B formed at a different time than Alpha Centauri C. Alpha Centauri A and Alpha Centauri B formed at the same time from a common collection of matter, and Alpha Centauri A was initially more massive than Alpha Centauri B. Alpha Centauri C formed later from a different, smaller collection of matter, and never became bigger than a red dwarf. At some point, the small Alpha Centauri C was attracted to the other two stars, resulting in a triple star system.

28. Based on Student 2's discussion, Alpha Centauri C is part of the Alpha Centauri system because of which of the following forces exerted on Alpha Centauri C by the original binary star system?

F. Electromagnetism
G. Gravitation
H. Strong nuclear interaction
J. Weak nuclear interaction

29. Based on Student 1's discussion and Fact 2, while matter flowed between Alpha Centauri C and Alpha Centauri A, Alpha Centauri C released most of its energy by fusing:

A. helium nuclei into hydrogen nuclei at its core.
B. hydrogen nuclei into helium nuclei at its core.
C. helium nuclei into hydrogen nuclei at its periphery.
D. hydrogen nuclei into helium nuclei at its periphery.

30. Suppose that stars that form from the same collection of matter have similar chemical composition, but that stars that form from different collections of matter have different chemical compositions. Student 2 would most likely agree with which of the following statements comparing chemical compositions of the stars in the current Alpha Centauri system at the time that they were formed.

F. Alpha Centauri A and Alpha Centauri B had the most similar compositions.
G. Alpha Centauri A and Alpha Centauri C had the most similar compositions.
H. Alpha Centauri B and Alpha Centauri C had the most similar compositions.
J. Alpha Centauri A, Alpha Centauri B, Alpha Centauri C all had the same compositions.

31. If the mass of the Sun is 2.0×10^{33} g, what is the mass of Alpha Centauri A?

A. 1.8×10^{33} g
B. 2.0×10^{33} g
C. 2.2×10^{33} g
D. 2.4×10^{32} g

32. Which of the following statements best explains why the process described in Fact 2 requires a high initial temperature and pressure?

F. All electrons are negatively charged, and like charges attract each other.
G. All electrons are negatively charged, and like charges repel each other.
H. All protons are positively charged, and like charges attract each other.
J. All protons are positively charged, and like charges repel each other.

33. Based on Fact 5 and Student 1's discussion, which of the 3 stars in the Alpha Centauri system, if any, is most likely to develop into a white dwarf?

   A. Alpha Centauri A
   B. Alpha Centauri B
   C. Alpha Centauri C
   D. The three stars will likely develop into white dwarves at the same time.

34. Based on Fact 5, would Student 2 agree that by the time Alpha Centauri B develops into a white dwarf, it will have spent as much time as a mid-sized star as Alpha Centauri A?

   F. Yes, because according to Student 2, Alpha Centauri A has always been less massive than Alpha Centauri B.
   G. Yes, because according to Student 2, Alpha Centauri A has always been more massive than Alpha Centauri B.
   H. No, because according to Student 2, Alpha Centauri A has always been less massive than Alpha Centauri B.
   J. No, because according to Student 2, Alpha Centauri A has always been more massive than Alpha Centauri B.

Electromagnets are used in a variety of industrial processes and often consist of a large *solenoid*, a helical coil of wire, that produces a uniform *magnetic field strength* B, when current I, passes through it (see Figure 1).

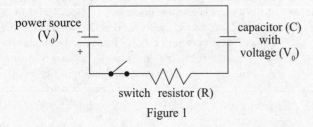

power source (V_0)

capacitor (C) with voltage (V_0)

switch   resistor (R)

Figure 1

The magnetic field of a solenoid is a factor of its resistance to changes in current, a property called *inductance* (L). The *relative permeability*, μ, is a property of the material within the solenoid coils which may magnify the magnetic field strength.

Figure 2 shows at 25°C, for specific values of μ and l (the length of the solenoid), how B varies with I and with the number of coils (N).

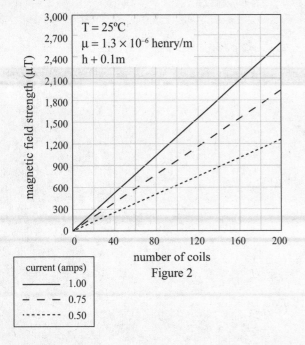

number of coils

Figure 2

current (amps)	
——	1.00
– – –	0.75
······	0.50

Figure 3 shows, for specific values of A (cross-sectional area of the solenoid) and N, how L varies with l and m at 25°C. In a separate experiment, the *average minimum solenoid length*, l_o, for a solenoid containing 100 coils was determined.

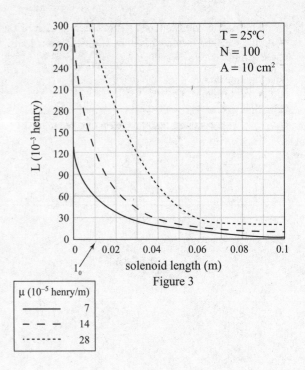

solenoid length (m)

Figure 3

μ (10^{-5} henry/m)	
——	7
– – –	14
······	28

35. For the conditions specified in Figure 2 and I = 0.75 Amps, the solenoid will attract iron metal particles most strongly when the number of coils is closest to which of the following?

A.   0 coils
B.   40 coils
C.   120 coils
D.   200 coils

36. According to Figure 3, does l_o vary with μ ?

F.   Yes; as μ increases, l_o decreases.
G.   Yes; as μ increases, l_o remains the same.
H.   No; as μ increases, l_o increases.
J.   No; as μ increases, l_o remains the same.

37. According to Figure 3, for $\mu = 14 \times 10^{-5}$ henry/m, as the length of the solenoid increases, L:

A.   increases only.
B.   decreases only.
C.   varies, but with no consistent trend.
D.   remains the same.

38. For a given solenoid length, what is the correct ranking of the values of μ in Figure 3, from the μ associated with the highest L to the μ associated with the lowest L?

F. 7×10^{-5} henry/m, 14×10^{-5} henry/m, 28×10^{-5} henry/m

G. 14×10^{-5} henry/m, 28×10^{-5} henry/m, 7×10^{-5} henry/m

H. 7×10^{-5} henry/m, 28×10^{-5} henry/m, 14×10^{-5} henry/m

J. 28×10^{-5} henry/m, 14×10^{-5} henry/m, 7×10^{-5} henry/m

39. What is the average minimum solenoid length of a solenoid of for the conditions given in Figure 3 ?

A. 0 m

B. 0.1 m

C. 0.2 m

D. 0.4 m

ANSWERS

Passage I
1. B
2. J
3. A
4. H
5. D
6. F

Passage II
7. B
8. H
9. A
10. F
11. B

Passage III
12. J
13. B
14. H
15. B
16. H
17. C

Passage IV
18. J
19. A
20. F
21. B
22. J

Passage V
23. C
24. F
25. A
26. H
27. B

Passage VI
28. G
29. B
30. F
31. C
32. J
33. C
34. J

Passage VII
35. D
36. J
37. B
38. J
39. B

EXPLANATIONS

Passage I

1. **B**   This question asks about Study 1, so we'll need to look at Figure 2. The color intensity for the moths in City *Y* is shown on the right side of the second graph in black, and the highest percentage of these moths had a color intensity of 8. Eliminate choices (C) and (D). The color intensity for the moths in City *X* is shown on the left side of the third graph in gray, and the highest percentage of these moths had a color intensity of 5. Eliminate choice (A), and the only remaining answer is choice (B).

2. **J**   The blurb in Study 2 contains the following information: *During dry years, pollutants are more likely to concentrate on tree bark, and the tree bark itself tends to become thicker.* Therefore, bark is thickest during dry years, and of the years listed on Figure 3, only 2003 is listed as a "dry" year, and therefore is the best answer from the given choices.

3. **A**   Study 1 contains the following information: *Scientists captured 100* B. betularia f. typica *and 100* B. betularia f. carbonaria *in City X.* Study 2 contains the following information: *During each visit* [from 1983 to 1992], *they captured at least 50* B. betularia f. typica *moths and measured their body color intensities.* Therefore, it can be assumed that they *did not* catch B. bethularia f. carbonaria in Study 2, making choice (A) the best answer. For color intensity, note the axes of each of the graphs. Color intensity is a variable plotted along the *x*-axis in Figure 2 and along the *y*-axis in Figure 3, meaning that it was measured in both studies.

4. **H**   Choices (H) and (J) are direct opposites, which means that one of them is likely to be true. You'll need to use a bit of science common sense here to choose between these two. In Study 1, the scientists are trying to count the number of moths in these various cities; therefore, in order to make this count accurate, they will need to make sure that each moth is only counted once, as in choice (H). Choice (F) is incorrect because *pollution* is measured in Study 2, and choice (G) is incorrect because *wingspan* is not measured in either study.

5. **D**   Figure 3 shows that 2005 was a wet year, and the average color intensity was 10. First, it is clear that moths with higher color intensities are more likely to survive in the wet years than the dry years, so the moth with a color intensity of 9.5 is more likely to survive than the moth with a color intensity of 6.5. Eliminate choices (A) and (B). Then, notice that Study 2 contains the following information: *During wet years, pollutants tend to be washed from the surfaces of tree bark.* This information agrees with choice (D).

6. **F**   This question is difficult to answer "Yes" or "No" immediately, so work with the reasons given in each of the answer choices. In City *X*, the coloration of *B. betularia f. typica* ranges from 5 to 10. In City *Y*, the coloration of *B. betularia f. typica* ranges from only 7 to 10. Eliminate choices (G) and (J). The hypothesis that a greater range in body coloration is produced by a diversity in the subspecies is therefore supported by this information, because City *X* contains two subpsecies and City *Y* contains only one. This question is tricky: You don't need to use the *y*-axis at all, because nothing in the question asks about the percent of captured moths. The only variable at play is body coloration.

Passage II

7. **B**   "Freezing point" does not appear on any of the figures, so you'll need a bit of outside knowledge here. Think about it this way: The freezing point is the point at which a substance turns from a liquid into a solid. The melting point is the point at which a substance turns from a solid into a liquid. Therefore, freezing point and melting point are one and the same. Use Figure 1. According to the passage, all readings are taking at atmospheric pressure 101.3 kPa, so you can disregard that part of the question. The melting point of the solution seems to be lowest around 70% EG. The closest of the answers is choice (B), 68%.

8. **H**   Use Figure 1. According to the passage, all readings are taking at atmospheric pressure 101.3 kPa, so you can disregard that part of the question. According to Figure 1, at 60% EG, the melting point is roughly −48°C, or choice (H).

9. **A**   The substance that will behave most like pure water and boil at the same temperature would be pure water itself. Choice (A), 0% EG, would mean a solution of no ethylene glycol and all water. Increasing the % EG, as in choices (B), (C), and (D), and therefore decreasing the percentage of water, would make the solution behave less like water.

10. **F**   This question requires a bit of outside knowledge: "density" and "mass per unit length" are one in the same. Therefore, you can use Figure 3 to answer this question even though the word "density" does not appear explicitly in this question. According to the passage, all density readings are taken at a temperature of 25°C, so you can disregard that temperature and just look at the graph. According to this graph, as % EG increases, the density steadily increases as well. The best answer, therefore, comes from choice (F).

11. **B**   According to Figure 2, a substance with a density of 1.09 g/mL has 40% EG. Use this EG value on Figure 3. According to Figure 3, a substance with 40% EG has a boiling point of approximately 104°C. Only choice (B) works.

Passage III

12. **J**   The axes given in Figure 3 are "Crystal mass (g)" and "Crystal volume (cm^3)." According to the key, different levels of radiation were measured. Nowhere in any of these axes or curves do we have any indication of the *number of crystals* measured. Without this information, and without any relevant information in the introduction, we can't determine how many crystals were measured, making choice (J) the only possible answer.

13. **B**   Although this question does not mention one specific figure, look at the variables to be compared. We'll need to make a prediction about Volume based on Radiation level. The only one of the three figures that compares these two variables is Figure 1. According to the information in Study 1, these readings were taken after *a period of 7 days*, so we can disregard that bit of information from the question. Now, the question asks about BGO(II), which is represented on Figure I by the darker of the two bars. According to the figure, as radiation level increases, crystal volume increases. Therefore, it is reasonable to assume that the volume of a crystal with a radiation level of 300 rads will be higher than that of a crystal with a radiation level of 150 rads and lower than that of a crystal with a radiation level of 450 rads. According to Figure 1, a BGO(II) crystal with a radiation level of 150 rads has a volume of 35 cm^3, and a BGO(II) crystal with a radiation level of 450 rads has a volume of 50 cm^3. Only choice (B) gives the appropriate range of values between these two volumes.

14. **H**   Plot the information from the problem onto Figure 3. A mass of 10 g and a volume of 100 cm^3 match most closely the curve appearing lowest on the figure. According to the key, this is the curve for 450 rads, or choice (H).

15. **B**   Figure 3 gives the curve for 150 rads, so find the plot in the answer choices that matches up most closely with the curve for 150 rads in Figure 3. Use POE. The curve starts at 0 cm^3, heads in an upward direction, and maxes out around 140 cm^3. Eliminate choices (A) and (D) because these curves decrease. Eliminate choice (C) because this curve does not start at 0 cm^3. Only choice (B) meets all the requirements and is therefore the best answer.

16. **H**   Use POE. Figure 1 contains a side-by-side comparison of the volumes of the crystals at different radiation levels. The BGO(I) crystals are represented by the lighter bar, and the BGO(II) crystals are represented by the darker bar. In all cases, the BGO(I) crystals had a smaller volume, so eliminate choices (F) and (G). Figure 2 contains the masses of BGO(II), but not BGO(I). According to the passage, though, *The average mass of the BGO(I) was determined to be about 13 gm*. Therefore, since the masses shown in Figure 2 are all well above this value, it can also be inferred that BGO(I)'s mass was smaller, eliminating choice (J).

17. **C**   According to the passage, *The average mass of the BGO(I) was determined to be about 13 gm*. Therefore, since there are 8 *whole* crystals left at the end of the experiment, their total mass can be found by multiplying the number of seeds by the mass of each: 13 gm × 8, or choice (C).

Passage IV

18. **J**   Make sure you are keeping the curves and axes straight. We're dealing with Figure 2, which shows the data for the *canopy* layer. The question asks about the leaf area index, so we need the solid line and the *y*-axis shown on the left side of the figure. Once all those elements are in place, you find that the leaf-area index in Year 5 was closest to 5.5. Make sure you are dealing with the correct figure and the correct axes given on that figure.

19. **A**   Table 1 shows a direct relationship: As precipitation goes up, leaf-area index goes up. Therefore, we can expect the leaf-area index at 1.70 mm/km^2/yr of precipitation to be below the leaf-area index at 1.80 mm/km^2/yr. The leaf-area index at 1.80 mm/km^2/yr is 5.2, and the only answer choice that gives a value in between is choice (A).

20. **F**   This problem asks about the *canopy* layer and the *understory* layer, so we will need to use Figures 2 and 3. Take a look at these two graphs: The two curves in the *canopy*-layer graph seem to go up and down at roughly the same rate, whereas the two curves in the *understory*-layer graph don't seem to have a consistent relationship. Because the *canopy*-layer graph shows a more consistent relationship, we can eliminate choices (G) and (J). A more consistent *canopy*-layer graph also *disagrees* with the botanist's statement from the problem, eliminating choice (H). Only choice (F) contains the correct answer to the question and the correct reason for that answer.

21. **B**   Use Figures 1, 2, and 3 to determine each of the annual precipitation values in Year 7. This is the dotted curve, and the values are on the *y*-axis on the right side of each figure. For the *emergent* layer shown in Figure 1, the annual precipitation was roughly 1.33. For the *canopy* layer shown in Figure 2, the leaf-area index was roughly 1.0. For the *understory* layer shown in Figure 3, the annual precipitation was roughly 0.67. You don't need to worry about exact figures: *emergent* should be the largest and *understory* should be the smallest. Only choice (B) works.

22. **J**   This question requires a bit of outside knowledge but can be solved with a little bit of common sense. First, sunlight is more likely to hit higher places than lower places, eliminating choices (F) and (G). Then, between choices (H) and (J), we need to choose between the ranges "30 to 45 m above the rainforest floor" in choice (H) and "45 to 55 m above the rainforest floor" in (J). Read the question carefully! It is asking about the *emergent* layer, which according to the introduction is found *45 to 55 m above the rainforest floor*, making choice (J) the only possible answer.

Passage V

23. **C**   According to Figure 1, when the volcano releases 100 km³ of ash, its diameter is approximately 0.1 km, or choice (C). If you had trouble with this problem, you may have been looking at the wrong axes.

24. **F**   Figure 2 shows a direct relationship. As "Average time elapsed" increases, "Volcano diameter" also increases. Only choice (F) adequately represents this trend.

25. **A**   Use POE. Pick any point on the graph: For 1–5% covered, for example, the bar showing the ash-flow of the Himalayas is lower than both the bars for the Cascades and the Appalachians. This same trend holds true for the other percentages as well. Only choice (A) accurately describes this trend.

26. **H**   The passage states that Figure 1 *shows the volume of the ash clouds released by of differing diameters*. It also states that the *ash flow around Mt. Mantu covered an area 30 times larger than the original size of the volcano*. Therefore, if the ash flow in the question is 30 km, the original size of the volcano must be 30 times smaller, or 1 km. According to Figure 1, a volcano with a diameter of 1 km will have an ash-cloud volume of approximately 54,000 km³. Choice (H) gives the best approximation of this value.

27. **B**   According to Figure 3, a volcano with a diameter of 30 km should have approximately 1,000,000 years between eruptions. Therefore, since this volcano erupted 500,000 years ago, it will not erupt for another 1,000,000 – 500,00 = 500,000 years, or choice (B).

Passage VI

28. **G**   This question requires a bit of outside knowledge. Student 2 concludes with the following sentence: *At some point, the small Alpha Centauri C was attracted to the other two stars, resulting in a triple star system.* Gravity is the attraction between two objects with mass, so attracted matches up most closely with choice (G), *gravitation*. If you picked one of the other answer choices, be careful—the correct answer must have textual support!

29. **B**   Student 1's hypothesis contains the following sentence: *The large Alpha Centauri C had more helium fusion than the other two stars, so it quickly became the smallest of the stars.* More of its matter flowed to Alpha Centauri A than to Alpha Centauri B. In other words, Alpha Centauri C released most of its matter by helium fusion. According to Fact 2, mid-sized stars fuse hydrogen nuclei (composed of protons) into helium nuclei at their centers, in a process known as helium fusion. It can therefore be inferred that Alpha Centauri C, in undergoing this process of helium fusion, was fusing hydrogen nuclei into helium nuclei at its center. Only choice (B) contains information consistent with Student 1 and Fact 2.

30. **F**   Student 2's hypothesis contains the following sentence: *Alpha Centauri A and Alpha Centauri B formed at the same time from a common collection of matter.* As the question suggests, stars that form from the same collection of matter have similar chemical compositions. Therefore, Student 2 would likely suggest that Alpha Centauri A and Alpha Centauri B have similar chemical compositions because they formed *from a common collection of matter.* Alpha Centauri C formed from a different collection of matter, eliminating choices (G), (H), and (J). Only choice (F) remains.

31. **C**   The introduction to this passage contains the following information: *Alpha Centauri A, a 1.10-solar-mass yellow dwarf star, where one solar mass unit is equivalent to the mass of the Sun.* The question states that the mass of the Sun is 2.0×10^{33} g. Therefore, the mass of Alpha Centauri A must be 1.10 times this value, given the definition of solar mass. Don't worry about calculating the exact value: You know that this value must be slightly greater than the mass of the sun, and only choice (C) gives a value greater than 2.0×10^{33} g.

32. **J**   Use POE. This question requires a bit of outside knowledge, but it can be solved easily with a bit of common sense. First of all, Fact 2 states that the nuclei being fused are *composed of protons.* It is therefore not likely that the answer to this question will have anything to do with *electrons*, eliminating choices (F) and (G). *Helium fusion* describes the process by which these protons are *fused*, or put together. Think about it this way: If these protons are attracted to each other to begin with, do you think it would take a bunch of extra energy to put them together? Not likely! Eliminate choice (H), and only choice (J) remains.

33. **C**   Fact 5 contains the following information: Red dwarves are smaller stars that can also carry out helium fusion. These stars can develop into white dwarves sooner than yellow and orange dwarves. Student 1 states, *The large Alpha Centauri C had more helium fusion than the other two stars, so it quickly became the smallest of the stars.* Therefore, according to this information, Alpha Centauri C is one of those smaller stars that can develop into white dwarves sooner. Choice (C) is our best answer. Also, Scientist 1 doesn't ever really talk about any differences between Alpha Centauri A and Alpha Centauri B, so it's unlikely that one would be correct and the other incorrect.

34. **J**   Use POE. If you're not sure how to answer "Yes" or "No," look at the reasons. Student 2's hypothesis contains the following information: *Alpha Centauri A was initially more massive than Alpha Centauri B.* This eliminates choices (F) and (H) immediately. Fact 5 contains the following information: *Red dwarves are smaller stars that can also carry out helium fusion. These stars can develop into white dwarves sooner than yellow and orange dwarves.* Therefore, since Alpha Centauri B is smaller, it is one of the *smaller stars* that *can develop into white dwarves sooner.* Therefore, it is not likely that it will spend the same amount of time as a white dwarf. Think about it this way: Fact 5 suggests that the main qualification for a *white dwarf* is its size. If Student 2 is correct about Alpha Centauri A and Alpha Centauri B having different sizes, their *white dwarf* qualifications can't be the same, so eliminate choice (G).

Passage VII

35. **D**   The words *magnetic field strength* don't appear explicitly in the question, but they are suggested by the word *attract*. Therefore, use Figure 2 to figure out the relationship between the number of coils and the magnetic field strength. According to this Figure, the magnetic field strength increases with increasing number of coils for all three curves shown. Therefore, in order to get the strongest possible magnetic field, we will need the maximum number of coils, or 200, as in choice (D).

36. **J**   Use POE. If you're not sure whether to answer "Yes" or "No," check the reasons. The variable l_0 appears on the *x*-axis of Figure 3 at a single point: solenoid length of 0.1 m. This point does stays the same, regardless of the other variables, eliminating choices (F) and (H). Then, l_0 cannot be said to vary with any of the variables on this Figure, including μ, eliminating choice (G). Only choice (J) remains.

37. **B**   Find $\mu = 14 \times 10^{-5}$ in the key for Figure 3. Notice, though, that all three of these curves follow the same trend: as solenoid length increases, L decreases and then levels off at the end. Only choice (B) offers an answer choice consistent with this information.

38. **J**   According to Figure 3, as solenoid length increases, L decreases. The μ curves don't follow quite so consistent a relationship. Pick a point and see how these μ values relate to one another. At a solenoid length of 0.2 m, the μ value associated with the largest L value is $\mu = 28 \times 10^{-5}$. The μ value associated with the smallest L value is $\mu = 7 \times 10^{-5}$. Therefore, the correct answer should have 28×10^{-5} as its first value and 7×10^{-5} as its last. Only choice (J) works.

39. **B**   According to the passage, *the average minimum solenoid length, l_0, for a solenoid containing 100 coils was determined*. Therefore, we need to determine the value of l_0. According to Figure 3, l_0 appears on the *x*-axis at solenoid length 0.1 m. Only choice (B) works.

Later Science
Passages from the
ACT

Passage I

In an experimental device known as a *cloud chamber*, protons and electrons act as *condensation nuclei* that get ionized by alcohol vapor inside the chamber to form a *high-energy mist*. When this mist acquires enough energy, it forms *tracks* that travel through the chamber. These tracks can then be accelerated when exposed to a magnetic field; with protons and electrons moving in opposite directions.

Two studies using cloud chambers were done at a research center in a temperate climate, using supercooled gaseous ethanol as a medium. The cloud chamber temperature ranged from 0°C to –150°C.

Study 1

Four types of anions (A–D) were used. Anions of each type, when released into the cloud chamber, emit groups of electrons into the chamber with a specific distribution of charges (see Table 1).

Anion Type	Percent of groups of electrons having charges (coulombs):			
	0.1–0.5	0.6–1.0	1.1–1.5	1.5–2.0
A	70	20	8	2
B	75	10	8	7
C	80	8	7	5
D	85	7	5	3
1 coulomb is the charge of 6.24×10^{18} electrons.				

Table 1

A device containing all 4 types of anions was placed next to the cloud chamber. A computer in the device determined whether or not to immediately release at least 1 anion, emitting electrons into the chamber. The computer also selected which type of anion to release, and how many anions to release to generate 10, 100, 1,000, or 10,000 condensation nuclei per cm³ within the chamber. The average number of tracks produced by each type of anion and at each concentration of condensation nuclei is shown in Figure 1.

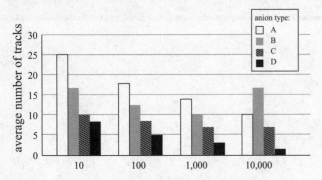

concentration of condensation nuclei
(nuclei/cubic centimeter)

Figure 1

Study 2

The magnetic force required to make each track to accelerate away from a straight line was recorded over an hour following the release of the four types of anions into two types of cloud chambers: one with ethanol vapor and one with water vapor. The averaged results for both types of cloud chambers are shown in Figure 2.

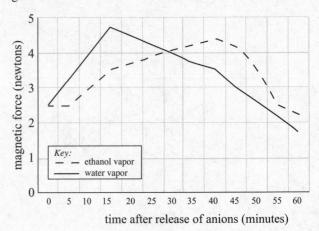

time after release of anions (minutes)

Figure 2

1. According to the results of Study 1, as the condensation nuclei concentration increased, the average number of tracks generated:

   A. increased for all 4 types of anions.
   B. increased for anion types A and B, but decreased for anion types C and D.
   C. decreased for all 4 types of anions.
   D. decreased for anion types A and B, but increased for anion types C and D.

2. Based on the passage, what is the correct order of tracks, subatomic particles, and condensation nuclei, according to their diameters, from smallest to largest?

   F. Subatomic particle, track, condensation nucleus
   G. Subatomic particle, condensation nucleus, track
   H. Track, subatomic particle, condensation nucleus
   J. Track, condensation nucleus, subatomic particle

3. According to the results of Study 2, how did the magnetic fields required in the cloud chamber with ethanol vapor differ from the magnetic fields required in the cloud chamber with water vapor with respect to their maximum strength?

A. It took more time for the magnetic field in the ethanol vapor to reach a maximum strength, and it reached a greater maximum strength.

B. It took less time for the magnetic field in the ethanol vapor to reach a maximum strength, and it reached a greater maximum strength.

C. It took more time for the magnetic field in the ethanol vapor to reach a maximum strength, and it reached a lesser maximum strength.

D. It took less time for the magnetic field in the ethanol vapor to reach a maximum strength, and it reached a lesser maximum strength.

4. The design of Study 1 differed from the design of Study 2 in that Study 1, the:

F. tracks of condensation nuclei were analyzed, whereas in Study 2, the concentration of condensation nuclei was analyzed.

G. strength of magnetic fields was measured, whereas in Study 2, the concentration of condensation nuclei was analyzed.

H. tracks of condensation nuclei were analyzed, whereas in Study 2, the strength of magnetic fields was analyzed.

J. strength of magnetic fields was analyzed, whereas in Study 2, tracks of condensation nuclei were analyzed.

5. Which of the following statements gives the most likely reason that data from the cloud chamber was not recorded below a temperature of $-150°C$? Below $-150°C$, there would be present:

A. only water vapor.
B. only alcohol vapor.
C. ice crystals but little water vapor.
D. solidified alcohol but little alcohol vapor.

6. Which of the following statements about the concentration of condensation nuclei in the 4 types of anions is supported by Table 1 ?

F. For all 4 types of anions, the majority of particles belonged to the largest charge category.

G. For all 4 types of anions, the majority of particles belong to the smallest charge category.

H. For anion types A and B, most anions belong to the largest charge category, whereas for anion types C and D, most anions belong to the smallest charge category.

J. For anion types A and B, most anions belong to the smallest charge category, whereas for anion types C and D, most anions belong to the largest charge category.

Passage II

Three experiments were conducted using the gases nitrogen (N_2), nitrogen dioxide (NO_2), and xenon (Xe). For each gas:

1. A cap was placed on a 2 L metal chamber, containing sensors to measure temperature and pressure and a vale to allow gas to enter.

2. Air was pumped out of the chamber until the pressure inside was measured to be 0.00 mmHg.

3. The chamber was placed on an analytical balance, which was then reset to 0.00 g.

4. Some of the gas was added to the chamber.

5. When the gas in the vessel reached room temperature (298 K), the mass and pressure inside were recorded.

6. Steps 4 and 5 were repeated for different masses.

The experiments were repeated using a 4 L metal chamber (see Figures 1 and 2).

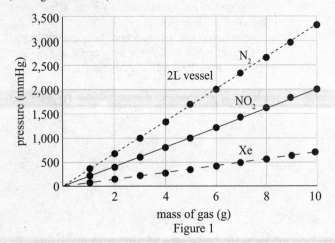

mass of gas (g)
Figure 1

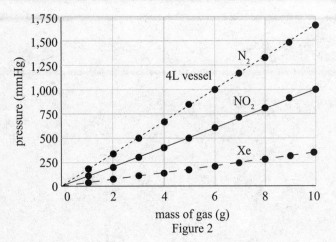

mass of gas (g)
Figure 2

7. Based on Figure 2, if 12 g of Xe had been added to the 4 L vessel, the pressure would have been:

   A. less than 300 mmHg.
   B. between 300 and 600 mmHg.
   C. between 600 mmHg and 900 mmHg.
   D. greater than 1200 mmHg.

8. Suppose the experiments had been repeated, except with a 3 L vessel. Based on Figures 1 and 2, the pressure exerted by 10 g of NO_2 would most likely have been:

   F. less than 1000 mmHg.
   G. between 1000 and 2000 mmHg.
   H. between 2000 and 2500 mmHg.
   J. greater than 2500 mmHg.

9. Based on Figures 1 and 2, for a given mass of N_2 at 298 K, how does the pressure exerted by the N_2 in a 4 L vessel compare to the pressure exerted by the N_2 in a 2 L vessel? In the 4 L vessel, the N_2 pressure will be:

   A. half as great as in the 2 L vessel.
   B. the same as in the 2 L vessel.
   C. twice as great as in the 2 L vessel.
   D. 4 times as great as in the 2 L vessel.

10. Which of the following best explains why equal masses of N_2 and NO_2 at the same temperature and in vessels of similar sizes had different pressures? The pressure exerted by the N_2 was:

F. greater, because there were fewer N_2 molecules per gram than there were NO_2 molecules per gram.

G. greater, because there were more N_2 molecules per gram than there were NO_2 molecules per gram.

H. less, because there were fewer N_2 molecules per gram than there were NO_2 molecules per gram.

J. less, because there were more N_2 molecules per gram than there were NO_2 molecules per gram.

11. Suppose the experiment involving N_2 and the 4 L vessel had been repeated, except at a temperature of 287 K. For a given mass of N_2, compared to the pressure measured in the original experiment, the pressure measured at 287 K would have been:

A. greater, because pressure is directly proportional to temperature.

B. greater, because pressure is inversely proportional to temperature.

C. less, because pressure is directly proportional to temperature.

D. less, because pressure is inversely proportional to temperature.

Passage III

Escherichia coli (E. coli) are commonly used in laboratories for the expression, replication, and purification of introduced circular pieces of DNA called *plasmids*. Engineered plasmids encode a gene of interest and often genes that confer resistances to select antibiotics. Antibiotic resistance may be analyzed using the *disk diffusion method*. During the disk diffusion method, bacteria from a single *colony*, or a cluster of genetically identical cells, are incubated in liquid growth media and spread on agar plates (see Figure 1). Small paper disks containing a known concentration of antibiotic are set on the agar plates and the bacteria are allowed to grow at optimal temperatures. Laboratory strains of *E. coli* lacking plasmids containing genes of resistance to select antibiotics will be unable to grow near the disk containing that antibiotic. Only bacteria that have received the introduced plasmid containing an antibiotic resistance gene should be able to grow in the presence of the antibiotic-containing disk.

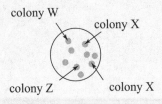

plate of
transformed colonies

Figure 1

Experiment 1

A biotech company has engineered new laboratory strains (A–E) of *E. coli* and is testing whether each strain could grow in the presence of a variety of common antibiotics—ampicillin (Amp), kanamycin (Kan), penicillin (Pen), and tetracycline (Tet). Each of the strains was incubated in a clear nutrient media containing either extra sugar (glucose) or an antibiotic at 37°C for 24 hr. After 24 hrs, the growth media was examined for *turbidity* or cloudiness, a signal of bacterial growth (see Table 1).

Table 1					
Strain	Nutrient Media				
	+Glu	+Amp	+Kan	+Pen	+Tet
A	+	+	−	+	−
B	+	−	−	+	−
C	+	−	−	+	+
D	+	+	+	−	−
E	+	−	+	+	−

Note: + indicates presence of turbidity;
− indicates no change in appearance

Experiment 2

The scientists at the biotech company tested strain B for growth after *transformation*, a process of introducing engineered plasmids, with antibiotic-resistance containing plasmids. Four different transformed colonies (W, X, Y, and Z) and untransformed strain B were incubated in liquid growth media and spread on agar plates. To identify which colonies had received which resistance genes, disks containing one of each of the common antibiotics were then placed on the agar plate and the bacteria were permitted to grow at 37°C (see Figure 2).

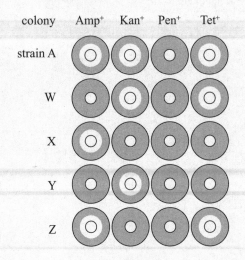

Figure 2

12. Suppose *E. coli* Strain D had been incubated on plates containing kanamycin and tetracycline (Kan⁺Tet⁺) disks and growth near both disks was observed. Do the data in Table 1 support this observation?

F. Yes; the results shown in Table 1 indicate that Strain D can grow in the presence of both Kan and Tet.

G. Yes; the results shown in Table 1 indicate that Strain D cannot grow in the presence of Kan.

H. No; the results shown in Table 1 indicate that Strain D can grow in the presence of both Kan and Tet.

J. No; the results shown in Table 1 indicate that Strain D cannot grow in the presence of Tet.

13. Which of the labeled colonies shown in Figure 2 is most likely to have received a plasmid containing resistance to tetracycline?

A. Colonies W and X
B. Colonies X and Z
C. Colonies Y and Z
D. Colonies X and Y

14. According to Table 1, how many strains tested in Experiment 1 were able to grow in nutrient media containing penicillin?

F. 0
G. 1
H. 2
J. 4

15. Based on Table 1 and Figure 2, which colonies, if any, likely received a plasmid with resistance genes to ampicillin and tetracycline?

A. Colony W only
B. Colony Y only
C. Colonies X and Y
D. Colonies Y and Z

16. Before beginning the experiments, the scientists sprayed the lab area down with a disinfectant. The most likely reason that the disinfectant was used was to avoid contaminating:

F. the nutrient growth media with strains that were lab generated.

G. the agar plates with strains that were lab generated.

H. both the nutrient growth media and agar plates with strains that were lab generated.

J. both the nutrient growth media and agar plates with strains that were not lab generated.

17. Which of the colonies shown in Figure 2 did NOT grow in the presence of penicillin?

A. Colony X
B. Colony Y
C. Colony Z
D. None of the strains

Passage IV

The *absolute threshold pressure for hearing* is the minimum air pressure at each audio frequency that can produce a sound that is detectable by the human ear. The *pain threshold pressure for hearing* is the maximum air pressure at each frequency that the human ear can withstand without sensing pain.

Figure 1 below displays the absolute and pain threshold pressures for hearing in two media: air and water. The figure also shows P, the percentage increase in compression of the air or water with increasing sound pressure. Audio frequency is given in cycles per second (cyc/sec), and sound pressure level is given in decibels (db).

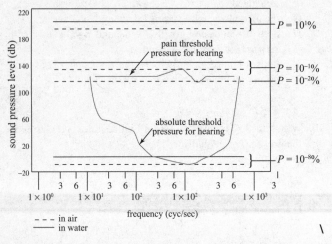

Figure 1

18. According to the figure, which of the following is the closest to the highest frequency that can be heard by a human being?

F. 1 cyc/sec
G. 10 cyc/sec
H. 100 cyc/sec
J. 1000 cyc/sec

19. Based on the figure, a sound of a given frequency will have the highest sound level pressure for which of the following sets of conditions?

	Sound in:	P
A.	Air	$10^{-8}\%$
B.	Air	$10^{-1}\%$
C.	Water	$10^{-8}\%$
D.	Water	$10^{-1}\%$

20. As humans grow older, there is often a loss in the ability to hear sounds at high frequencies. Which of the following figures best illustrates this?

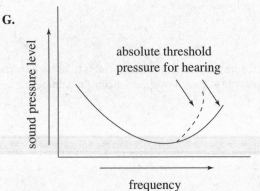

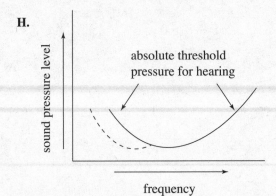

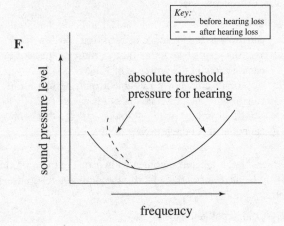

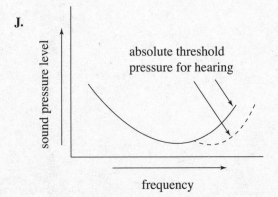

21. A scientist developed a hypothesis that sounds with any sound pressure level would be painful to humans if the frequency were 10^4 cyc/sec. Do the data from the figure support this hypothesis?

A. No, because humans are unable to hear sounds over 10^4 cyc/sec.

B. No, because the absolute threshold of pain for hearing is relatively constant with changes in frequency.

C. Yes, because the absolute threshold of pain for hearing is relatively constant with changes in frequency.

D. Yes, because as frequency increases above 10^4 cyc/sec, the absolute threshold of pain for hearing also increases.

22. Based on the figure, does P depend on the frequency of sound at a given sound pressure level?

F. No, because as frequency increases, P increases.

G. No, because as frequency increases, P remains constant.

H. Yes, because as frequency increases, P increases.

J. Yes, because as frequency increases, P remains constant.

Passage V

A group of students added 100 mg of Salt A to an Erlenmeyer flask containing 100 mL of water at 20°C. The mixture was heated over a *Bunsen burner* and a thermometer placed in the flask to acquire temperature readings (Figure 1).

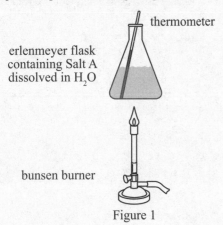

thermometer

erlenmeyer flask containing Salt A dissolved in H_2O

bunsen burner

Figure 1

The mixture was heated and temperature readings acquired every 30 sec until the solution reached a full boil and the solid had completely dissolved. The boiling temperature for the solution was measured to be 104°C. The procedure was repeated with Salt B, which resulted in a boiling temperature of 110°C.

The teacher asked 3 of the students in the group to explain why the solutions had different boiling temperatures.

Student 1

The solution containing Salt B had a higher boiling point because Salt B produces more ions in solution than Salt A. As the solid dissolves, the salt ionizes and interacts with water molecules. This causes more interactions between the ions and water thus requiring more energy for water molecules to break these interactions and become a gas (boiling). Since salts become ions in solution, salts that produce more ions will have more interactions with water than salts producing fewer ions. Thus, if two salts of equal amounts are added to water, the solution containing the salt that produces more ions will boil at the higher temperature.

Student 2

The solution containing Salt B had a higher boiling point because it had a lower *molar mass* (the mass of 6.02×10^{23} particles). Consider equal amounts of two salts with different molar masses. More mass is required of the salt with the greater molar mass to result in the same number of particles. Since more heat energy is required to boil water with more interactions, the solution with more salt particles will boil at a higher temperature. Thus, if equal amounts of two salts with different molar masses are added, the salt with the lower molar mass will result in more particles and a greater solution boiling point than a salt with a greater molar mass.

Student 3

The solution containing Salt B had a higher boiling point because Salt B releases more heat upon dissolving than Salt A. The *enthalpy change of dissolution* ($\Delta H°_{diss}$) is a measure of the net amount of heat energy absorbed in the process of dissolving a salt. Salts that absorb more energy to dissolve will have more positive $\Delta H°_{diss}$ values and will make the solution cooler. Salts that absorb less energy than they release will have more negative $\Delta H°_{diss}$ values and will make the solution warmer. If equal amounts of two salts with different $\Delta H°_{diss}$ values are dissolved in solution, the solution containing the salt with the more negative $\Delta H°_{diss}$ value will release more heat and thus result in a greater boiling point.

The number of ions produced, molar mass, and enthalpy change dissolution ($\Delta H°_{diss}$) of some common salts are shown in Table 1.

Table 1			
Salt	Ions Produced	Molar Mass (g/mol)	$\Delta H°_{diss}$ (kJ/mol)
Sodium chloride	2	58.4	+ 3.9
Calcium chloride	3	111.0	− 81.2
Ammonium nitrate	2	80.1	+ 25.7
Potassium hydroxide	2	56.11	− 57.6
Magnesium sulfate	2	120.38	− 91.0

23. Suppose that Salt A had been potassium hydroxide and Salt B had been magnesium sulfate. The results of the experiment would have supported the explanation(s) provided by which student(s)?

   A. Student 2 only
   B. Student 3 only
   C. Students 1 and 3 only
   D. Students 2 and 3 only

24. Suppose that the students also tested ammonium nitrate in the experiment and found it to have resulted in a boiling temperature in solution of 107°C. Student 2 would claim that ammonium nitrate:

   F. has a greater molar mass than Salt A, but a smaller molar mass than Salt B.
   G. has a greater molar mass than Salt B, but a smaller molar mass than Salt A.
   H. has a greater enthalpy change of dissolution than Salt A, but a smaller enthalpy change of dissolution than Salt B.
   J. has a greater enthalpy change of dissolution than Salt B, but a smaller enthalpy change of dissolution than Salt A.

25. Which of the following graphs of the relative number of particles produced is most consistent with Student 2's explanation?

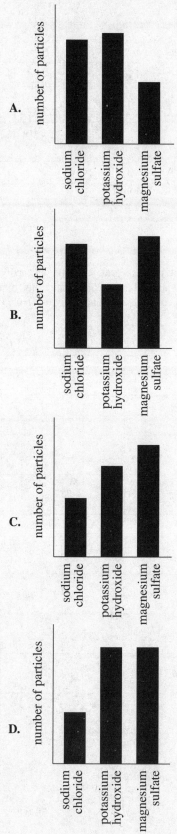

A.

B.

C.

D.

26. During the experiment, the temperature reading in the thermometer as readings were taken every 30 sec:

F. increased only.
G. decreased only.
H. increased, then decreased.
J. decreased, then increased.

27. Based on Student 3's explanation, which of the salts in Table 1 would result in the greatest solution boiling temperature?

A. Calcium chloride
B. Ammonium nitrate
C. Potassium hydroxide
D. Magnesium sulfate

28. Consider the data for cesium hydroxide shown in the table below:

Ions Produced	Molar Mass (g/mol)	ΔH°_{diss} (kJ/mol)
2	149.91	−71.6

Which student(s), if any, would predict that cesium hydroxide would produce a solution with a lower boiling temperature than calcium chloride?

F. Student 1 only
G. Students 2 and 3 only
H. Students 1, 2, and 3
J. None of the students

29. Is the claim "If equal amounts of salt are dissolved, sodium chloride will result in a greater boiling point than ammonium nitrate" consistent with Student 2's explanation?

A. No, because sodium chloride has a smaller molar mass than ammonium nitrate.
B. No, because sodium chloride has a more negative enthalpy change of dissolution.
C. Yes, because sodium chloride has a smaller molar mass than ammonium nitrate.
D. Yes, because sodium chloride has a more negative enthalpy change of dissolution.

Passage VI

Ions in seawater, such as Cl^-, SO_4^{2-}, Na^+, and Mg^{2+}, are carried down to the ocean floor through a process known as *marine deposition*. SO_4^{2-} and Mg^{2+} primarily come from the erosion of rocks, while Cl^- and Na^+ come from both mineral erosion and underwater volcanoes and hydrothermal vents.

Study 1

A fluid motion sensor was placed on a section of the seabed in the Atlantic Ocean, and data were collected over 12 months. At 6:00 a.m. every morning, the movement of water past the sensor was recorded, and a small amount of water was sequestered. Figure 1 shows the water movement that was measured in m^3 per second.

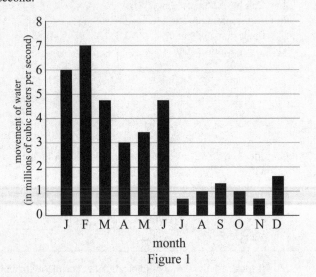

Figure 1

At the end of each month, the sequestered water was extracted by a science research crew, and a portion was analyzed for the concentrations of Cl^- and SO_4^{2-} ions. Using these data, the marine deposition was measured in kilograms (kg) per cubic meter (m^3) for each substance in each month (see Figure 2).

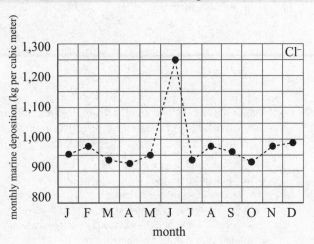

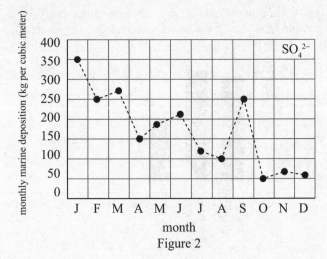

Figure 2

Study 2

Another portion of the monthly water sample was analyzed for concentrations of Na^+ and Mg^{2+} ions. The monthly marine deposition was calculated for each substance in equivalents (Eq) per m^3 (see Figure 3).

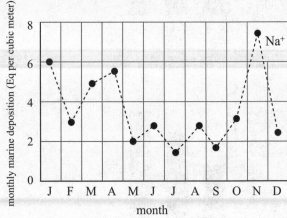

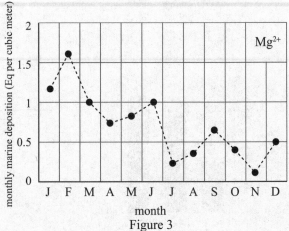

Figure 3

Study 3

The annual marine deposition of Cl^- and SO_4^{2-} ions over the 12-month period was calculated in kg/m^3 at the test site, and also at two sites in the Arctic Ocean, located 2,000 and 4,000 miles north, respectively (see Figure 4).

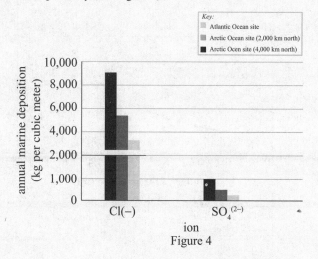

Key:
- Atlantic Ocean site
- Arctic Ocean site (2,000 km north)
- Arctic Ocen site (4,000 km north)

ion

Figure 4

30. According to Figure 1, during the year over which data were collected, the movement of water was greatest in February and least in November. According to Figures 2 and 3, the marine deposition of which ion was also greatest in February and least in November?

F. Cl^-
G. Mg^{2+}
H. Na^+
J. SO_4^{2-}

31. Based on the results from Study 1, the mean monthly marine deposition for Cl^- over the year of the study was:

A. less than 900 kg/m^3.
B. between 900 kg/m^3 and 1,000 kg/m^3.
C. between 1,000 kg/m^3 and 1,200 kg/m^3.
D. over 1,200 kg/m^3.

32. A student states, "The marine deposition of Na^+ is highest in the winter and lowest in the summer, since the winter features greater activity of volcanoes and hydrothermal vents." Is this statement supported by the results of Study 2 ?

F. No, because marine deposition of Na^+ was, on average, greater between November and January than it was between June and August.

G. No, because marine deposition of Na^+ was, on average, less between November and January than it was between June and August.

H. Yes, because marine deposition of Na^+ was, on average, greater between November and January than it was between June and August.

J. Yes, because marine deposition of Na^+ was, on average, less between November and January than it was between June and August.

33. Suppose that the fluid motion sensor was placed in an underwater cave in the Atlantic Ocean where there is no net movement of water during one month of the 12-month study. The information provided indicates that during that month, there would have been:

A. no marine deposition of any of the 4 substances.
B. no marine deposition of Cl^- and SO_4^{2-}, but a high level of marine deposition of Na^+ and Mg^{2+}.
C. high marine deposition of Cl^- and SO_4^{2-}, but no marine deposition of Na^+ and Mg^{2+}.
D. high marine deposition of all 4 substances.

34. According to Study 3, as the distance from the fluid motion sensor in the Atlantic Ocean decreased, the annual marine deposition:

F. decreased for both Cl^- and SO_4^{2-}.
G. decreased for Cl^- but increased for SO_4^{2-}.
H. increased for Cl^- but decreased for SO_4^{2-}.
J. increased for both Cl^- and SO_4^{2-}.

35. Which of the following variables remained constant in Study 2 ?

A. Marine deposition of SO_4^{2-}
B. Marine deposition of Mg^{2+}
C. Movement of water during the month
D. Location of the study

Passage VII

Oxidation-reduction titration is a method in which precise volumes of a *titrant* (an oxidizing or reducing agent) are added dropwise to a known volume of an *analyte* (a reducing or oxidizing agent, respectively). This process can be monitored by adding a *redox indicator* (a substance that changes color over a certain range of electrode potentials) to the analyte or by measuring the sample's *voltage* using a potentiometer. Voltage (measured in kilovolts, kV) is a measure of the force of an electrical current that could be transmitted by the solution.

Two titration experiments were performed at 298 K using a 0.10 M iodine (I_2) solution and either a 0.0010 M sulfur dioxide (SO_2) solution or a 0.0010 M sodium thiosulfate solution (where M is the number of moles of oxidizing or reducing agent per liter of solution). All solutions were aqueous. A redox indicator solution of *starch* was also used. Starch and I_2 form a complex with a deep blue color, but when I_2 is reduced to 2 iodide (I^-) ions, the complex dissipates and the solution becomes colorless.

Experiment 1

A drop of starch solution was added to an Erlenmeyer flask containing 100.0 mL of the SO_2 solution. A potentiometer, which acts as a control input for electronic circuits, was placed in the solution. The I_2 solution was incrementally added to the SO_2 solution. After each addition, the SO_2 solution was stirred and the solution's color and voltage were recorded (see Figure 1).

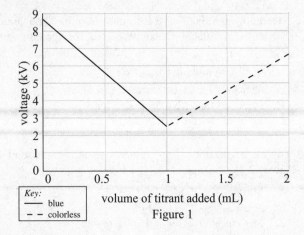

Key:
— blue
-- colorless

volume of titrant added (mL)

Figure 1

Experiment 2

Experiment 1 was repeated, except that the sodium thiosulfate solution was used instead of the SO_2 solution (see Figure 2).

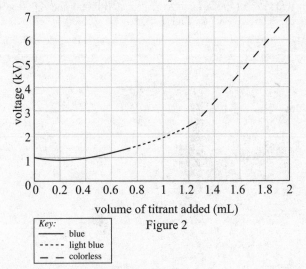

Key:
— blue
----- light blue
– – colorless

volume of titrant added (mL)

Figure 2

36. In Experiment 1, the analyte was blue at which of the following volumes of titrant added?

F. 0.7 mL
G. 1.1 mL
H. 1.5 mL
J. 1.9 mL

37. In Experiment 2, the analyte was in its reduced form for which of the following volumes of titrant added?

A. 0.3 mL
B. 0.6 mL
C. 0.9 mL
D. 1.2 mL

38. In Experiment 1, if 2.5 mL of titrant was added to the analyte, the voltage would most likely have been:

F. less than 1 kV.
G. between 1 kV and 4 kV.
H. between 4 kV and 7 kV.
J. more than 7 kV.

39. In Experiment 2, which solution was the analyte and which solution was the titrant?

	titrant	sample solution
A.	Sodium thiosulfate	I
B.	SO_2	I_2
C.	I_2	Sodium thiosulfate
D.	I_2	SO_2

40. In Experiments 1 and 2, the potentiometer that was placed in the analyte most likely did which of the following?

F. Detected the concentration of starch in the solution
G. Conducted an electric current initiated by ions in the solution
H. Heated the solution to its boiling point
J. Cooled to solution to its freezing point

41. A chemist states that in Experiment 2, the analyte was fully reduced with 0.2 mL of titrant added, but not with 1.8 mL of titrant added. Do the results of Experiment 2 support this claim?

A. Yes; at a value of 0.2 mL of titrant added, the analyte was blue, while at a value of 1.8 mL of titrant added, the analyte was colorless.
B. Yes; at a value of 0.2 mL of titrant added, the analyte was colorless, while at a value of 1.8 mL of titrant added, the analyte was blue.
C. No; at a value of 0.2 mL of titrant added, the analyte was blue, while at a value of 1.8 mL of titrant added, the analyte was colorless.
D. No; at a value of 0.2 mL of titrant added, the analyte was colorless, while at a value of 1.8 mL of titrant added, the analyte was blue.

ANSWERS

Passage I
1. C
2. G
3. C
4. H
5. D
6. G

Passage II
7. B
8. G
9. A
10. G
11. C

Passage III
12. J
13. D
14. J
15. B
16. J
17. D

Passage IV
18. J
19. D
20. G
21. A
22. G

Passage V
23. B
24. G
25. A
26. F
27. D
28. H
29. C

Passage VI
30. G
31. B
32. H
33. A
34. J
35. D

Passage VII
36. F
37. D
38. J
39. C
40. G
41. C

EXPLANATIONS

Passage I

1. **C** In Figure 1, all four anions follow the same trend, so eliminate choices (B) and (D) immediately. From left to right in the graph, the concentration of condensation nuclei is increasing for all four anions, and as this value increases, the average number of tracks decreases for all four anions. Only choice (C) accurately reflects this trend.

2. **G** The first paragraph states the following: *protons and electrons act as condensation nuclei that get ionized by alcohol vapor inside the chamber to form a high-energy mist. When this mist acquires enough energy, it forms tracks that travel through the chamber.* Since tracks form the last part of the process, it can be inferred that they are made from the other two parts, and therefore the largest of the three. Only choice (G) offers an answer choice that correctly places tracks as the largest of the three components.

3. **C** Notice from the answer choices that this question has two components: time to maximum magnetic force and maximum magnetic force itself. Notice also that all the answer choices focus on the *ethanol vapor*. According to Figure 2, the ethanol vapor took about 40 minutes to reach its maximum magnetic field where the water vapor took only about 15 minutes. Therefore, the ethanol vapor took more time, eliminating choices (B) and (D). The ethanol vapor reached a maximum magnetic field of approximately 4.25 Newtons, where the water vapor reached a maximum magnetic field of approximately 4.75 Newtons. Therefore, the ethanol vapor's magnetic field reached a lesser maximum strength, eliminating choice (A) and making choice (C) the correct answer.

4. **H** Note the axes on each of the graphs. "Magnetic field" appears only in Study 2, which eliminates choices (G) and (J) immediately. Then, since magnetic field is the primary focus of Study 2, eliminate choice (F) because it contains no mention of magnetic field. Only choice (H) remains and contains accurate information regarding both studies.

5. **D** This requires a bit of logical thinking and some outside knowledge. Only Study 2 is concerned with *water vapor*, whereas the general introduction discusses *alcohol vapor*. Therefore, it can be inferred that the entire experiment deals with *alcohol vapor*, making changes in water vapor only partially relevant, eliminating choices (A) and (C). Then, between the two answer choices, which is more likely to be the case at temperatures *below* –150°C? Alcohol in this temperature range is colder and therefore more likely to be solid than vapor. Only choice (D) reflects this information correctly.

6. **G** According to Table 1, 75–80% of all four types of anions fit in to the 0.1–0.5 category, or the "smallest charge category." There are no exceptions in Table 1, so the only answer choice that can work is choice (G).

Passage II

7. **B**   Figure 2 only gives the information up to 10 g of gas added, but fortunately, all these curves have a very consistent relationship: As mass of gas goes up, the pressure goes up. In the 4 L vessel, when 10 g of Xe is added, the pressure is approximately 300 mmHg. At 12 g of Xe, the pressure should be slightly higher, somewhere around 450 mmHg. Only choice (B) gives a range that contains this value.

8. **G**   As you compare Figures 1 and 2, notice how much higher the pressure values are in Figure 1. It can therefore be assumed that the 2 L vessel has higher pressure values than the 4 L vessel, shown in Figure 2. The pressure values in a 3 L vessel should therefore be greater than those of the 4 L vessel but less than those of the 2 L vessel. In the 2 L vessel, 10 g of NO_2 gives a pressure of approximately 2000 mmHg. In the 4 L vessel, 10 g of NO_2 gives a pressure of approximately 1000 mmHg. Therefore, in a 3 L vessel, 10 g of NO_2 should give a pressure between 1000 and 2000 mmHg, as in choice (G).

9. **A**   There's a new value in this problem, but as Step 5 of the introduction indicates, *298 K* is merely the temperature at which the mass and pressure were recorded. It is therefore already implied in Figures 1 and 2, so you don't have to worry about it. Since we need to compare the N_2 values from Figures 1 and 2, it's best to find values as exact as possible. Notice that at mass 6 g, the 2 L vessel has a pressure of 2000 mmHg, and the 4 L vessel has a pressure of 1000 mmHg. Therefore, the pressure in the 4 L vessel is *half as great as* the pressure in the 2 L vessel. Only choice (A) works.

10. **G**   Use POE. In Figures 1 and 2, the pressure when N_2 is used is consistently greater than the pressure when the NO_2 is used. Eliminate choices (H) and (J). Then, you'll need a bit of outside knowledge to complete the question. Simply stated, an N_2 molecule has fewer components than an NO_2 molecule, so it has a smaller mass. Therefore, in order to get the same mass of both molecules, we will need more N_2 molecules per gram, eliminating choice (F).

11. **C**   This question requires a bit of outside knowledge. You need to know the relationship between pressure and temperature: As pressure increases, so does temperature. This is a *direct* relationship, eliminating choices (B) and (D). Because of this relationship, as the temperature decreases from 298 K to 287 K, the pressure will decrease also, as in choice (C).

Passage III

12. **J** Use POE. If you're not sure whether to answer "Yes" or "No," check the reasons. According to Table 1, Strain D can grow in the presence of Glu, Amp, and Kan. Eliminate choice (G), which states that Strain D cannot grow in the presence of Kan. Also according to Table 1, Strain D cannot grow in the presence of Pen or Tet. Eliminate choices (F) and (H), which suggest that Strain D can grow in the presence of Tet. Only choice (J) remains.

13. **D** The question says that you only need Figure 2, but the presence of Strain A at the top of the figure links the figure back to Figure 1. According to Figure 1, Strain A can grow in the presence of Glu, Amp, and Pen. It cannot grow in the presence of Kan or Tet. It can be inferred that if a colony *can* grow in the presence of one of these substances, the colony pictured will have a larger white region. Therefore, the colonies that have received a "plasmid containing resistance to tetracycline" should have a smaller white region in the "Tet" column. Colonies X and Y have this small white region, making choice (D) the best answer.

14. **J** According to Table 1, Strains A, B, C, and E were able to grow in the presence of penicillin, or "+Pen." Choice (J) gives the correct number.

15. **B** According to Figure 1, Strain A can grow in the presence of Glu, Amp, and Pen. It cannot grow in the presence of Kan or Tet. It can be inferred that if a colony *can* grow in the presence of one of these substances, the colony pictured will have a larger white region. Therefore, the colonies that have received a plasmid "with resistance genes to ampicillin and tetracycline" should have a smaller white region in the Amp and Tet columns. Only Strain Y shows a resistance to *both* substances, making choice (B) the only acceptable answer.

16. **J** This question requires a bit of outside knowledge about why scientists do what they do when setting up experiments. Use POE and common sense. Notice choices (F), (G), and (H) all contain mention of substances that are "lab generated." Only choice (J) contains mention of strains that are "not lab generated." Think about it this way: Scientists are trying to control the environment of their experiment, so they don't want things from outside (things that are "not lab generated") to contaminate the things in the experiment. Also, notice that choices (H) and (J) are direct opposites, a good indication that one of them will be correct.

17. **D** According to Figure 1, Strain A can grow in the presence of Glu, Amp, and Pen. It cannot grow in the presence of Kan or Tet. It can be inferred that if a colony *can* grow in the presence of one of these substances, the colony pictured will have a larger white region. None of the strains in Figure 2 have this large white region under "Pen+," suggesting that none of them are able to grow in the presence of penicillin, making choice (D) the correct answer. Also, notice that all the colonies in the "Pen+" column look the same. Therefore, they're clearly not acting any differently from one another in the presence of this substance, so the only possible answer is (D).

Passage IV

18. **J**   The first line of the passage states the following: The absolute threshold pressure for hearing is the minimum air pressure at each audio frequency that can produce a sound that is detectable by the human ear. In other words, the absolute threshold pressure for hearing gives the highest pressure and frequency at which humans can hear. In order to answer this question, we'll need to use Figure 1 and the curve labeled "Absolute pressure threshold for hearing," and we will need to find its maximum frequency, listed on the x-axis. According to Figure 1, this curve maxes out right around 1×10^3 cyc/sec, or 1000 cyc/sec, as in choice (J). If you selected choice (H) be careful, this is the point of minimum Sound Pressure Level, not the maximum frequency.

19. **D**   Use POE. Note the key at the bottom of Figure 1. According to this key, "Water" is shown on the graph with a solid line, and "Air" is shown on the graph with a dotted line. The solid line is consistently higher than the dotted, suggesting that "Water" can withstand higher frequencies, eliminating choices (A) and (B). Then, note the P-values on the right side of the graph. According to the graph, these P-values increase with increasing sound pressure level, so in order to increase the sound pressure level, we will want the highest possible P-value, which in the list of remaining answer choices is 10^{-1}%, as in choice (D).

20. **G**   Use POE. According to this question, some change happens at high frequencies. Accordingly, whichever graph we choose will need to show a change at high frequency, rather than low frequency. Based on this information alone, we can eliminate choices (F) and (H). Then, the dotted curve ("After hearing loss") should indicate some kind of hearing *loss* at high frequencies, so it should show a curve that does not quite reach the highest frequencies, as only choice (G) does. If you selected choice (J), you may have reversed the two curves.

21. **A**   The frequency of 10^4 cyc/sec doesn't appear on the graph, but according to Figure 1, the absolute threshold of hearing is around 10^3 cyc/sec. The pain threshold of hearing is within the absolute threshold, so if 10^4 cyc/sec isn't within the absolute threshold, it won't be within the pain threshold either. Think of it this way: In order for something to hurt when you hear it, you need to be able to hear it first. Therefore, only choice (A) can work because it is the only answer choice with a reason consistent with the information in Figure 1.

22. **G**   Use POE. If you're unsure whether to answer "Yes" or "No," check the reasons. Use Figure 1. Frequency appears on the x-axis, and Pressure appears on the y-axis. According to the lines showing the pressure "in Air" and "in Water," the increasing frequency has no effect on the pressure values. Eliminate choices (F) and (H). Therefore, the pressure does *not* depend on the frequency, making choice (G) the correct answer.

Passage V

23. **B** According to Table 1, potassium hydroxide produced 2 ions, had a molar mass of 56.11 g/mol, and had a $\Delta H°_{diss}$ of –57.6 kJ/mol. Magnesium sulfate produced 2 ions, had a molar mass of 120.38 g/mol, and had a $\Delta H°_{diss}$ of –91.0 kJ/mol. Use POE. Student 1 writes, *The solution containing Salt B had a higher boiling point because Salt B produces more ions in solution than Salt A.* These findings do not agree with Table 1 for the given substances, which produced the same number of ions. Eliminate choice (C). Student 2 writes, *The solution containing Salt B had a higher boiling point because it had a lower molar mass (the mass of 6.02×10^{23} particles).* "Salt B" in this question is magnesium sulfate, which does not have a lower molar mass than potassium hydroxide, so you can eliminate choices (A) and (D). This leaves only choice (B), and the findings in the table do agree with Student 3's hypothesis.

24. **G** The passage gives the following information: The boiling temperature for the solution of Salt A was measured to be 104°C. The procedure was repeated with Salt B, which resulted in a boiling temperature of 110°C. According to this question, ammonium nitrate has a boiling point of 107°C, right between Salts A and B. According to Student 2, the solution containing Salt B had a higher boiling point because it had a lower molar mass. Therefore, because ammonium nitrate has a higher boiling point than Salt A, it must have a lower molar mass. Only choice (G) can work. Choices (H) and (J) can be eliminated because Student 2 does not discuss enthalpy change.

25. **A** According to Student 2, *the salt with the lower molar mass will result in more particles.* In other words, the lower the molar mass of a substance the more particles it will produce. According to Table 1, sodium chloride has a molar mass of 58.4 g/mol, potassium hydroxide has a molar mass of 56.11 g/mol, and magnesium sulfate has a molar mass of 120.38 g/mol. Since potassium hydroxide has the lowest molar mass, it should produce the *most* particles. With this information alone, you can eliminate choices (B), (C), and (D). Only choice (A) remains and puts the substances in the correct relation to one another.

26. **F** The passage states, the mixture was heated and temperature readings acquired every 30 sec until the solution reached a full boil and the solid had completely dissolved. Since the mixture is only heated, it can be inferred that its temperature increases only. There's no indication that the substance is ever cooled, so choice (F) is the only answer supported by information from the passage.

27. **D** Student 3 offers the following hypothesis: The solution containing the salt with the more negative $\Delta H°_{diss}$ value will release more heat and thus result in a greater boiling point. According to Table 1, magnesium sulfate has the most negative $\Delta H°_{diss}$ value at –91.0 kJ/mol. Therefore, according to student 3, this substance should have the greatest boiling point of the substances listed.

28. **H**   Compare the new values given in the question to those for calcium chloride given in Table 1. Cesium hydroxide produces 2 ions, where calcium chloride produces 3. Student 1 writes, *The solution containing Salt B had a higher boiling point because Salt B produces more ions in solution than Salt A.* According to this hypothesis, calcium chloride produces more ions, so it should have a higher boiling point. The findings therefore support the hypothesis of Student 1, eliminating choices (G) and (J). Cesium hydroxide has a molar mass 149.91 g/mol, where calcium chloride has a molar mass of 111.0 g/mol. Student 2 writes, *The solution containing Salt B had a higher boiling point because it had a lower molar mass (the mass of 6.02×10^{23} particles).* According to this hypothesis, calcium chloride has a lower molar mass, so it should have a higher boiling point. The findings therefore support the hypothesis of Student 2, eliminating choice (F). There's no need to test the findings against Student 3's hypothesis: The only option left is choice (H).

29. **C**   According to Student 2, the salt with the lower molar mass will result in more particles and a greater solution boiling point than a salt with a greater molar mass. Student 2 is not concerned with "enthalpy change," so you can eliminate choices (B) and (D) immediately. According to Table 1, sodium chloride has a molar mass of 58.4 g/mol and ammonium nitrate has a molar mass of 80.1 g/mol. Therefore, because sodium chloride has a smaller molar mass it should have a greater boiling point, as suggested in choice (C).

Passage VI

30. **G**   According to Figure 3, the marine deposition of Mg^{2+} is highest in February and lowest in November, making choice (G) the correct answer. The marine deposition of Cl^- is highest in June and lowest in October, eliminating choice (F). The marine deposition of Na^+ is highest in November and lowest in July, eliminating choice (H). The marine deposition of SO_4^{2-} is highest in January and lowest in October, eliminating choice (J).

31. **B**   Look carefully at Figure 2. The marine deposition of Cl^- is around 950 kg/m³ except in June, at which point it is much higher. Because it has only this single outlier, we can reasonably expect that the *mean*, or *average*, monthly deposition will be closer to 950, as choice (B) suggests.

32. **H**   This question is difficult to answer "Yes" or "No" immediately, so work with the reasons given in each of the answer choices. Use Figure 3 to check these reasons. According to Figure 3, the monthly deposition of Na^+ is highest in the winter months and lowest in the summer months. We can therefore eliminate choices (G) and (J), which give information that contradicts Figure 3. This information then *supports* the statement in the problem that the *marine deposition of Na⁺ is highest in the winter and lowest in the summer*, thus making choice (H) the correct answer.

33. **A**   The introduction to the passage gives the following information: *Ions in seawater, such as Cl⁻, SO₄²⁻, Na⁺, and Mg₂⁺, are carried down ocean floor through a process known as* marine deposition. Therefore, in order for there to be *marine deposition*, ions must be *carried down* somewhere. If the water does not move during an entire month, then the ions will not move and no marine deposition will occur doing this month.

34. **J** Make sure you pay careful attention to the key in Figure 4. According to Figure 4, the annual marine depositions of both ions were lower in the Arctic Ocean, the site farthest from the Atlantic Ocean. The annual marine depositions of both ions increase as the sensor gets closer to the Atlantic Ocean site.

35. **D** According to Figure 3, the marine deposition of SO_4^{2-} was not studied, eliminating choice (A). The marine deposition of Mg^{2+} changed during the study, eliminate choice (B). According to Figure 1, the movement of water during the month changed every month during the twelve-month period, eliminating choice (C). Only the location of the study, the Atlantic Ocean, was held constant, making choice (D) the correct answer. The location of the study was not changed until Study 3.

Passage VII

36. **F** Use Figure 1. The key in the corner of the graph says that the anything graphed with a solid line is *blue* and anything graphed with a dotted line is *colorless*. The curve shown in this graph changes from solid to dotted at 1 mL of titrite added, meaning that all the solution at all values less than 1 mL will be blue and the solution at all values greater than 1 mL will be colorless. The only one of the answer choices that gives a value less than 1 mL is choice (F).

37. **D** The blurb contains the following sentence: Starch and I_2 form a complex with a deep blue color, but when I_2 is reduced to 2 iodide (I^-) ions, the complex dissipates and the solution becomes colorless. In other words, when the solution is reduced, it becomes colorless. According to Figure 2, the solution is colorless (and therefore reduced) above 1 mL of titrite added. Only choice (D) gives a value greater than 1 mL.

38. **J** Figure 2 does not show the voltage at 2.5 mL of titrite added, but the curve follows a clear trend. As the volume of titrant added increases, the voltage increases as well. At 2 mL of titrite added, the voltage is equivalent to 7 kV. Therefore, at 2.5 mL of titrant added, the voltage will most likely be greater than 7 kV, as in choice (J).

39. **C** The experiment detailed in this passage is described in the first line as follows: Oxidation-reduction titration is a method in which precise volumes of a titrant (an oxidizing or reducing agent) are added dropwise to a known volume of an analyte (a reducing or oxidizing agent, respectively). In other words, one substance (the titrant) is added gradually to a certain amount of another substance (the analyte). Therefore, when Experiment 1 says that the I_2 solution was incrementally added to the SO_2 solution, it can be inferred that the I_2 is the titrant and the SO_2 is the analyte. In Experiment 2, the sodium thiosulfate solution was used instead of the SO_2 solution; therefore, in Experiment 2, the I_2 is still the titrant, and the sodium thiosulfate solution is the analyte, as in choice (C). If you picked choice (D), be careful—you may not have noticed the change from Experiment 1 to Experiment 2.

40. **G**   Use POE. Experiment 1 contains the following information: *A potentiometer, which acts as a control input for electronic circuits, was placed in the solution.* The key word here is *electric currents*. There's nothing to suggest that the potentiometer has anything to do with *concentration*, eliminating choice (F), or *freezing* or *boiling point*, eliminating choices (H) and (J). Only choice (G) contains any reference to *electric currents* and is therefore the best answer.

41. **C**   Use POE. If you're not sure how to answer "Yes" or "No," have a look at the reasons. According to the blurb, starch and I_2 form a complex with a deep blue color, but when I_2 is reduced to 2 iodide (I^-) ions, the complex dissipates and the solution becomes colorless. In other words, when the solution is reduced, it becomes colorless. At 0.2 mL of titrant added, the solution is blue, and at 1.8 mL of titrant added, the solution is colorless. Eliminate choices (B) and (D), whose reasons contradict this information. Then, answer the question: Do these findings agree with the scientist's hypothesis? They don't, because the titrant is not reduced at values below 1 mL, so the answer must be "No," eliminating choice (A). Only choice (C) remains.

Math for the ACT

In some ways, the Math test of the ACT is the content-heaviest of all the tests: In other words, there are many problems on the Math that test concepts similar to those you've learned in your Math classes. In fact, ACT makes a big deal about how "curricular" the exam is, claiming that the Math test is "designed to assess the mathematical skills students have typically acquired in courses taken up to the beginning of grade 12." They even go so far as to offer a list of how the topics will break down in any given administration.

Topic	Number of Questions
Pre-algebra	14
Elementary Algebra	10
Intermediate Algebra	9
Plane Geometry	14
Coordinate Geometry	9
Trigonometry	4

But as with all things ACT, these distinctions may not mean a ton to you, the test-taker. Nor should they. At best, this chart should help to drive home one main point:

The ACT Math test is in Order of Difficulty. Keep an eye on the question numbers!

> The Math test of the ACT is roughly half Algebra and half Geometry.

Algebra on the ACT

So you've got roughly 33 algebra questions to tackle on any given Math test. It's probably a good idea to comb the test looking for those 14 pre-algebra questions first, and then to track down the 10 elementary-algebra questions, and then to go back and look for the intermediate-algebra questions, right? No way! That would be a tremendous waste of time, and even a nearly impossible task—what are the distinctions among these three categories anyway?

For our money, it's best to think of Algebra problems (and really all Math problems) as broken down into two categories: *Plug-and-Chug* and *Word Problems*. Many of the Math skills you use in these problems will be the same, but each will require a slightly different approach, for the obvious reason that Word Problems require that you deal with, well, words.

But let's start with a nice, straightforward, "Plug and Chug" problem:

MADSPM
(Multiply/Add, Divide/Subtract, Power/Multiply)

When you *multiply* two bases, you *add* their exponents.

$$e.g., \ x^2 \times x^3 = x^5$$

When you *divide* two bases, you *subtract* their exponents.

$$e.g., \ \frac{x^5}{x^3} = x^2$$

When you raise a base to a *power*, you *multiply* the exponents.

$$e.g, \ \left(x^2\right)^3 = x^6$$

25. The expression $-4y^2\left(9y^7 - 3y^5\right)$ is equivalent to:

   A. $-36y^9 + 12y^7$

   B. $-36y^9 - 12y^7$

   C. $-36y^{14} + 12y^{10}$

   D. $-36y^{14} - 12y^{10}$

   E. $-24y^4$

Here's How To Crack It

Sure, there are words in this problem, but all it's really asking you to do is to match up the expression in the question with one of the expressions in the answer choices. Remember to distribute and use MADSPM.

Let's see how this works with the equation given in question 25.

$$-4y^2(9y^7 - 3y^5) = y^2(-36y^7 + 12y^5)$$
$$= -36y^9 + 12y^7$$

This matches up with choice (A). If you worked through this problem and got one of the other answer choices, think about what you may have done wrong. If you chose (B), you may have forgotten to distribute the negative sign when you multiplied the −4. If you chose (C), you may have multiplied the exponents rather than adding them together. If you chose (D), you may have multiplied the exponents and forgotten to distribute the negative. If you chose (E), you may have forgotten that you can only add and subtract exponents when the bases are the same.

Whatever the case may be, don't sell these problems short. Even though they don't take as long, they're worth just as much as the "harder" problems. Recall from the introduction how few questions you really need to pull up your math score. Make sure you work carefully on all your Now and Later questions. There is no partial credit on the ACT, so a careless error leaves you with an answer just as wrong as a random guess.

> Fixing a few careless math errors can improve your ACT Math score significantly by ensuring that you get all the points on questions you know how to do.

Let's have a look at another.

43. $4x^2 + 20x + 24$ is equivalent to:

    A. $(4x+4)(x+6)$
    B. $(4x-4)(x-6)$
    C. $(4x+24)(x-1)$
    D. $2(2x-4)(x-3)$
    E. $2(2x+4)(x+3)$

This one looks a lot like the last one, but the math is a good deal more difficult. In fact, even if you're pretty good at factoring quadratic equations, you might still find this one to be a bit of an issue. If you can do the factoring quickly and accurately, great, but if not, help is on the way!

PLUGGING IN

When you look at the topic breakdown for the ACT, what is it about "Pre-algebra" that sounds so much easier than "Intermediate" or even "Elementary Algebra"? Well, for one thing, with Algebra inevitably come *variables*. You probably remember first hearing about these things in sixth or seventh grade and thinking to yourself how much easier life was when math was just plain numbers.

Here's the good news. Many of the algebra problems on the ACT, even the most complex, can be solved with what we like to call *Plugging In*. What Plugging In enables you to do is to solve difficult variable problems using basic arithmetic.

First, you'll need to identify whether you can Plug In.

Plug In when:

      there are variables in the answer choices.

      there are variables in the question.

      the question is dealing with fractions, percents, or other relational numbers.

Here's How to Crack It

Plugging In works with both Word Problems and Plug and Chug questions. Question 43 may look like it requires a "content-based" approach, but let's see how much easier it is if we Plug In.

First, let's Plug In a number for the variable. The best numbers to Plug In are usually small and easy to deal with: numbers like 2, 5, and 10. Let's try 2 in this problem. If $x = 2$,

$$4(2)^2 + 20(2) + 24 = 4(4) + 20(2) + 24$$
$$= 16 + 40 + 24$$
$$= 56 + 24$$
$$= 80$$

So if we Plug In 2 everywhere there's an x, the expression gives us 80. Now, since the question is merely asking for an equivalent expression, we will want the same result as we plug our value into the answer choices. In this case, 80 is our *target answer*. Let's go to the answer choices and see which one matches up:

43. $4(2)^2 + 20(2) + 24$ is equivalent to $\boxed{80}$.

    A. $(4(2) + 4)((2) + 6) = (12)(8) = 96$
    B. $(4(2) - 4)((2) - 6) = (4)(-4) = -16$
    C. $(4(2) - 24)((2) - 1) = (-16)(1) = -16$
    D. $2(2(2) - 4)((2) - 3) = 2(0)(-1) = 0$
    E. $2(2(2) + 4)((2) + 3) = 2(8)(5) = 80$

The only one that matches up is choice (E), the correct answer. No quadratic formula or difficult factoring required!

Let's review the steps:

> Once you've determined that you can Plug In, follow these steps.
>
> 1. Plug In an easy-to-use value for your variable or variables.
>
> 2. Work the information in the question using the numbers you've Plugged In to find a *target answer*.
>
> 3. Plug the variables into the answer choices to find the one that matches up with the target.
>
> 4. Make sure you check all the answer choices. If more than one answer choice works, plug in a new set of numbers and try again.

Let's try another one.

28. As part of an analysis to determine how summer vacations affect students' retention of school materials, scientists conducted an experiment. As shown in the chart below, they showed the time, d days, since the student had finished and the number of facts, f, that the student remembered from the previous year.

d	1	3	5	7	9
f	96	72	48	24	0

Which of the following equations represents all the data found in this study?

F. $f = 9 - d$

G. $f = 3(9 - d)$

H. $f = 3d + 3$

J. $f = 3(36 - 4d)$

K. $f = 96d$

Here's How to Crack It

This problem looks very different from our last two, but notice that it has some important features in common with them. Most important for our purposes are the variables in the answer choices. With these we know that we can Plug In on this question.

This problem is much bulkier than the last two, though, and in many ways more intimidating. This is because it's a *Word Problem*. As we mentioned earlier in this chapter, even though Word Problems often use the same mathematical concepts, they ask about them in much more convoluted ways. Here's a simple Basic Approach for dealing with Word Problems.

When dealing with Word Problems on the ACT Math test:

1. **Know the question.** Read the whole problem before calculating anything, and underline the actual question.

2. **Let the answers help.** Look for clues on how to solve and ways to use POE (Process of Elimination).

3. **Break the problem into bite-sized pieces.** Watch out for tricky phrasing.

Let's use these steps to solve this problem.

1. **Know the question.** We need to find an equation that can accommodate all of the information in the table for d and f. The question in this problem is below the chart. How much of the other stuff do we need? Not much.
2. **Let the answers help.** Remember how important the answers have been in what we've done so far in this chapter. If there are variables in those answer choices, we can usually Plug In. We have variables in these answer choices, so we'll plan to Plug In here.
3. **Break the problem into bite-sized pieces.** We know we need an equation that will work for all the points in this chart. Let's pick one set of points that will be easy to test, and then a second set to confirm our answers. Go easy on yourself! There's no reason to pick the biggest numbers. Let's try first the point to the far right of the chart: $d = 9$, $f = 0$. We want an equation that will work for these points, so let's try the answers:

$$
\begin{array}{lll}
\textbf{F.} & 0 = 9 - 9 & \checkmark \\
\textbf{G.} & 0 = 3(9 - 9) & \checkmark \\
\textbf{H.} & 0 = 3(9) + 3 & \times \\
\textbf{J.} & 0 = 3(36 - 4(9)) & \checkmark \\
\textbf{K.} & 0 = 96(9) & \times
\end{array}
$$

Okay, we've eliminated two of the answer choices. Now let's try another set of points: $d = 7, f = 24$.

> **F.** $24 = 9 - 7$ ✕
> **G.** $24 = 3(9 - 7)$ ✕
> **H.** $f = 3d + 3$
> **J.** $24 = 3(36 - 4(7))$ ✓
> **K.** $f = 96d$

Only one remains, and our best answer is (J). All using basic arithmetic in the formulas provided.

PLUGGING IN THE ANSWERS

Now, what happens when we don't have the hallmarks of easy Plugging In problems: variables in the answer choices or in the problem? Like question 45:

> **45.** A high-school basketball player has shot 170 free throws and has made 100 of those free throws. Starting now, if she makes each free throw she attempts, what is the least number of free throws she must attempt in order to raise her free-throw percentage to at least 70% ?
>
> **A.** 19
> **B.** 20
> **C.** 63
> **D.** 64
> **E.** 70

In this problem, there are no variables anywhere to be seen. Still, we're going to need to put together some kind of equation or something that will enable us to answer the question. For this one, we can *Plug in the Answers* (PITA).

PITA when:

the question asks for a specific amount. Look for "How many?" or "How much?" or "What is the value of?"

there are no variables in the answer choices.

Question 45 is a Word Problem, so let's go through the steps:

1. **Know the question.** We need to figure out how many additional free throws this player will need to have a free-throw percentage of 70%. Also, when ACT italicizes or capitalizes a word, pay special attention. In this case, they've italicized the word *least*. Keep this in mind, it tells you that a number of the answer choices may work, but the correct will be the *least* of these. The phrase "What is the least number?" is the kind of very specific question that usually makes for a good PITA problem.

2. **Let the answers help.** There are no variables in these answer choices, and that coupled with the fact that it asks for a specific value is a good indication that we'll be using these answer choices to PITA. Notice the answer choices are listed in ascending order, which means it might be smart to start with the middle choice. That way we can eliminate answers that are too high or too low.

3. **Break the problem into bite-sized pieces.** With many PITA problems, it can help to create columns building on the information given in the answer choices and the problem. Start with the question that's being asked: You've already got five possible answers to that question.

45. A high-school basketball player has shot 170 free throws and has made 100 of those free throws. Starting now, if she makes each free throw she attempts, <u>what is the least number of free throws she must attempt in order to raise her free-throw percentage to at least 70% ?</u>

Free-throws	Total free-throws	Total completed	Percentage free-throws
A. 19			
B. 20			
C. 63	233	163	69.9%
D. 64			
E. 70			

Here's How To Crack It

As choice (C) has shown, 63 additional free throws only raises the percentage to 69.9%. We know this is wrong because we want to raise it to 70%. Therefore, since choice (C) gives a value that is too small, choices (A) and (B) must be too small as well. Let's try choice (D).

Our best answer here is choice (D), because it produces a free-throw percentage of 70.1%. Choice (E) will produce a percentage greater than 70% as well, but remember, this question is asking for the *least*.

45. A high-school basketball player has shot 170 free throws and has made 100 of those free throws. Starting now, if she makes each free throw she attempts, <u>what is the least number of free throws she must attempt in order to raise her free-throw percentage to at least 70% ?</u>

Free-throws	Total free-throws	Total completed	Percentage free-throws
A. ~~19~~	189	89	47.1
B. ~~20~~	190	90	47.4%
C. ~~63~~	233	163	69.9%
D. 64	234	164	70.1%
E. 70			

Let's review what we've learned about this type of question so far.

When you've identified a problem as a PITA problem:

Start with the middle answer choice. This can help with POE (process of elimination).

Label your answer choices—they answer the question you underlined in the problem.

When you find the correct answer, stop! But make sure you're answering the right question.

Make sure you account for all the relevant information. PITA is most effective in simplifying difficult Word Problems, but make sure you've got everything you need!

Let's try another problem.

18. The product of two distinct integers is 192. If the sum of those same two integers is 28, what is the value of the larger of the two integers?

F. 18
G. 16
H. 12
J. 10
K. 8

Here's How to Crack It

Let's go through the steps.

1. Know the question. "What is the value of the larger of the two integers?" The key word here is *larger*. The numbers in the answer choices will be possibilities for this *larger* value. Notice this is asking for a specific value, which means we can PITA.
2. Let the answers help. We've got a list of non-variable answers in ascending order. Each one offers a possible answer to the specific question posed in the problem. Let's PITA, and use the answers to work backwards through the problem.
3. Break the problem into bite-sized pieces. Even though this is a short problem, there's a lot of information here, so we should use columns to help us keep all the information straight. The problem says that the *sum* of the two integers is 28, so let's start there. Begin with answer choice (C) to help with Process of Elimination.

---

18. The product of two distinct integers is 192. If the sum of those same two integers is 28, <u>what is the value of the larger of the two integers?</u>

Larger integer	Smaller integer	(Larger Smaller) = 192?
F. 18		
G. 16		
H. 12	16	CAN'T WORK
J. 10		
K. 8		

We can eliminate choice (H) right off the bat. Just from what we've found, 12 can't be the *larger* integer if 16 is the *smaller* integer. We will therefore need a number larger than 12, so we can eliminate choices (J) and (K) as well. Let's try choice (G).

---

18. The product of two distinct integers is 192. If the sum of those same two integers is 28, <u>what is the value of the larger of the two integers?</u>

Larger integer	Smaller integer	(Larger Smaller) = 192?
F. 18		
G. 16	12	16 × 12 = 192 Yes!
~~**H.** 12~~	~~16~~	~~CAN'T WORK~~
~~**J.** 10~~		
~~**K.** 8~~		

Choice (G) works, so we can stop there. Notice how PITA and Plugging In have enabled us to do these problems quickly and accurately without getting bogged down in generating difficult algebraic formulas.

A NOTE ON PLUGGING IN AND PITA

Plugging In and PITA are not the only ways to solve these problems, and it may feel weird using these methods instead of trying to do these problems "the real way." You may have even found that you knew how to work with the variables in Plugging In problems or how to write the appropriate equations for the PITA problems. If you can do either of those things, you're already on your way to a great Math score.

But think about it this way. We've already said that ACT doesn't give any partial credit. So do you think doing it "the real way" gets you any extra points? It doesn't: On the ACT, a right answer is a right answer, no matter how you get it. "The real way" is great, but unfortunately, it's often a lot more complex and offers a lot more opportunities to make careless errors.

The biggest problem with doing things the real way, though, is that it essentially requires that you invent a new approach for every problem. Instead, notice what we've given you here: two strategies that will work toward getting you the right answer on any number of questions. You may have heard the saying, "Give a man a fish and you've fed him for a day, but teach a man to fish and you've fed him for a lifetime." Now, don't worry, our delusions of grandeur are not quite so extreme, but Plugging In and PITA are useful in a similar way. Rather than giving you a detailed description of how to create formulas and work through them for these problems that won't themselves ever appear on an ACT again, we're giving you a strategy that will help you to work through any number of similar problems in future ACTs.

Try these strategies on your own in the drill that concludes this chapter.

PLUGGING IN DRILL

2. If $\dfrac{3n}{4} - 7 = 2$, then $n =$

   F.   −9

   G. $-\dfrac{7}{3}$

   H. $\dfrac{7}{3}$

   J.   9

   K. 12

3. If $f(a) = \dfrac{a^2 - 24}{a + 8}$, what is the value of $f(12)$?

   A.   6
   B.   8
   C. 12
   D. 20
   E. 120

4. $-x^3 + 24x + 75 + 34x^3 - 36x$ is equivalent to:

   F. $99x$
   G. $-35x^3$
   H. $24x + 75$
   J. $33x^3 - 12x + 75$
   K. $35x^3 + 12x + 75$

11. If b is a positive integer greater than 1, what is the smallest integer value of a for which there exists a value of b such that $\sqrt{a} - b^2 > 0$?

   A.   5
   B. 16
   C. 25
   D. 36
   E. 49

13. Which of the following expressions is equivalent to $n^3 - n^2$?

   A. $n^2(n + 1)$
   B. $n(n - 1)$
   C. $n^2(n - 1)$
   D. n
   E. $n(n^2 - 1)$

18. Amethyst's route to work is 48 miles long. Along the way, she stops for coffee and notices that the ratio of the number of miles she's driven so far to the number of miles left to go is 3:1. How many miles does she have left to drive?

   F.   6
   G. 12
   H. 24
   J. 30
   K. 36

22. If $a + b = 42$ and $a - b = 16$, what is the value of b ?

   F.   8
   G. 13
   H. 24
   J. 29
   H. 58

24. A salesman earns \$600 per week in base salary. For each successful sale, he receives \$125 in commission. Which of the following represents the amount of money, in dollars, the salesman earns in a given week in which he makes s successful sales?

   F. $725s$
   G. $125s - 600$
   H. $600s + 125$
   J. $600 - 125s$
   K. $600 + 125s$

27. The expression $(n^2 - 6n + 5)(n + 4)$ is equivalent to:

   A. $n^3 - 2n^2 - 19n + 20$
   B. $n^3 - n^2 + 9n + 20$
   C. $n^3 - 2n^2 - 7n + 20$
   D. $n^3 + 2n^2 - 24n + 20$
   E. $n^3 - 2n^2 - 29n + 20$

28. If $|n - 6| = 17$, what are the possible values of n ?

   F.   −23 and 11
   G. −23 and 23
   H. −11 and 23
   J. −11 and 11
   K.   28 only

31. If the area of a circle is 36π inches, what is the diameter of the circle, in inches?

A. 4
B. 6
C. 12
D. 18
E. 36

32. If $f(a) = a^2 + 3$ and $g(a) = 3a - 1$, which of the following is an expression for $g(f(a))$?

F. $a^2 + 3a + 2$
G. $3a^2 - 3$
H. $-a^2 + 3a - 2$
J. $3a^2 + 9a - 3$
K. $3a^2 + 8$

40. In a professional sports league consisting of x teams, y represents the number of teams that qualify for the playoffs in a given season. Which of the following could be used to determine the fraction of teams that does NOT make the playoffs in a given season?

F. $\dfrac{x-y}{x}$

G. $\dfrac{y-x}{x}$

H. $\dfrac{y}{x}$

J. $\dfrac{x-y}{y}$

K. $\dfrac{x+y}{x}$

41. If n is an integer, which of the following is a factor of the sum of $5n$ and $12n$?

A. 5
B. 12
C. 17
D. 34
E. 60

45. Which of the following gives the solution set for $\sqrt[3]{(n^2 - 6n)} = 3$?

A. $\{3\}$
B. $\{2 \pm \sqrt{3}\}$
C. $\{-3, 9\}$
D. $\{3, -9\}$
E. $\{27\}$

46. If $x > y$, then $-|y - x|$ is equivalent to which of the following?

F. $\sqrt{y - x}$
G. $x - y$
H. $|y - x|$
J. $-(x - y)$
K. $|x - y|$

48. If x is a negative integer, which of the following must be a positive integer?

F. 0^x
G. x^0
H. $x + 4$
J. $-x^4$
K. x^x

49. If n is a real number, what is the solution of the equation $9^{1-n} = 3^{1+n}$?

A. $-\dfrac{2}{3}$

B. $-\dfrac{1}{3}$

C. $\dfrac{1}{3}$

D. $\dfrac{1}{2}$

E. $\dfrac{4}{3}$

55. Which of the following is an irrational value of n that is a solution to the equation $|n^2 - 30| - 6 = 0$?

A. $\sqrt{6}$
B. 6
C. $2\sqrt{6}$
D. $3\sqrt{6}$
E. $4\sqrt{6}$

59. Consider all pairs of positive integers a and b whose sum is 6. For how many values of a does $a^b = b^a$?

A. None
B. 1
C. 2
D. 3
E. 6

ANSWERS

2. K
3. A
4. J
11. C
13. C
18. G
22. G
24. K
27. A
28. H
31. C
32. K
40. F
41. C
45. C
46. J
48. G
49. C
55. C
59. D

EXPLANATIONS

2. **K**   Plug In the Answers on this one. No harm in starting with the middle answer choice, but if you want this problem to be as easy as possible (and it is question 2, so it should be relatively easy), you might try the whole numbers in the answers first. With choice (J), it means that $\frac{3(9)}{4} - 2 = 7$. Since $\frac{3(9)}{4} = 6.75$, you can eliminate it. Try choice (K): $\frac{3(12)}{4} - 2 = 7$. $\frac{3(12)}{4} = 9$, and $9 - 2 = 7$, so you've found your answer.

3. **A**   Here, ACT is telling you what to Plug In: When you see a function and you're given a number inside the parentheses, Plug In that number everywhere in the function that you see the variable. So, $f(12) = \frac{12^2 - 24}{12 + 8}$. That results in $\frac{120}{20}$, which means the answer is 6.

4. **J**   While algebra works on this one, the safest bet is to Plug In. Since there are exponents, pick a small number, like 2. $-2^3 + 24(2) + 75 + 34(2)^3 - 36(2)$. This simplifies to $-8 + 48 + 75 + 272 - 72$. When you combine all those numbers, you get a target answer of 331. When you go to the answer choices, look for that same number. In choice (J), you have $33(2)^3 - 12(2) + 75$. Since $264 - 12 + 75 = 331$, you have your answer.

11. **C**   This is a tricky and confusing problem made simple by Plugging In the Answers. Since the problem asks for the smallest possible value of a, start with the smallest answer choice. Work your way up to 25, and the problem reads $\sqrt{25} - b^2 > 0$. The question becomes, "Is there a value of b (remember, b must be an integer greater than 1) that makes that equation true?" Sure there is: If $b = 2$, then $5 - 4 > 0$.

13. **C**   Plug In your own number since you see variables in the answers. If $x = 3$, then the expression is $3^3 - 3^2 = 27 - 9$; your target answer is 18. Plugging in $x = 3$, the only answer choice that matches the target is choice (C): $3^2(3-1) = 9(2) = 18$.

18. **G**   Note that the problem is asking for the number of miles left to go. Plug In the Answers starting with choice (H). If she has 24 miles left, then she's halfway there—that's not far enough along, so eliminate choice (H) and any answer with higher mileage. Plug in choice (G). If she's got 12 miles left to go, that means $48 - 12 = 36$, meaning she's driven 36 miles so far. Since the ratio of 36:12 is 3:1, this is your answer.

22. **G**   Plug In the Answers starting with choice (H). You'll know you've found the answer when you get the same value for a in both equations. This works with choice (G): If $a + 13 = 42$, then $a = 29$, and if $a - 13 = 16$, then $a = 29$.

24. **K** Plug In a small number for the number of sales he's completed so the math is as easy as possible. If he completed 2 sales, then he's made $250 commission to go with his $600 base salary, for total earnings of $850. Choice (K) gets you the same value.

27. **A** Play it safe and Plug In 2. $(2^2 - 6(2) + 5)(2 + 4)$ means $(4 - 12 + 5)(6)$, which gives you -18 as a target answer. Choice (A) will read $2^3 - 2(2)^2 - 19(2) + 20$. Simplified, $8 - 8 - 38 + 20 = -18$.

28. **H** When the absolute value of an expression is equal to a number, you can set up two separate equations, one equal to the positive value and one equal to its negative equivalent. In this case, $n - 6 = 17$ and $n - 6 = -17$. Plug In each pair of numbers in the answer choices. In choice (H), $23 - 6 = 17$ and $-11 - 6 = -17$.

31. **C** Plug in the circle's area into the area formula: $r^2 = 36$ to determine the radius is 6. The question asks for the diameter, which is twice the radius, so the answer is choice (C). Be careful not to pick choice (B), which is a partial answer.

32. **K** When you have one function inside another, start with the one on the inside and work your way out. And of course...Plug In! So Plug In 2, and start with $f(2) = 2^2 + 3$. That means $f(2) = 7$. That's now the value you can Plug In to the other function. $g(7) = 3(7) - 1$, so your target answer is 20. Plug 2 into the answer choices, and choice (K) will read $3(2)^2 + 8$, which is 20.

40. **F** Plug In values for the number of teams in the league and the number of teams that qualify for the playoffs. Say there are 15 teams in the league (represented by x) and 8 of them qualify (represented by y). That leaves 7 for the number of teams that do not qualify, which means that your target answer is $\frac{7}{15}$. Choice (F) becomes $\frac{15-8}{15}$, or $\frac{7}{15}$.

41. **C** Here, you may need to Plug In multiple times. Make $n = 2$, and the sum of $12(2)$ and $5(2)$ is 34. Both choices (C) and (D) work. But make $n = 1$, and the sum of $12(1)$ and $5(1)$ is 17, eliminating choice (D).

45. **C** To make things a little easier, you can cube both sides to get rid of the radical. The right side of the equation is now 27. Now, Plug In the Answers and see which one works. In choice (C), $(-3)^2 - 6(-3) = 9 - (-18) = 27$, and $(9)^2 - 6(9) = 81 - 54 = 27$.

46. **J** Plug In anything you want as long as $x > y$, such as $x = 3$ and $y = 2$. In the original problem, $-|2 - 3| = -|-1|$, so the target answer is -1. Try this out in the answer choices. Choice (J) works: $-(3 - 2) = -1$.

48. **G** Plug In any negative integer for x and try each answer choice out. Since any number, positive or negative, raised to the power of 0 is 1, that's the only answer that works.

49. **C** Plug In the Answers to avoid the confusing algebra with exponents. Starting with choice (C), use your calculator to determine whether the equation $9^{1\frac{1}{3}} = 3^{1+\frac{1}{3}}$.

55. **C** The problem asks for an irrational solution, so while choice (B) would work, it is rational, so cross it off. Then Plug In the Answers. When you Plug In the value in choice (C), the equation reads $\left|(2\sqrt{6})^2 - 30\right| - 6 = 0$. When you square $2\sqrt{6}$, you get 24, so it's $\left|24 - 30\right| - 6 = 0$. The value inside the absolute value symbol becomes -6, the absolute value of which is 6. The final equation is now much simpler: $6 - 6 = 0$.

59. **D** First, figure out all the pairs of positive integers which add up to 6 and Plug them In. 1^5 and 5^1 aren't equal, so try 2 and 4. $2^4 = 4^2$. Be sure to keep track of what the problem asks: how many values of a satisfy the equation. Consider that a could occupy the place of either the 2 or the 4, so those are 2 possible values for a. The last pair of numbers is 3 and 3. Since $3^3 = 3^3$, 3 is the third value for a.

Geometry on the ACT

We've seen in the Algebra chapter that a smart test-taking strategy, in and of itself, can improve your Math score. That is no less true for Geometry problems, but for these you typically have to bring a bit more to the table. ACT doesn't give you the formulas like SAT does, so you need to have them stored in your brain (or your calculator) when test day rolls around. Remember, counting trigonometry, Geometry makes up about half of any given ACT Math test.

THE BASIC APPROACH

Let's try a straightforward geometry problem.

22. In right triangle $\triangle STU$ shown below, V is the midpoint of $\overline{TU}$.
    In inches, what is the length of $\overline{UV}$?

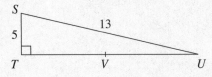

   F. 6
   G. 9
   H. 12
   J. 72
   K. 144

1. Ballpark

First, ACT has actually done us a big favor on this problem. While they claim that "illustrative figures are NOT necessarily drawn to scale," it's usually safe to assume that they are at least close. Remember what we're looking for here, the length of $\overline{UV}$. Look closely at this figure: You can tell just by looking at it that the longest side is $\overline{SU}$, which has a length of 13, so it's not likely that any smaller part of the triangle will have a longer length, eliminating choices (J) and (K). We can probably eliminate (H) as well, because $\overline{SU}$ is so much longer than $\overline{UV}$. This way, if we were running short on time and had to guess, we have improved our chances of guessing from 20% to 50%. Not bad for no work, huh?

2. Write on the Figure

Now, let's dig in to get our final answer. Rather than trying to keep everything in your mind, make sure you are writing all over your figure. The problem says that V is the midpoint of $\overline{TU}$, so make sure you mark that on your figure. It's probably worth emphasizing the portion, $\overline{UV}$, that you are looking for as well.

3. Write Down Formulas

As for the formulas, get those down before you begin working the problem as well. For this problem, you are dealing with the sides of a right triangle, so it is likely that you will need the Pythagorean theorem: $a^2 + b^2 = c^2$, where c is the longest side. Plug in the information you have, and write anything new that you find on the figure:

$$a^2 + b^2 = c^2$$
$$(5)^2 + \left(\overline{TU}\right)^2 = (13)^2$$
$$\left(\overline{TU}\right)^2 = (13)^2 - (5)^2$$
$$= 169 - 25$$
$$= 144$$
$$\overline{TU} = 12$$

Don't make your brain work any harder than it needs to! Make sure you're writing everything down. Hopefully by now your scratch paper looks something like this:

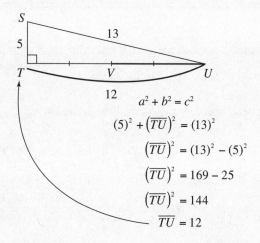

$$a^2 + b^2 = c^2$$
$$(5)^2 + \left(\overline{TU}\right)^2 = (13)^2$$
$$\left(\overline{TU}\right)^2 = (13)^2 - (5)^2$$
$$\left(\overline{TU}\right)^2 = 169 - 25$$
$$\left(\overline{TU}\right)^2 = 144$$
$$\overline{TU} = 12$$

Now, once you've got all the information on the figure, it's probably very clear that the answer is choice (F), because $\overline{TU}$ is 12, and $\overline{UV}$ is one half of this value. If you know your Pythagorean triples, you may have found $\overline{TU}$ even more quickly, but make sure you're reading the question carefully. If you don't read all the way, you might fall into the trap and pick choice (H).

Pythagorean triples are easy-to-remember, commonly tested ratios for the sides of a right triangle. Memorizing them can save you a lot of time by enabling you to bypass the Pythagorean theorem. The most common Pythagorean triples are 3:4:5, 6:8:10, and 5:12:13, each listed from the shortest to the longest side. Which one does question 22 use?

So let's review the basic approach for Geometry problems.

> The Basic Approach on Geometry questions suggests:
>
> 1. Use ballparking to eliminate wrong answers on questions in which a figure is given.
>
> 2. Write any information given by the question on the provided figure.
>
> 3. Write down any formulas you need and Plug In any information you have.
>
> 4. If the question doesn't provide a figure, draw your own.

THE FORMULAS

Here are some of the formulas you may find useful on Geometry questions.

Circles

Think CArd! (Circumference, Area, radius, diameter)

If you have one of these, you can always find the other three.

$$d = 2r \qquad C = \pi d = 2\pi r \qquad A = \pi r^2$$

When dealing with the parts of a circle, set up a ratio.

$$\frac{part}{whole} = \frac{central\ angle}{360°} = \frac{arc}{2\pi r} = \frac{sector\ area}{\pi r^2}$$

For Coordinate Geometry, be able to recognize the equation of a circle:

$$(x - h)^2 + (y - k)^2 = r^2$$

where (h, k) is the center of the circle, and (x, y) is any point on the circle.

Triangles

$$\text{Area} = A = \frac{1}{2}bh$$

Perimeter: P = sum of the sides

Sum of all angles: 180°

Similar triangles have congruent angles and proportional sides.

Right Triangles

The Triangle rules apply, but there are some special rules for right triangles.

Pythagorean theorem, where a, b, and c are the sides of the triangle where c is the hypotenuse:

$$a^2 + b^2 = c^2$$

SOHCAHTOA (ratios between sides and angles of right triangles)

$$\sin\theta = \frac{\text{Opposite}}{\text{Hypotenuse}} \qquad \cos\theta = \frac{\text{Adjacent}}{\text{Hypotenuse}} \qquad \tan\theta = \frac{\text{Opposite}}{\text{Adjacent}}$$

Special Right Triangles

When you've determined the angles of your right triangle, use the following ratios to bypass the Pythagorean theorem:

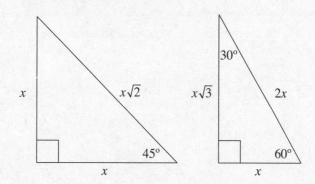

If a triangle problem contains a $\sqrt{2}$ or a $\sqrt{3}$, you can most likely use one of these special triangles.

If you don't know the angles, you can often bypass the Pythagorean theorem with the Pythagorean triples:

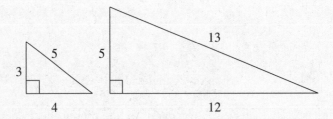

These Pythagorean triples are basic ratios, so they can be multiplied to be used with larger numbers.

6:8:10 is commonly cited as a Pythagorean triple, but it is just the 3:4:5 multiplied by 2.

Four-Sided Figures (Quadrilaterals)

Parallelogram: Opposite sides are parallel, opposite sides and angles are equal.

Rhombus: Opposite sides parallel, ALL sides equal, opposite angles equal.
    A rhombus is a *parallelogram* in which all four sides are equal.

Rectangle: Opposite sides parallel, opposite sides equal, ALL angles 90°.
    A rectangle is a *parallelogram* with four right angles.

Square: Opposite sides parallel, ALL sides equal, ALL angles 90°.
    A square is a type of *parallelogram*, *rhombus*, and *rectangle*.

For any of these four shapes:

Area: $A = bh$, where b and h are perpendicular

Perimeter: $P =$ the sum of all sides

Coordinate Geometry Formulas

All points are written (x,y) where x gives the x-coordinate and y gives the y-coordinate.

Two lines *intersect* when they meet at a single point.

$$\text{Slope: } \frac{rise}{run} = \frac{y_2 - y_1}{x_2 - x_1}$$

where (x_1, y_1) and (x_2, y_2) are two points on a line.

$$\text{Slope-intercept formula: } y = mx + b$$

where (x, y) is a point on the line, m is the slope, and b is the y-intercept, or the point at which the line crosses the y-axis.

Use the slope-intercept form when a question asks for the slope of a *perpendicular* line. The slope of a line perpendicular to it will be the opposite reciprocal or $-\dfrac{1}{m}$. That is, if slope of a line is 2, the slope of a perpendicular will be $-\dfrac{1}{2}$.

Parallel lines have equal slopes.

THE PROBLEMS

Plane Geometry

Let's use these formulas and the Basic Approach to solve some problems.

44. A circle has a diameter of 8 inches. What is the area of the circle, to the nearest 0.1 square inch?

    F. 12.6
    G. 25.1
    H. 50.3
    J. 64.0
    K. 201.1

Here's How To Crack It

Remember the Basic Approach. There's no figure, so draw your own. Once you've done that, mark it up with information from the problem, and get all your formulas down. Think CArd! Your paper should look something like this:

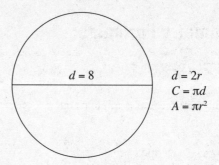

$$d = 8$$

$$d = 2r$$
$$C = \pi d$$
$$A = \pi r^2$$

Now work the formulas to get the answer. We know that the diameter of this circle is 8, which means its radius is 4. Use the radius in the Area formula, and use your calculator to find this Area:

$$A = \pi r^2$$
$$A = \pi (4)^2$$
$$A = 16\pi$$
$$A \approx 50.3$$

This matches up nicely with choice (H). If you don't have a calculator, or you're not especially handy with it, no problem. Use ballparking. You know that π is roughly equivalent to 3, so your answer will need to be close to 16×3 or 48. Only choice (H) is close enough.

Coordinate Geometry

Let's try a Coordinate Geometry problem. ACT likes to make a big deal about the distinction between Plane and Coordinate Geometry, but as we'll see, your approach won't really differ at all.

23. In the standard (x,y) coordinate plane, point G lies at $(-3,-4)$ and point H lies at $(2,5)$. What is the length of $\overline{GH}$ in coordinate units?

A. 7

B. 4

C. $\sqrt{14}$

D. $\sqrt{45}$

E. $\sqrt{106}$

Here's How To Crack It

Your first impulse here will probably be to whip out the distance formula and complete this problem in lightning-fast time. The only problem is that the distance formula looks like this:

$$d = \sqrt{(x_2 - x_1)^2 + (y_2 - y_1)^2}$$

Yikes. If you've got this formula stored away in the RAM of your brain, great. Unfortunately, for most of us, this is a really easy formula to forget, or worse, to remember incorrectly. What you'll find about ACT Geometry is that for 90% of the problems, you're best off just dealing with the basics. For weird shapes in Plane Geometry, this will mean carving things up into recognizable shapes and working from there. On Coordinate Geometry, you will find that simple formulas and the Basic Approach can get you plenty of points.

Let's use the Basic Approach. First and foremost, this is a Geometry problem, and they haven't given you a figure. Draw your own. It should look something like this:

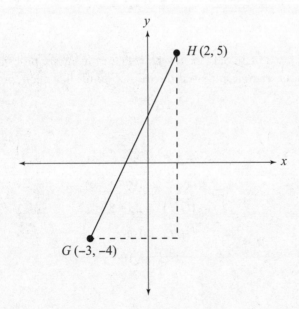

Now, look carefully at the line you've drawn for $\overline{GH}$. Remind you of anything? How about the hypotenuse of a right triangle? Remember, you want to work with the basics, and you know your triangles, so let's turn this thing into a right triangle.

Draw in the sides and find the lengths of those sides. To find the base of the triangle, figure out how much you're moving from one x-coordinate to the other. The points are (–3, –4) and (2, 5), so the x-coordinate will go from –3 to 2, or 5 units. The y-coordinate will go from –4 to 5, or 9 units. After you've drawn all this in and marked up your figure, you should have something like this:

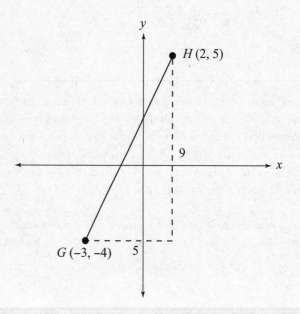

And now this is just a plain old ("plane" old?) Plane Geometry problem. You know two sides of a right triangle and need the third. Sounds like a job for the Pythagorean theorem.

$$a^2 + b^2 = c^2$$
$$(5)^2 + (9)^2 = \left(\overline{GH}\right)^2$$
$$\left(\overline{GH}\right)^2 = 25 + 81$$
$$\left(\overline{GH}\right)^2 = 106$$
$$\overline{GH} = \sqrt{106}$$

The answer is choice (E). And no distance formula required.

Trigonometry

There's a common misconception about the ACT regarding trigonometry. Many believe that if you don't have a solid foundation in trigonometry, you can't get a good score on the ACT Math Test. However, let's think back to the chart from the beginning of this lesson. Remember, there are only 4 trig questions on any given ACT.

What's more, two of these questions will deal with basic SOHCAHTOA, which you clearly don't need a whole semester or year of trig to learn. The other two questions may deal with radians, or the unit circle, or some of the trig identities, but you shouldn't worry about these until you've solidified a math score of at least 28.

So let's have a look at one of these basic SOHCAHTOA questions.

Don't worry about Advanced Trigonometry concepts unless you are consistently scoring a 28 or higher on the ACT Math Test. It's way too much to learn for only two questions!

42. According to the measurements given in the figure below, which of the following expressions gives the distance, in meters, from the house to the garage?

    F. $40\tan38°$

    G. $40\cos38°$

    H. $40\sin38°$

    J. $\dfrac{40}{\cos38°}$

    K. $\dfrac{40}{\sin38°}$

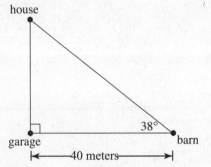

Here's How To Crack It

They've already written most of the information you'll need on the figure, but it can be worth noting the side that you are looking for: the side that shows the distance from the house to the garage.

Let the answer choices help. These choices tell you a lot more than you may think: First of all, they offer the main indication that this will be a SOHCAHTOA problem by showing that you will need to choose sine, cosine, or tangent. Next, they tell you that you'll only be dealing with one angle, the 38° one. Finally, they tell you that you won't need to do any weird rounding with decimals because they just want the sine, cosine, or tangent expression.

Have a close look at the sides you're dealing with. Where are they relative to the 38° angle? The base of the triangle is touching the 38° angle, so it's *adjacent*, and the side you're looking for is *opposite* the 38° angle. It looks like we won't be dealing with the *hypotenuse* at all. So which trig function deals with the *opposite* and *adjacent* sides? Remember SOHCAHTOA. The function we'll need is tangent. And don't do more work than you need to. Only choice (F) offers an expression featuring the tangent function, so it must be the correct answer.

Shapes Within Shapes: What's the Link?

ACT's favorite way to ask hard Geometry questions is to put shapes within shapes. You know the drill: Some shape inscribed in some other shape, or two shapes share a common side. They've got all kinds of ways to ask these questions. But when you see a shape drawn within another shape, there's usually one question that will blow the question wide open: *What's the link between the two shapes?* Let's try a few.

1. A square inscribed in a circle

2. A triangle inscribed in a rectangle

3. A square overlapping with a circle

So, what's the link?

1. What's the link? The diagonal of the square is the diameter of the circle.

2. What's the link? The base of the triangle is the long side of the rectangle, and the height of the triangle is the short side of the rectangle.

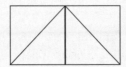

3. What's the link? The side of the square is equivalent to the radius of the circle.

Let's try a problem that deals with these concepts.

37. In the square shown below, points E and F are the midpoints of sides $\overline{AB}$ and $\overline{CD}$, respectively. Two semicircles are drawn with centers E and F. What is the perimeter, in feet, of the shaded region?

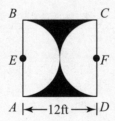

A. $12 + 12\pi$
B. $24 + 12\pi$
C. $24 + 24\pi$
D. $48 + 12\pi$
E. $48 + 24\pi$

Here's How To Crack It

Make sure you write everything you need on the figure, including the relevant square and circle formulas. Since you are dealing with shapes within shapes, now is also a good time to figure out what the link is, what these two (or three, in this case) shapes have in common. Don't worry about digging up a formula for the perimeter of that hourglass-shaped thing. Stick with the shapes you know.

For this problem, the links occur on the right and left sides of the figure: The left and right sides of the square are the same as the diameters of each of the semi-circles. We can therefore say that if all sides of a square are equal, each of these sides is 12. Since the diameter of each semi-circle is equivalent to a side of the square, then the diameters of both semicircles must also be 12.

Let's use this information to find the perimeters of each of these semi-circles. Remember, when you're dealing with circles, the perimeter is called the *circumference*, which can be found with the formula $C = \pi d$. Since you're dealing with a semi-circle here, you'll need to divide its circumference in half. Let's find the circumference of the semicircle with center E.

$$\frac{C_E}{2} = \frac{\pi d}{2}$$
$$= \frac{\pi(12)}{2}$$
$$= 6\pi$$

The semicircle with center F will have the same circumference because it has the same diameter. Now all we need to do is add up our perimeters to find our answer. You know the sides of the square will each be 12 and the circumference of each semicircle will be 6π, so the total perimeter of the shaded region will be $12 + 12 + 6\pi + 6\pi = 24 + 12\pi$, choice (B).

So let's hear it once more:

> Don't do more work than you have to on Geometry problems by trying to remember every weird formula you've ever learned. Stick to the formulas you know, and work with the Basic Approach.

Now go ahead and give some of these concepts a try in the drill at the end of this chapter.

GEOMETRY DRILLS

Plane Geometry

6. In $\triangle XYZ$, $\angle X$ and $\angle Z$ are congruent, and the measure of $\angle Y$ is 122°. What is the measure of $\angle X$?

 F. 29°
 G. 60°
 H. 61°
 J. 58°
 K. 122°

14. The 8-sided figure below is divided into 6 congruent squares. The total area of the 6 squares is 96 square centimeters. What is the perimeter, in centimeters, of the figure?

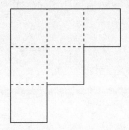

 F. 16
 G. 28
 H. 48
 J. 56
 K. 96

20. The base of a triangle is 4 times the base of a smaller triangle. The 2 triangles have the same height. The area of the larger triangle is N square units. The area of the smaller triangle is xN square units. Which of the following is the value of x ?

 F. $\dfrac{1}{16}$

 G. $\dfrac{1}{8}$

 H. $\dfrac{1}{4}$

 J. 4

 K. 16

24. What is the area, in square meters, of the figure below?

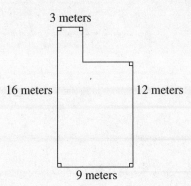

 F. 40
 G. 50
 H. 108
 J. 120
 K. 144

27. In right triangle $\triangle FHK$ below, $\overline{GJ}$ is parallel to $\overline{FK}$, and $\overline{GJ}$ is perpendicular to $\overline{HK}$ at J. The length of $\overline{HK}$ is 12 inches, the length of $\overline{GJ}$ is 6 inches, and the length of $\overline{GH}$ is 10 inches. What is the length, in inches, of $\overline{FK}$?

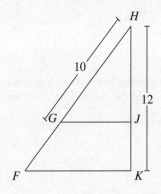

 A. 7
 B. 8
 C. 9
 D. 10
 E. 11

31. In the figure below, *JKLM* is a square. Points *N*, *O*, *P*, and *Q* are the midpoints of the sides of *JKLM*. Points *R*, *S*, *T*, and *V* are the midpoints of the sides of *NOPQ*. A side of *JKLM* is how many times as long as a side of *RSTV* ?

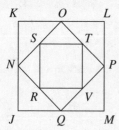

A. $\sqrt{2}$
B. 2
C. 3
D. 6
E. 8

37. The circle below has an area of 36π square meters. The circle is inscribed in the square and is tangent to the square at *W, X, Y,* and *Z*. What is the area, in square meters, of the square?

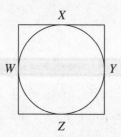

A. 6
B. 12
C. 18
D. 36
E. 144

48. In the figure below, the circle with center *X* has a radius of 8 centimeters and the measure of $\angle SRX$ is 70°. What is the measure of $\overarc{RS}$?

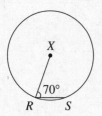

F. 20°
G. 40°
H. 50°
J. 55°
K. 70°

54. The side of an equilateral triangle is *s* inches longer than the side of a second equilateral triangle. How many inches longer is the altitude of the first triangle than the altitude of the second triangle?

F. $\dfrac{\sqrt{3}}{2}s$

G. $\sqrt{2}s$

H. $2s$

J. $3s$

K. s^3

55. In the figure below, the circles centers at *N* and *O* intersect at *X* and *Y*, and points *N*, *X*, *Y*, and *O* are collinear. The lengths of $\overline{MN}$, $\overline{OP}$, and $\overline{XY}$ are 10, 8, and 3 inches, respectively. What is the length, in inches, of $\overline{NO}$?

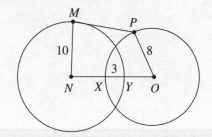

A. 10
B. 11
C. 12
D. 15
E. 18

Coordinate Geometry

3. A point at $(5, 4)$ in the standard (x,y) coordinate plane is shifted left 3 units and up 6 units. What are the new coordinates of the point?

- **A.** $(11, \ 7)$
- **B.** $(\ 8, \ \ 2)$
- **C.** $(\ 8, 10)$
- **D.** $(\ 2, \ \ 2)$
- **E.** $(\ 2, 10)$

13. The points $A(-6,8)$ and $B(10,2)$ lie in the standard (x,y) coordinate plane. What is the midpoint of $\overline{AB}$?

- **A.** $(-3, \ 4)$
- **B.** $(\ 2, \ 5)$
- **C.** $(\ 4,10)$
- **D.** $(\ 5, \ 1)$
- **E.** $(\ 8,-3)$

17. What is the slope-intercept form of $5x - y + 2 = 0$?

- **A.** $y = -5x - 2$
- **B.** $y = -5x + 2$
- **C.** $y = 2x - 5$
- **D.** $y = 5x - 2$
- **E.** $y = 5x + 2$

24. Points $O(5,3)$ and $P(-3,8)$ lie in the standard (x,y) coordinate plane. What is the slope of $\overline{OP}$?

- **F.** $-\dfrac{5}{8}$
- **G.** $\dfrac{5}{8}$
- **H.** $-\dfrac{2}{11}$
- **J.** $\dfrac{2}{11}$
- **K.** $\dfrac{11}{2}$

33. What are the quadrants of the standard (x,y) coordinate plane below that contain points on the graph of the equation $8x + 4y = 12$?

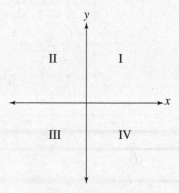

quadrants of the standard (x,y) coordinate plane

- **A.** II and IV only
- **B.** I, II, and III only
- **C.** I, II, and IV only
- **D.** I, III, and IV only
- **E.** II, III, and IV only

39. On a map in the standard (x,y) coordinate plane, the cities of Everton and Springfield are represented by the points $(-3,-5)$ and $(-6,-8)$, respectively. Each unit on the map represents an actual distance of 20 kilometers. Which of the following is closest to the distance, in kilometers, between these 2 cities?

- **A.** 316
- **B.** 120
- **C.** 85
- **D.** 60
- **E.** 49

41. Which of the following equations, when graphed in the standard (x,y) coordinate plane, would cross the x-axis at $x = -3$ and $x = 6$?

- **A.** $y = 3(x - 3)(x + 6)$
- **B.** $y = 3(x - 3)(x - 6)$
- **C.** $y = 3(x + 3)(x + 6)$
- **D.** $y = 6(x - 3)(x - 6)$
- **E.** $y = 6(x + 3)(x - 6)$

48. The graph of $f(x) = x^3$ is shown in the standard (x,y) coordinate plane below. For which of the following equations is the graph of the cubic function shifted 4 units to the left and 3 units up?

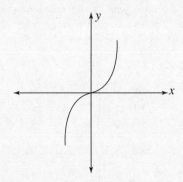

F. $f(x) = (x-4)^3 - 3$
G. $f(x) = (x-4)^3 + 3$
H. $f(x) = (x+3)^3 - 4$
J. $f(x) = (x+4)^3 + 3$
K. $f(x) = (x+4)^3 - 3$

52. In the standard (x,y) coordinate plane, the graph of which of the following equations is a circle with center $(3,5)$ and radius 4 coordinate units?

F. $(x-3)^2 + (y+5)^2 = 4$
G. $(x+3)^2 + (y-5)^2 = 4$
H. $(x+3)^2 + (y+5)^2 = 16$
J. $(x-3)^2 + (y+5)^2 = 16$
K. $(x+3)^2 + (y-5)^2 = 16$

56. The graph below shows the distance a hot-air balloon is from the ground for a period of 10 minutes. A certain order of 3 of the following 5 actions describes the balloon's movement in relation to the position of the ground. Which order is it?

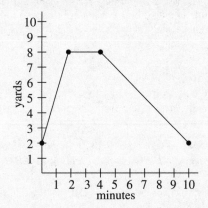

I.   Remains stationary for 2 minutes
II.   Moves away at 3 yards per minute
III.   Moves toward at 3 yards per minute
IV.   Moves away at 1 yard per minute
V.   Moves toward at 1 yard per minute

F.   I, II, II
G.   II, I, V
H.   III, I, IV
J.   IV, I, III
K.   V, I, II

Trigonometry

21. In right triangle $\triangle LMN$ below, $\sin L = \dfrac{3}{8}$. Which of the following expressions is equal to $\sin M$?

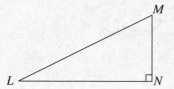

A. $\dfrac{8}{3}$

B. $\dfrac{\sqrt{73}}{3}$

C. $\dfrac{\sqrt{55}}{3}$

D. $\dfrac{\sqrt{73}}{8}$

E. $\dfrac{\sqrt{55}}{8}$

22. The dimensions of the right triangle shown below are given in meters. What is $\tan\theta$?

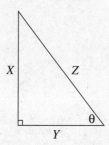

F. $\dfrac{X}{Y}$

G. $\dfrac{X}{Z}$

H. $\dfrac{Y}{Z}$

J. $\dfrac{Y}{X}$

K. $\dfrac{Z}{X}$

24. The right triangle shown below has a height of 6 feet. The measure of the angle indicated is 8°. Which of the following is closest to the length, in feet, of the side opposite the 8° ?

(Note: $\sin 8° \approx 0.1392$ $\sin 82° \approx 0.9903$
  $\cos 8° \approx 0.9903$ $\cos 82° \approx 0.1392$
  $\tan 8° \approx 0.1405$ $\tan 82° \approx 7.1154$)

F. 0.141
G. 0.835
H. 0.843
J. 5.942
K. 42.692

29. For the polygon below, which of the following represents the length, in inches, of FK ?

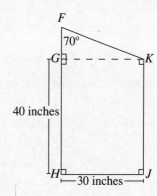

A. 10

B. 30

C. $\dfrac{10}{\sin 70°}$

D. $\dfrac{30}{\sin 70°}$

E. $\sin 70°$

35. A right triangle is shown in the figure below. Which of the following expressions gives θ ?

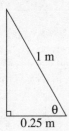

1 m

θ

0.25 m

A. $\cos^{-1}\left(\dfrac{1}{4}\right)$

B. $\sin^{-1}\left(\dfrac{1}{4}\right)$

C. $\tan^{-1}\left(\dfrac{1}{4}\right)$

D. $\cos^{-1}(4)$

E. $\tan^{-1}(4)$

37. A person stands on level ground holding a kite string. The string 128 meters long is attached to the center of the kite and makes an angle of 64° with the ground, as shown in the figure below. Which of the following expressions gives the distance, in meters, from the center of the kite to the ground?

A. $128\tan 64°$

B. $128\cos 64°$

C. $128\sin 64°$

D. $\dfrac{128}{\cos 64°}$

E. $\dfrac{128}{\sin 64°}$

53. In $\triangle XYZ$, the measure of $\angle X$ is 57°, the measure of $\angle Y$ is 72°, and the length of $\overline{XZ}$ is 12 inches. Which of the following is an expression for the length, in inches, of $\overline{YZ}$?

(Note: The law of sines states that for any triangle, the ratios of the lengths of the sides to the sines of the angles opposite those sides are equal.)

A. $\dfrac{\sin 57°}{12\sin 72°}$

B. $\dfrac{\sin 72°}{12\sin 57°}$

C. $\dfrac{12\sin 72°}{\sin 57°}$

D. $\dfrac{12\sin 57°}{\sin 72°}$

E. $\dfrac{(\sin 57°)(\sin 72°)}{12}$

56. Triangles $\triangle LMN$ and $\triangle WXY$ are shown below. The given side lengths are in inches. The area of $\triangle LMN$ is 40 square inches. What is the area of $\triangle WXY$, in square inches?

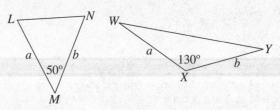

F. 15
G. 18
H. 20
J. 40
K. 45

58. The angle in the standard (x,y) coordinate plane shown below has its vertex at the origin. One side of this angle includes the positive x-axis, and the other side with measure θ passes through $(-12,-5)$. What is the sine of θ ?

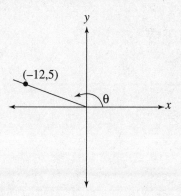

F. $-\dfrac{13}{5}$

G. $-\dfrac{12}{13}$

H. $-\dfrac{5}{13}$

J. $\dfrac{5}{13}$

K. $\dfrac{12}{5}$

59. The domain of the function $f(x) = 4\sin(3x - 1) + 2$ is all real numbers. Which of the following is the range of the function $f(x)$?

A. $-4 \leq f(x) \leq 4$

B. $-6 \leq f(x) \leq 2$

C. $-5 \leq f(x) \leq 3$

D. $-2 \leq f(x) \leq 6$

E. All real numbers

ANSWERS

Plane Geometry

6. F
14. H
20. H
24. J
27. C
31. B
37. E
48. G
54. F
55. D

Trigonometry

21. E
22. F
24. H
29. D
35. A
37. C
53. D
56. J
58. H
59. D

Coordinate Geometry

3. D
13. B
17. E
24. F
33. C
39. C
41. E
48. J
52. K
56. G

EXPLANATIONS

Plane Geometry

6. **F** The sum of the angles of a triangle is 180°, so $\angle X + \angle Z = 180° - 122° = 58°$. Congruent angles have equal measure so $\angle X$ and $\angle Z$ are each $\frac{58°}{2} = 29°$. Choice (J) neglects to divide the remaining measure by two. Choice (G) makes all three, rather than two, angles congruent. Choice (H) incorrectly assumes $\angle X$ is half of $\angle Y$. Choice (K) makes $\angle X$ congruent to $\angle Y$, rather than to $\angle Z$.

14. **H** Since the area of the six congruent squares is 96, the area of each square is $\frac{96}{6} = 16$. It might be tempting to select choice (F) here, but remember you're looking for the perimeter of the entire figure, not the area of each square. The area of a square is equal to s^2, so the length of the side of each square is $\sqrt{16} = 4$. The perimeter of the figure consists of 12 sides of congruent squares, so the perimeter is $12 \times 4 = 48$. Choice (G) confuses the sides of the square with the sides of the figure. Choice (J) misuses the fact that the figure is 8-sided; choice (K) finds the perimeter if all 4 sides of the 6 squares were exposed.

20. **H** Since N is the area of the larger triangle, we'll have to multiply by a fraction less than 1 to get a smaller area, eliminating choices (J) and (K). If we choose 5 for the height of both triangles and 8 for the base of the larger, the base of the smaller will be 2. Now the area of the smaller triangle is $\frac{1}{2}(2)(5) = 5$, and the area of the larger is $\frac{1}{2}(8)(5) = 20$, so choice (H) is correct—the smaller triangle's area is $\frac{1}{4}$ that of the larger. Careful—choices (F) and (G) incorrectly multiply and square the ratio of the side lengths.

24. **J** Carve up the weird figure into two rectangles. The larger rectangle has dimensions 9 meters by 12 meters. Since the left side of the figure is 4 more meters than the right side, the smaller rectangle must have dimensions 4 meters by 3 meters. Calculate the area of each rectangle: $A_L = 9 \times 12 = 108$ and $A_S = 4 \times 3 = 12$, then add find the total area: $108 + 12 = 120$. Choices (F), (G), and (H) are too small. Choice (K) finds the area of a 16×9 rectangle without the indentation.

27. **C** Given $\overline{GJ}$ is parallel to $\overline{FK}$, ΔFHK and ΔGHJ are similar triangles, so they have proportional sides. ΔGHJ is a right triangle, so you can either use the Pythagorean theorem or identify the sides as the Pythagorean triplet $6 - 8 - 10$ to determine $\overline{HJ}$ is 10. Then set up the proportion $\frac{\overline{FK}}{\overline{GJ}} = \frac{\overline{HK}}{\overline{HJ}}$ to determine $\overline{FK}$: $\frac{\overline{FK}}{6} = \frac{12}{8}$, so $\overline{FK}$ is 9 inches.

31. **B**   Use the figure to ballpark and eliminate choices (D) and (E). Plug in a value for the side lengths of square $JKLM$. If $\overline{JK}$ is 4 units, $\overline{KN}$ and $\overline{OK}$ are each 2 units and $\overline{ON}$ is $2\sqrt{2}$. Because N, O, P, and Q are the midpoints of a square, $NOPQ$ is also a square with side lengths of $2\sqrt{2}$. Therefore, $\overline{NR}$ and $\overline{NS}$ are $\sqrt{2}$ and $\overline{RS}$ is $\sqrt{2}\left(\sqrt{2}\right) = 2$. Therefore, $\dfrac{JK}{RS} = \dfrac{4}{2} = 2$. Choice (A) compares a side of $JKLM$ to a side of $NOPQ$.

37. **E**   Use the circle area formula to determine the radius: $A = 36\pi = \pi r^2$. Because the radius of the circle is 6, the diameter $\overline{WY}$ is 12. $\overline{WY}$ is congruent to the side of the square, so the area of the square is $A = 12^2 = 144$. Choices (A) and (B) are the radius and diameter of the circle, not the area of the square. Choices (C) and (D) use the incorrect side lengths for the square.

48. **G**   Both $\overline{RX}$ and $\overline{SX}$ are radii of the circle, making them congruent. The triangle $\triangle RSX$, therefore, is isosceles, and $\angle SRX$ and $\angle RSX$ are congruent, each measuring 70°. The third angle $\angle RSX = 180° - 2(70°) = 40°$ and is equal to the measure of $\overset{\frown}{RS}$. Choices (J) and (K) make the incorrect pair of angles congruent.

54. **F**   Plug in values for the sides of the triangles: Triangle 1 can have a side length of 8 and triangle 2 can have a side length of 6, making $s = 2$. Equilateral triangles can be split into two 30°–60°–90° triangles, thus their altitudes are $\dfrac{1}{2}(\text{side length}) \times \sqrt{3}$. Triangle 1's altitude is $4\sqrt{3}$ and triangle 2's altitude is $6\sqrt{3}$, making the answer $4\sqrt{3} - 3\sqrt{3} = \sqrt{3}$. Choice (G) confuses 30°–60°–90° with 45°–45°–90°, and choices (H), (J), and (K) do not have a $\sqrt{3}$.

55. **D** $\overline{MN}$ and $\overline{OP}$ are the radii of their respective circles, so the radius $\overline{NY}$ of circle N is 10 inches and radius $\overline{OP}$ of circle O is 8 inches. Given $\overline{XY}$ is 3 inches long, $\overline{NX}$ is $10 - 3 = 7$ inches and $\overline{OY}$ is $8 - 3 = 5$ inches. Adding the three segments $\overline{NX}$, $\overline{XY}$, and $\overline{OY}$, the length of $\overline{NO}$ is $7 + 3 + 5 = 15$ inches. Choices (A) and (B) are too small, choice (C) calculates the length with $\overline{XY}$, and choice (E) doesn't consider the radii overlapping in $\overline{XY}$.

Coordinate Geometry

3. **D** To shift left, subtract from the x-coordinate: $5 - 3 = 2$; to shift up, add to the y-coordinate: $-4 + 6 = 2$. Choice (A) confuses the x- and y-coordinates, and choices (B), (C), and (E) confuse the addition and subtraction.

13. **B** The coordinates for midpoint are the averages of the endpoints: $\left(\dfrac{x_1 + x_2}{2}, \dfrac{y_1 + y_2}{2}\right)$. For segment $\overline{AB}$ the midpoint is at $\dfrac{6+10}{2} = 2, \dfrac{8+2}{2} = 5$. Choices (A) and (D) incorrectly take half the coordinate of one of the endpoints. Choice (C) adds, rather than averages, the endpoints. Choice (E) subtracts, rather than adds, the endpoint coordinates.

17. **E** The slope-intercept form is $y = mx + b$. Isolate the y variable by subtracting $5x$ and 2 from both sides of the equation to get $-y = -5x - 2$. Then divide both sides by -1 to get the slope-intercept equation $y = 5x + 2$. Choice (A) forgets to divide both sides by -1, choices (B) and (D) confuse the positive and negative signs, and choice (C) confuses the coefficient and constant values.

24. **F** Use the slope formula $\dfrac{y_2 - y_1}{x_2 - x_1} : \dfrac{8-3}{-3-5} = -\dfrac{5}{8}$. Choice (G) confuses the positive and negative signs; choices (H) and (J) add rather than subtract the coordinates; and choice (K) attempts to calculate $\dfrac{\text{run}}{\text{rise}}$.

33. **C** To determine the graph of the equation, you must isolate the y by subtracting $8x$ and dividing by 4. The resulting equation is $y = -2x + 3$, which is a line with a slope of -2 and the y-intercept of 3. Because the y-intercept is positive, the line crosses y-axis from Quadrant II to Quadrant I and extends into Quadrant IV. The line never passes through Quadrant III, eliminating choices (B), (D), and (E). Choice (A) is a partial answer and does not include Quadrant I. Alternatively, once the equation is in slope-intercept form, just plug it into your graphing calculator and look at the graph.

39. **C** Find the distance between the points using the distance formula: $d = \sqrt{(x_1 - x_2)^2 + (y_1 - y_2)^2} = \sqrt{[(-3) - (-6)]^2 + [(-5) - (-8)]^2} = \sqrt{(3)^2 + (3^2)} = \sqrt{18} = 3\sqrt{2}$. Multiply the coordinate distance by 20 to get the distance in kilometers. Choices (A) and (E) incorrectly calculate the distance by adding the coordinates and forgetting to square the differences, respectively. Choices (B) and (D) result when the distance formula is not used. If you have trouble remembering the distance formula, sketch a figure and use the Pythagorean theorem as detailed in the Introductory chapter.

41. **E** The graph crosses the x-axis when $y = 0$, and the x values at those points are called the solutions of the equation. Plug the solution values for x into the answers to determine which expressions give $y = 0$. Substituting $x = -3$, you can eliminate choices (A), (B), and (D) because they do not result in $y = 0$. Substituting $x = 6$, you can eliminate choice (C) because it does not result in $y = 0$.

48. **J** For any function $f(x + h) + k$, h indicates horizontal shifts and k indicates vertical shifts. Because the horizontal shift is 4, not 3, you can eliminate choice (H). A negative h indicates a shift right, not left, eliminating choices (F) and (G). A negative k indicates a shift down, not up, eliminating choice (K).

52. **K** The general equation of a circle is $(x - h)^2 + (y - k)^2 = r^2$, in which (h, k) is the center of the circle and r is the radius. Note that h and k are *subtracted* in the formula. Because the radius is 4, r^2 is 16, eliminating choices (F) and (G). Choices (H) and (J) confuse the signs of h and k.

56. **G** The balloon remains stationary in the middle stage, so action (I) should be second in the order of events, eliminating choice (F). In the first stage, the graph is increasing which means the distance between the balloon and the ground increases, so the balloon is moving away, eliminating choices (H) and (K). The rate of increase is greater than the rate of decrease in the third stage, so choice (J) is incorrect. Only choice (G) gives the correct actions in the correct order.

Trigonometry

21. **E** Draw a triangle and use SOHCAHTOA to label the known sides: leg $\overline{MN}$ is 3 and hypotenuse $\overline{LM}$ is 8. Use the Pythagorean theorem to determine the third side: $\overline{LN}^2 + 3^2 = 8^2$, so $\overline{LN} = \sqrt{55}$, eliminating choices (B) and (D). Since $\sin = \dfrac{\text{opposite}}{\text{adjacent}}$, $\sin M = \dfrac{\overline{LN}}{\overline{LM}} = \dfrac{\sqrt{55}}{8}$. Choice (A) gives $\csc M$, Choice (C) gives $\tan M$.

22. **F** In SOHCAHTOA, Tan is Opposite over Adjacent relative to the angle, thus $\tan \theta = \dfrac{X}{Y}$. Choice (G) is $\sin \theta$; choice (H) is $\cos \theta$; choice (J) is $\cot \theta$; choice (K) is $\csc \theta$.

24. **H** We know side adjacent the angle $8°$ and are trying to determine the side opposite the angle $8°$, so use TOA: $\tan 8° = \dfrac{x}{6}$, so $x = 6 \tan 8°$. Choices (F), (G), and (J) do not use tan, and choice (K) incorrectly calculates $6 \tan 82°$.

29. **D** Because quadrilateral $GHJK$ has four right angles, it is a rectangle and $\overline{GK}$ measures 30 inches. We must use SOHCAHTOA to determine the side lengths of right triangle FGK, eliminating choices (A) and (B). Since we know the measure of $\angle F$, use SOH: $\sin 70° = \dfrac{30}{FK}$, which rearranges to give $\overline{FK} = \dfrac{30}{\sin 70°}$.

35. **A** We know the side adjacent the angle θ and the hypotenuse, so use CAH to set up the problem: $\cos\theta = \dfrac{0.25}{1} = \dfrac{1}{4}$. To determine the measure of angle θ, use the inverse function $\cos^{-1}$, eliminating choices (B), (C), and (E). Choice (D) incorrectly uses the reciprocal of $\dfrac{\text{adjacent}}{\text{hypotenuse}}$.

37. **C** The distance between the kite and the ground is opposite to the angle of $64°$. Since we also know the length of the hypotenuse, we're using SOH, eliminating choices (A), (B), and (D). Since $\sin 64° = \dfrac{\text{opposite}}{128}$, the distance is $128\sin 64°$. Choice (E) incorrectly sets up the ratio of sides.

53. **D** Draw the triangle to determine that side $\overline{YZ}$ is opposite $\angle X$ and side $\overline{XZ}$ is opposite $\angle Y$. Using the law of sines, set up the proportion $\dfrac{12 \text{ inches}}{\sin 72°} = \dfrac{\overline{YZ}}{\sin 57°}$. Multiply both sides by $\sin 57°$ to get $\overline{YZ} = \dfrac{12\sin 57°}{\sin 72°}$. Choice (C) does not use the correct angle-side pairs, and choices (A), (B), and (E) uses the incorrect proportions.

56. **J** To determine the area of non-right triangles, use the formula $A = \dfrac{1}{2}ab\sin\theta$, in which θ is the angle between sides a and b. For ΔLMN, $A = 40 = \dfrac{1}{2}ab\sin 50°$, so $ab = 104.4$. Since ΔWXY has the same side lengths a and b, we can substitute $ab = 104.4$ for the area $A = \dfrac{1}{2}(ab)\sin 130°$. The area of ΔWXY is $\dfrac{1}{2}(104.4)(0.766) \approx 40$.

58. **J** In the standard (x,y) coordinate plane, the sine of an angle in Quadrant II is always positive, eliminating choices (F), (G), and (H). Make a right triangle with the x-axis, which gives you a 5–12–13 triangle. The angle θ is at the origin, so the leg opposite the angle is 5 and the hypotenuse is 13. Sine is defined as opposite over hypotenuse, which in this case gives $\dfrac{5}{13}$, choice (J).

59. **D** The range of $\sin x$ is normally between -1 to 1, inclusive; however, the range can change depending on the graph's amplitude and vertical shift. In the general form $A\sin(Bx + C) + D$, amplitude is indicated by A, vertical shift is indicated by D, and the range is between $-A + D$ and $A + D$. The range for this function, therefore, is $-4 + 2 \le f(x) \le 4 + 2$. Choice (A) neglects the vertical shift of the graph; choice (B) subtracts rather than adding the vertical shift of $+D$; choice (C) uses the horizontal rather than vertical shift value; choice (E) gives the domain, not the range of the function.

Comprehensive Math Drill for the ACT

ACT MATHEMATICS TEST

60 Minutes—60 Questions

DIRECTIONS: Solve each problem, choose the correct answer, and then darken the corresponding oval on your answer document.

Do not linger over problems that take too much time. Solve as many as you can; then return to the others in the time you have left for this test.

You are permitted to use a calculator on this test. You may use your calculator for any problems you choose, but some of the problems may best be done without using a calculator.

Note: Unless otherwise stated, all of the following should be assumed:

1. Illustrative figures are NOT necessarily drawn to scale.
2. Geometric figures lie in a plane.
3. The word line indicates a straight line.
4. The word average indicates arithmetic mean.

---

1. Bob's Burgers charges $8 dollars for a hamburger and $5 for an order of French fries. Last month, h hamburgers and f orders of fries were purchased. Which of the following expressions gives the total amount of money, in dollars, Bob's Burgers earned on hamburgers and fries last month?

   A. $5h + 8f$
   B. $8h + 5f$
   C. $13(h + f)$
   D. $40(h + f)$
   E. $8(h + f) + 5f$

2. If $a = 8$, $b = -2$, and $c = 3$, what does $(a - b + c)(b + c)$ equal?

   F. -65
   G. -13
   H. 9
   J. 13
   K. 65

3. An artist at the State Fair paints 40 portraits per day. A second artist paints 50 portraits per day. The second artist opens for business three days after the first. Both remain open until the Fair closes, which is 11 days after the first artist began. Together, the two artists have painted how many portraits?

   A. 400
   B. 440
   C. 720
   D. 840
   E. 900

4. Josh has been a professional baseball player for four years. His home run totals each year have been 30, 39, 51, and 44, respectively. In order to maintain his current average number of home runs per season, how many home runs must Josh hit next year?

   F. 31
   G. 39
   H. 41
   J. 44
   H. 51

DO YOUR FIGURING HERE.

GO ON TO THE NEXT PAGE.

5. A craftswoman is paid $9.00 per necklace for making up to 30 necklaces per week. For each necklace over 30 that she is asked to make in a week, she is paid 1.5 times her regular pay. How much does she earn in a week in which she is asked to make 34 necklaces?

   A. $162
   B. $270
   C. $306
   D. $324
   E. $459

6. Which of the following mathematical expressions is equivalent to the verbal expression "The square root of a number, n, is 19 less than the value of 5 divided by n"?

   F. $n^2 = \dfrac{5}{n} - 19$

   G. $n^2 = \dfrac{n}{5} - 19$

   H. $\sqrt{n} = 19 - \dfrac{n}{5}$

   J. $\sqrt{n} = \dfrac{y}{n} - 19$

   K. $\sqrt{n} = \dfrac{5}{n} - 19$

7. If $12(y - 3) = -7$, then $y = ?$

   A. $-\dfrac{43}{12}$

   B. $-\dfrac{10}{12}$

   C. $-\dfrac{7}{12}$

   D. $\dfrac{29}{12}$

   E. $\dfrac{43}{12}$

8. At a department store, purses sell for $12 each during a one-day sale. Rita spent $84 on purses during the sale, $38.50 less than if she had bought the purses at the regular price. How much do purses cost at the regular price?

   F. $ 5.50
   G. $15.50
   H. $16.00
   J. $17.50
   K. $20.00

DO YOUR FIGURING HERE.

GO ON TO THE NEXT PAGE.

9. $(2a - 5b^2)(2a + 5b^2) =$

   A. $4a^2 - 25b^4$
   B. $4a^2 - 10b^4$
   C. $4a^2 + 25b^4$
   D. $2a^2 - 25b^4$
   E. $2a^2 - 10b^4$

DO YOUR FIGURING HERE.

10. A rectangle's perimeter is 18 feet and its area is 18 square feet. What is the length of the longest side of the rectangle?

   F. 10
   G. 8
   H. 6
   J. 3
   K. 2

11. In $\triangle XYZ$, $\angle X$ is 64°. What is the sum of $\angle Y$ and $\angle Z$?

   A. 26°
   B. 64°
   C. 116°
   D. 126°
   E. 128°

12. Each morning, a glee club member chooses her outfit among 4 plaid skirts, 5 pairs of argyle socks, 3 sweaters, and 4 headbands. How many different outfits are possible for her to put together on any given morning consisting of one skirt, one pair of socks, one sweater, and one headband?

   F. 4
   G. 15
   H. 16
   J. 120
   K. 240

13. Positive integers x, y, and z are consecutive such that $x < y < z$. The sum of x, $2y$, and $\dfrac{z}{2}$ is 59. What are the values of x, y, and z, respectively?

   A. 10, 11, 12
   B. 11, 12, 13
   C. 14, 15, 16
   D. 16, 17, 18
   E. 18, 19, 20

14. A function $h(x)$ is defined as $h(x) = -5x^3$. What is $h(-2)$?

   F. −1,000
   G. −40
   H. 30
   J. 40
   K. 1,000

GO ON TO THE NEXT PAGE.

DO YOUR FIGURING HERE.

15. If $z = \sqrt[4]{97}$, then which of the following must be true?

A. $2 < z < 3$
B. $3 < z < 4$
C. $4 < z < 5$
D. $5 < z < 6$
E. $6 < z$

16. What is the greatest common factor of 96, 108, and 144 ?

F. 12
G. 18
H. 24
J. 36
K. 48

17. Cowan Cola is holding a contest to develop a new, more environmentally efficient can for its soft drink. The winning can is a cylinder ten inches tall, with a volume of 40π in^3. What is the radius, in inches, of the can?

A. 1
B. 2
C. 4
D. 5
E. 8

18. A clock has 12 numbered points. Four points W, X, Y, Z lie on the clock representing certain numbers. W represents 3:00. X is 4 units clockwise from W. Y is 9 units counterclockwise from W. Z is 5 units counterclockwise from W and 7 units clockwise from W. What is the order of points, starting with W and working clockwise around the circle?

F. W, X, Y, Z
G. W, X, Z, Y
H. W, Y, X, Z
J. W, Y, Z, X
K. W, Z, Y, X

19. Tribbles reproduce at a rate described by the function $f(a) = 12(3)^a$, here a represents the number of days and $f(a)$ represents the number of tribbles. At this rate, how many tribbles will there be at the end of Day Four?

A. 48
B. 96
C. 240
D. 972
E. 1,296

GO ON TO THE NEXT PAGE.

20. The height of a triangle is half the height of a larger triangle. The two triangles have the same base. The area of the larger triangle is Y square feet. The area of the smaller triangle is xY square units. Which of the following is the value of x ?

F. $\dfrac{1}{4}$

G. $\dfrac{1}{2}$

H. 1

J. 2

K. 4

DO YOUR FIGURING HERE.

21. $(2x+3y+4z)-(6x-7y+8z)$ is equivalent to:

A. $-4x+10y-4z$

B. $-4x+10y+12z$

C. $-4x-4y-4z$

D. $-8x+10y+12z$

E. $-8x-4y+12z$

22. The right triangle shown below has lengths measured in inches. What is $\cos\theta$?

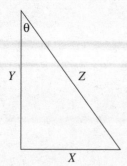

F. $\dfrac{X}{Y}$

G. $\dfrac{X}{Z}$

H. $\dfrac{Y}{X}$

J. $\dfrac{Y}{Z}$

K. $\dfrac{Z}{Y}$

GO ON TO THE NEXT PAGE.

23. On a dead-end street, 8 houses are evenly spaced around a circular cul-de-sac. A newspaper delivery person bikes around the cul-de-sac and tosses the newspapers onto the driveway of each house. The delivery person bikes rapidly enough that the person can only toss to every third house. On which lap around the cul-de-sac will the delivery person have delivered newspapers to all 8 houses on the street?

A. 2nd
B. 3rd
C. 4th
D. 8th
E. 11th

DO YOUR FIGURING HERE.

24. Lines q and m are in the standard (x,y) coordinate plane. The equation for line q is $y = 23x + 500$. The y-intercept of line m is 10 less than the y-intercept of line q. What is the y-intercept of line m ?

F. 2.3
G. 13
H. 50
J. 490
K. 510

25. The expression $-9a^5(8a^7 - 4a^3)$ is equivalent to:

A. $-36a^9$
B. $-72a^{12} + 36a^8$
C. $-72a^{12} - 36a^8$
D. $-72a^{35} + 36a^{15}$
E. $-72a^{35} - 36a^{15}$

26. $-4|-9+2| = ?$
F. −44
G. −28
H. 3
J. 28
K. 44

GO ON TO THE NEXT PAGE.

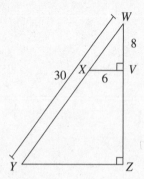

27. In right triangle $\triangle WYZ$ shown below, $\overline{XV}$ is perpendicular to $\overline{WZ}$ at point V and is parallel to $\overline{YZ}$. Line segments $\overline{WY}$, $\overline{XV}$, and $\overline{WV}$ measure 30 inches, 6 inches, and 8 inches, respectively. What is the measurement, in inches, of $\overline{YZ}$?

A. 15
B. 18
C. 20
D. 24
E. 27

DO YOUR FIGURING HERE.

28. As an experiment in botany class, students tracked a plant growing at a constant rate upward perpendicular to the ground. As shown in the table below, they measured the height, h inches, of the plant at 1-week intervals from $w = 0$ weeks to $w = 4$ weeks.

w	0	1	2	3	4
h	7	10	13	16	19

Which of the following equations expresses this data?

F. $h = w + 7$
G. $h = 3w + 4$
H. $h = 3w + 7$
J. $h = 7w + 3$
K. $h = 10w$

29. The inequality $4(n - 3) < 5(n + 2)$ is equivalent to which of the following inequalities?

A. $n > -22$
B. $n > -14$
C. $n > -13$
D. $n > -2$
E. $n > 2$

GO ON TO THE NEXT PAGE.

30. The sides of an equilateral triangle are 4 inches long. One vertex of the triangle is at (1,1) on a coordinate graph labeled in inch units. Which of the following could give the coordinates of another vertex of the triangle?

F.   (–4, 1)
G.   (0, 1)
H.   (2, 3)
J.   (1,–3)
K.   (5,–3)

DO YOUR FIGURING HERE.

31. For ΔLMN, shown below, which of the following expresses the value of m in terms of n ?

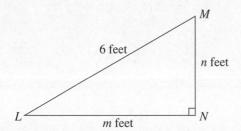

A. $6-n$
B. $\sqrt{6-n}$
C. $\sqrt{12+n^2}$
D. $\sqrt{36-n^2}$
E. $\sqrt{36+n^2}$

32. A jar holds 10 pear jellybeans, 16 cherry jellybeans, and 19 watermelon jellybeans. How many extra pear jellybeans must be added to the 45 jellybeans currently in the jar so that the probability of randomly selecting a pear jellybean is $\frac{3}{8}$?

F.   9
G.   11
H.   21
J.   35
K.   45

GO ON TO THE NEXT PAGE.

33. The graph of the equation $6x + 3y = 12$ is found in which quadrants of the standard (x,y) coordinate plane below?

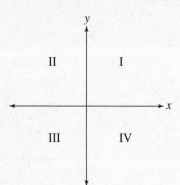

A. II and IV only
B. I, II, and III only
C. I, II, and IV only
D. I, III, and IV only
E. II, III, and IV only

34. The graph of $y = -2x^2 + 10$ contains the point $(3, 4n)$ in the standard (x,y) coordinate plane. What is the value of n ?

F.   7
G.   1
H. −2
J. −4
K. −8

35. Jennifer, Kelly, and Meredith split their apartment rent. Jennifer paid $\frac{2}{3}$ of the rent, Kelly paid $\frac{1}{4}$ of the rent, and Meredith paid the rest. What is the ratio of Jennifer's contribution to Kelly's contribution to Meredith's contribution?

A.   1:3:8
B.   3:8:1
C.   3:1:8
D.   8:3:1
E.   8:1:3

GO ON TO THE NEXT PAGE.

DO YOUR FIGURING HERE.

36. In the standard (x,y) coordinate plane, a circle has an equation of $x^2 + (y+4)^2 = 28$. Which of the following gives the center and radius of the circle, in coordinate units?

	center	radius
F.	$(0, -4)$	$\sqrt{28}$
G.	$(0, -4)$	14
H.	$(0, -4)$	28
J.	$(0, \ 4)$	$\sqrt{28}$
K.	$(0, \ 4)$	14

37. An equilateral triangle and 2 semicircles have dimensions as shown in the figure below. What is the perimeter, in inches, of the figure?

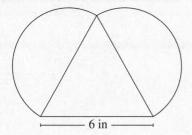

— 6 in —

- **A.** $3 + 3\pi$
- **B.** $6 + 6\pi$
- **C.** $6 + 12\pi$
- **D.** $18 + 6\pi$
- **E.** $18 + 12\pi$

38. In the figure below, points H, J, K, and L bisect the sides of rhombus $DEFG$, and point M is the intersection of $\overline{HK}$ and $\overline{JL}$. The area enclosed by $DEFG$ except the area enclosed by $HEFM$ is shaded. What is the ratio of the area of $HEFM$ to the area of the shaded area?

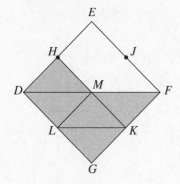

- **F.** $1:2$
- **G.** $3:4$
- **H.** $3:5$
- **J.** $3:8$
- **K.** Cannot be determined from the given information

GO ON TO THE NEXT PAGE.

DO YOUR FIGURING HERE.

39. In the standard (x,y) coordinate plane, the endpoints of $\overline{FG}$ lie on the coordinates $(-6,10)$ and $(8,-2)$. What is the y-coordinate of the midpoint of $\overline{FG}$?

A. 1
B. 2
C. 4
D. 6
E. 8

40. What is the volume, in cubic feet, of a cube with a side of length 9 feet?

F. 729
G. 486
J. 243
H. 81
K. 27

41. The system below has linear equations, in which r, s, t, and v are positive integers.

$$rx + sy = t$$
$$rx + sy = v$$

Which of the following best describes a possible graph of such a system of equations in the standard (x,y) coordinate plane?

   I.   2 lines intersecting at only 1 point
   II. 1 single line
   III. 2 parallel lines

A. I only
B. III only
C. I and II only
D. II and III only
E. I and III only

GO ON TO THE NEXT PAGE.

42. Given the dimensions in the figure below, which of the following expresses the distance, in feet, from the tree to the house?

DO YOUR FIGURING HERE.

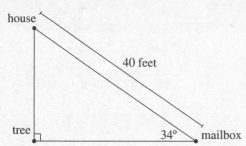

F. 40 sin 34°

G. 40 cos 34°

H. 40 tan 34°

J. $\dfrac{40}{\sin 34°}$

K. $\dfrac{40}{\cos 34°}$

43. The chart below shows the percentage of students, by grade, enrolled in a school. A student is picked randomly in a lottery to win a new graphing calculator. What are the odds (in the grade:not in the grade) that the winning student is in Grade 6 ?

Grade	5	6	7	8	9
Percentage of total number of students	12	22	25	27	14

A. 1:4

B. 1:5

C. 7:25

D. 11:39

E. 11:50

GO ON TO THE NEXT PAGE.

DO YOUR FIGURING HERE.

Use the following information to answer questions 44–46.

The figure below shows the pattern of a square tile mosaic to decorate the wall of Chelsea's Mexican Café. Grout fills the small spaces between individual tile pieces. All white triangular tiles are equilateral and share a vertex with each adjacent triangular piece. A green square piece is at the center of the mosaic. The length of the mosaic is 3 meters.

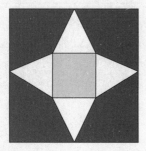

44. How many lines of symmetry in the plane does the pattern of the tile mosaic have?

F. 2
G. 3
H. 4
J. 8
K. Infinitely many

45. What is the length of the diagonal of the mosaic, to the nearest 0.1 meters?

A. 2.4
B. 3.0
C. 3.4
D. 4.2
E. 5.7

46. Joe wants to put a tile mosaic on the wall of his office. The pattern of the mosaic will be identical to that in the restaurant. The length of the office wall is 20% shorter than the length of the mosaic. The office wall is how many meters long?

F. 0.6
G. 2.4
H. 2.8
J. 3.6
K. 6.0

GO ON TO THE NEXT PAGE.

DO YOUR FIGURING HERE.

47. In the figure below, $\overline{DE} \parallel \overline{FG}$, $\overline{DG}$ bisects $\angle HDE$, and $\overline{HG}$ bisects $\angle FGD$. If the measure of $\angle EDG$ is 68°, what is the measure of $\angle DHG$?

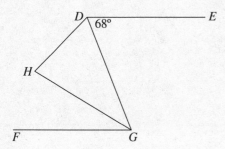

A. 68°
B. 78°
C. 80°
D. 82°
E. Cannot be determined from the given information

48. In the figure shown below, points A, B, and C lie on the circle with an area of 16π square meters and center O (not shown). $\overline{AC}$ is the longest chord in the circle, and the measure of $\overline{AB}$ is 4 meters. What is the degree measure of minor arc BC ?

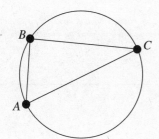

F. 60°
G. 90°
H. 120°
J. 145°
K. Cannot be determined from the given information

49. For which of the following values of b would the system of equations below have no solutions?

$$12x + 8y = 16$$

$$3x + by = 2$$

A. 2
B. 4
C. 8
D. 16
E. 32

GO ON TO THE NEXT PAGE.

DO YOUR FIGURING HERE.

Use the following information to answer questions 50–52.

Rebecca and Scott make and sell pies and cookies for school bake sales. It takes them 1 hour to make a dozen cookies and 3 hours to make a pie. The shaded triangular region shown below is the graph of a system of inequalities representing school-week constraints Rebecca and Scott have on their baking. For making and selling d dozen cookies and p pies, they make a profit of $12d + 25p$ dollars. They sell all the goods they bake.

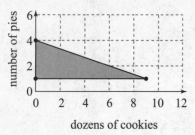

50. The constraint represented by the horizontal line segment containing (9,1) means that each school-week Rebecca and Scott make a minimum of:

F. 1 pie
G. 9 pies
H. 1 dozen cookies
J. 9 dozen cookies
K. 10 dozen cookies

51. What is the maximum profit Rebecca and Scott can earn from the baking they do in 1 school-week?

A. $100
B. $109
C. $122
D. $133
E. $237

52. During the third week of October each year, school is closed for Fall Break, and Rebecca and Scott have more time than usual to bake. During that week, for every hour that they spend baking, they donate $2 to the school's fund for after-school reading programs. This year, they baked 5 pies and 3 dozen cookies during Fall Break. Which of the following is closest to the percent of that week's profit they donated to the reading program fund?

F. 5%
G. 9%
H. 15%
J. 18%
K. 22%

GO ON TO THE NEXT PAGE.

DO YOUR FIGURING HERE.

53. The *determinant* of a matrix $\begin{bmatrix} a & c \\ b & d \end{bmatrix}$ equals $ad - bc$. What must be the value of w for the matrix $\begin{bmatrix} w & w \\ w & 10 \end{bmatrix}$ to have a determinant of 25 ?

   A. 5

   B. $\dfrac{10}{3}$

   C. $\dfrac{5}{2}$

   D. $-\dfrac{5}{3}$

   E. -5

54. Henry discovers that the population of the bacterial colony in his lab can be calculated using the equation $x = B(1 + .2g)^n$ where x is the current population, B is the original number of bacteria, g is a growth rate constant for that species, and n is the number of days elapsed. Which of the following is an expression for B in terms of g, n, and x ?

   F. $x - .2g^n$

   G. $x + .2g^n$

   H. $\left(\dfrac{x}{1 + .2g} \right)^n$

   J. $\dfrac{x}{(1 - .2g)^n}$

   K. $\dfrac{x}{(1 + .2g)^n}$

55. If m and n are real numbers such that $m < -1$ and $n > 1$, then which of the following inequalities *must* be true?

   A. $\dfrac{n}{m} > 1$

   B. $|n|^2 > |m|$

   C. $\dfrac{n}{7} + 2 > \dfrac{m}{7} + 2$

   D. $n^2 + 1 > m^2 + 1$

   E. $n^{-2} > m^{-2}$

GO ON TO THE NEXT PAGE.

56. Triangles *TVW* and *XYZ* are shown below. The given side lengths are in inches. The area of $\triangle TVW$ is 45 square inches. What is the area of $\triangle XYZ$ in square inches?

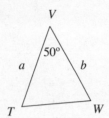

F. 22.5
G. 27
H. 30
J. 45
K. 50

57. Triangle *JKL* is shown in the figure below. The measure of $\angle K$ is 50°, $JK = 9$ cm, and $KL = 6$ cm. Which of the following is the lengths, in centimeters, of *LJ* ?

(Note: For a triangle with sides of length *a*, *b*, and *c* opposite angles $\angle A$, $\angle B$, and $\angle C$, respectively, the law of sines states

$$\frac{\sin \angle A}{a} = \frac{\sin \angle B}{b} = \frac{\sin \angle C}{c}$$ and the law of cosines states $c^2 = a^2 + b^2 - 2ab\cos \angle C$.)

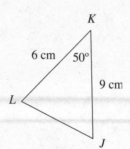

A. $9 \sin 50°$

B. $6 \sin 50°$

C. $\sqrt{9^2 - 6^2}$

D. $\sqrt{9^2 + 6}$

E. $\sqrt{9^2 + 6^2 - 2(9)(6)\cos 50°}$

58. What is the sum of the first 3 terms of the arithmetic sequence in which the 7th term is 13.5 and the 11th term is 18.3 ?

F. 15.9
G. 22.5
H. 25.5
J. 32.4
K. 43.5

GO ON TO THE NEXT PAGE.

59. In the equation $w^2 - pw + q = 0$, p and q are integers. The *only* possible value for w is 8. What is the value of p ?

A. 8
B. −8
C. 16
D. −16
E. 64

60. The solution set of which of the following equations is the set of real numbers that are 4 units from −1 ?

F. $|x+1| = 4$

G. $|x-1| = 4$

H. $|x+4| = 1$

J. $|x-4| = 1$

K. $|x+4| = -1$

END OF TEST.
STOP! DO NOT TURN THE PAGE UNTIL TOLD TO DO SO.

ANSWERS

1. B		31. D	
2. J		32. G	
3. D		33. C	
4. H		34. H	
5. D		35. D	
6. K		36. F	
7. D		37. B	
8. J		38. H	
9. A		39. C	
10. H		40. F	
11. C		41. D	
12. K		42. F	
13. D		43. D	
14. J		44. H	
15. B		45. D	
16. F		46. G	
17. B		47. B	
18. H		48. H	
19. D		49. A	
20. G		50. F	
21. A		51. B	
22. J		52. K	
23. B		53. A	
24. J		54. K	
25. B		55. C	
26. G		56. J	
27. B		57. E	
28. H		58. G	
29. A		59. C	
30. J		60. F	

EXPLANATIONS

1. **B**   Since *h* represents the number of hamburgers, multiply it by $8 to get the total amount of money paid for burgers; since *f* represents the number of orders of fries, multiply it by $5 to get the total amount of money paid for fries. You want the total amount of money earned, so you need to add the two expressions together: $8h + 5f$. You can also just plug in values for *h* and *f* and see which answer choice matches the target answer you get for those values—only choice (B) will work for all values of *h* and *f*.

2. **J**   Plug in the values given in the question. The problem should then read $(8 - [-2] + 3)(-2 + 3)$. Follow the order of operations and do the arithmetic within each parenthesis individually before multiplying: $(13)(1) = 13$.

3. **D**   Figure out the two artists separately, and then combine. The first one paints 40 portraits a day for 11 days, so 440 total. The second paints 50 per day for 8 days, so 400 total. Add them up, and there are 840 portraits.

4. **H**   If you add together all the home runs, you get 164. Divide that by four seasons and his average number of home runs per season is 41. The question is simply asking you how to keep a 41 home run average going after a fifth year. Simple: Hit 41 home runs exactly in year five.

5. **D**   The trick here is that you must calculate the first 30 necklaces at the regular rate of $9.00 each: She makes $270 for the first 30. Then figure out what 1.5 times her usual rate is (it's $13.50) and multiply that by the extra four necklaces. She gets $54 for the extras; add that to the $270, and she makes a total of $324 for the week.

6. **K**   This question is about translating English into math. The trickiest part is remembering to subtract 19 from $\frac{5}{n}$ instead of the other way around. Read closely and make sure you take the square root and not the square of *n*.

7. **D**   Those answer choices are ugly, but if you have a good calculator and are comfortable with all the fractions and parentheses, you can PITA. Otherwise, just solve for the variable. First, distribute the 12 on the left side, and you get $12y - 36 = -7$. Add 36 to both sides and you get $12y = 29$. Divide both sides by 12, and you're done.

8. **J**   First, calculate how many $12 purses you get for $84—you can buy seven of them. The difference between the prices is $38.50, so divide this by 7, and you get the value of the discount per purse, which turns out to be $5.50. Now add that to the sale price of a single purse, and you get $17.50 as the non-discount price.

9. **A** You can Plug In, though the numbers will get fairly large once you start taking things to the 4th power. Or you can solve it as a quadratic, using FOIL. You may recognize it as a twist on $(x + y)(x - y)$. You know that when one binomial is a sum and the other a difference, their product will be the difference of two squares, so eliminate choice (C). After that, just make sure everything gets squared, coefficients as well as variables, and you wind up with choice (A).

10. **H** The formula for a rectangle's area is base × height. PITA to find which answer choice fits the parameters in the question. Remember to start with the middle value! If we use 6 for the longer side of the rectangle, that means the short side will be 3, since we need an area of 18. Adding all four sides together gives us $6 + 6 + 3 + 3 = 18$, the perimeter given in the question, so choice (H) is the correct answer.

11. **C** The sum of all the angles in any triangle is 180. Since $\angle X$ is 64°, the sum of $\angle Y$ and $\angle Z$ is calculated by subtracting 64° from 180°, leaving 116°.

12. **K** Every possibility must be accounted for. For each of the four skirts, there are five sock options. $4 \times 5 = 20$, so there are 20 skirt/sock combinations. For each of those 20 combinations, there are three sweater options. $20 \times 3 = 60$, so there are 60 skirt/sock/sweater combinations. Finally, for each of these 60 combinations, there are 4 headband options. $60 \times 4 = 240$ total outfit combinations.

13. **D** Use PITA. Start with the middle answer, choice (C), and you'll get $14 + 2(15) + \frac{16}{2} = 52$, so you know you need a higher set of numbers. Go to choice (D), and you'll get $16 + 2(17) + \frac{18}{2} = 59$.

14. **J** When ACT gives you a function and then identifies a number inside the parentheses, it means to plug that number in for x every time it appears in the question. In this case, $x = -2$, so the function will end up reading $h(x) = -5(-2)^3$. Then you get $h(x) = -5(-2)^3$. $(-2)^3 = -8$, and when you multiply that by -5, you get 40. Watch out for the traps in choices (J) and (K), which involve cubing the -5 along with the x.

15. **B** Don't overcomplicate here. Grab your calculator and see what the 4th root of 97 is (it's in the "Math" menu of your TI 80-series calculator). Another approach would be to recognize that $z = \sqrt[4]{97}$ could be altered to read $z^4 = 97$. This way, you can PITA. Since $3^4 = 81$, and $4^4 = 256$, the value of z must be between 3 and 4.

16. **F** The simplest approach is to PITA. Grab your calculator and divide each of the numbers in the question by each answer choice, starting with the highest answer choice, since the question asks for the greatest. 24 and 48 are factors of 96 and 144, but not of 108, so choices (H) and (K) must be eliminated. 18 and 36 are factors of 108 and 144, but not of 96, so choices (G) and (J) must be eliminated. That leaves choice (F) as the correct answer, because 12 divides evenly into all three numbers.

17. **B**   You'll need to know the formula for volume of a cylinder: $V = \pi r^2 h$. So plug the known height (10") into the formula and set it equal to the known volume. $40\pi = \pi r^2$ (10). $6\pi = \pi r^2$ (4). Solve from here, and you will find that $r = 2$. You can also PITA, since the answer choices represent the radius in that formula.

18. **H**   This problem is very difficult to visualize, so make sure you draw a figure. Since W represents 3:00, count the hours in the directions indicated in the problem and mark the points that you reach. X will be 7:00; Y will be 6:00, and Z will be 10:00. So the order, clockwise, will be W, Y, X, Z.

19. **D**   The trouble with this problem is that it looks more complicated than it is. Since a represents the number of days and the problem asks you about Day Four, plug 4 in for a and solve the equation. 3^4 is 81 and 81(12) is 972 tribbles.

20. **G**   The best approach is to Plug In. You need the formula for area of a triangle: $\frac{1}{2}bh$. The two triangles have the same base, so start there—plug in 5, for instance. Then Plug In for the heights; try 4 for the larger and 2 for the smaller. Now you can compute the respective areas. For the larger, $\frac{1}{2}(5)(4) = 10$ square feet (the problem calls this y), and for the smaller, $\frac{1}{2}(5)(2) = 5$ square feet. So the final step is to re-read the problem and make sure what you're being asked for. $Y = 10$, and $xY = 5$, so $x = \frac{1}{2}$.

21. **A**   To simplify the expression, distribute the negative to every term in the second set of variables and drop the parentheses: $2x + 3y + 4z - 6x + 7y - 8z$. Combine like terms to get $-4x + 10y - 4z$. Choices (B), (C), (D), and (E) forget to distribute the negative to at least one of the terms.

22. **J**   Use SOHCAHTOA for right triangles: CAH means $\cos\theta = \frac{adjacent}{hypotenuse}$, which is $\frac{y}{z}$. Remember to identify the adjacent and opposite legs of the triangle relative to angle θ. Choice (G) incorrectly gives the adjacent leg as x rather than y; choice (F) gives $\tan\theta$; choice (H) gives $\cot\theta$; choice (K) gives $\sec\theta$.

23. **B**   Draw a diagram with numbers 1–8 evenly spaced around a circle. On the first run, the paper is delivered to houses 1, 4, and 7; on the second run, the paper is delivered to houses 2, 5, and 8; on the third run, the paper is delivered to houses 3 and 6. Therefore, by the third lap, the paper has been delivered to all the houses.

24. **J**   In the equation of a line $y = mx + b$, the y-intercept is given by constant b, thus line q has a y-intercept of 500. The y-intercept of line m is 10 less than line q, so subtract 10 from 500 to get 490. Choice (K) incorrectly adds 10; choice (H) calculates the y-intercept as 10 *times* less, rather than 10 less than that of line m. Choices (F) and (G) use the slope rather than the y-intercept.

25. **B**   Simplify the expression by multiplying $-9a^5$ to each term in the parentheses. Remember MADSPM. When bases are multiplied, exponents are added. Therefore, the equation should look like this: $-9a^5(8a^7 - 4a^3) = -72a^{(5+7)} + 36a^{(5+3)} = -72a^{12} + 36a^8$. Choices (D) and (E) incorrectly multiply the exponents. Choice (C) doesn't distribute the negative sign to the second term. Choice (A) incorrectly subtracts non-combinable terms inside the parentheses and then multiplies $-9a^5$.

26. **G**   Consider PEMDAS and first combine the terms inside the absolute value: $-4|-9 + 2| = -4|-7|$. Then take the absolute value of -7, which is $+7$, and multiply by -4 to get -28. Choices (F) and (K) incorrectly take the absolute value of -9 and 2 first and then combine. Choice (H) adds rather than multiplying -4 and $+7$. Choice (J) neglects to take the absolute value of -7.

27. **B**   Given YZ is parallel to XV, $\triangle WXV$ and $\triangle WYZ$ are similar triangles, thus they have proportional sides. First use Pythagorean theorem $WX^2 = 6^2 + 8^2$ to calculate WX is 10, or remember that this is one of the special right triangles. Then set up the proportion $\dfrac{WX}{WY} = \dfrac{XV}{YZ}$ to find YZ: $\dfrac{10}{30} = \dfrac{6}{YZ}$, and YZ is 18 inches. Choices (A), (C), and (E) do not use the correct proportions; choice (D) is the length of WZ, not YZ.

28. **H**   Plug in a w value from the table and eliminate equations that do not give the corresponding h value. When you plug in $w = 0$, choices (G), (J), and (K) do not give $h = 7$. When you plug in $w = 1$, choice (F) gives $h = 8$, not 10, and also can be eliminated.

29. **A**   Simplify the expression by distributing the coefficients on both sides of the inequality: $4(n - 3) < 5(n + 2)$ becomes $4n - 12 < 5n + 10$. Combine like terms to get $-n < 22$ and divide by -1, remembering to flip the inequality sign. Choices (B), (C), (D), and (E) all result from either neglecting to distribute the coefficient completely through the parentheses or mixing up the positive and negative signs.

30. **J**   The other vertices of the triangle must be 4 inches from (1,1). Use POE. Choice (F) is 5 units to the left and choice (G) is only 1 unit to the left. Using either right triangles or distance formula, you can determine choice (H) is not long enough and choice (K) is too long. Choice (J) is 4 units due south from (1,1). If you have trouble remembering the distance formula, just sketch and ballpark!

31. **D**   Use the Pythagorean theorem: $m^2 + n^2 = 6^2$. Isolate m by subtracting n^2 and square rooting both sides. Choices (A), (B), and (C) do not correctly square each side length before isolating m. Choice (E) treats side m as the hypotenuse rather than one of the legs of the right triangle. If you get stuck with the algebra, plug in a value for n and use your calculator.

32. **G** Probability is the fraction of what you want (pear jellybeans) over total number of possibilities (all jellybeans). Use PITA. There are currently $10 + 16 + 19 = 45$ jellybeans in the jar. Start with choice (H). If 21 pear jellybeans are added, then there will be a total of 66 jellybeans in the jar. The probability of selecting a pear jellybean will be $\frac{21}{66}$, which is too low. Go to choice (G). If 11 jellybeans are added, there will be a total of 56 jellybeans in the jar. The probability of selecting a pear jellybeans will be $\frac{21}{56}$, which simplifies to $\frac{3}{8}$, making choice (G) the correct answer.

33. **C** To determine the graph of the equation, you must isolate the y by subtracting $6x$ *and* dividing by 3. The resulting equation is $y = -2x + 4$, which is a line with a slope of -2 and the y-intercept of $+4$. Because the y-intercept is positive, the line crosses y-axis from Quadrant II to Quadrant I and extends into Quadrant IV. The line never passes through Quadrant II, eliminating choices (B), (D), and (E). Choice (A) is a partial answer and does not include Quadrant I. Remember, in order to avoid doing any figuring, once you've got the equation in slope-intercept form, you can just plug it in to your graphing calculator.

34. **H** Substitute the values $(3, 4n)$ in for (x, y) in the equation to get $4n = -2(3)^2 + 10$. Remember PEMDAS: $4n = -2(9) + 10$, so $4n = -8$ and $n = -2$. Choice (F) results when you mix up the positive and negative signs. Choices (G) and (J) result when you do not use PEMDAS correctly. Choice (K) is a partial answer and gives the value of $4n$, not n.

35. **D** Plug In! Make sure you choose a value for the rent that divides evenly by 3 and 4. Let's say the rent is $24. Then, Jennifer pays $16, Kelly pays $6, and Meredith pays the remainder, or $2. The ratio of Jennifer's contribution to Kelly's contribution to Meredith's contribution is then 16:6:2, which simplifies to 8:3:1, or choice (D).

36. **F** The general equation of a circle is $(x - h)^2 + (y - k)^2 = r^2$, for which (h, k) are the coordinates for the center of the circle and r gives the radius length. For the given equation, the $h = 0$ and $k = -4$; choices (J) and (K) confuse the sign in front of k. Since $r^2 = 28$, the radius of the circle is $\sqrt{28}$. Choice (G) divides by 2 rather than square rooting 28. Choice (H) gives the value of r^2, not r.

37. **B** The perimeter of the figure consists of one side of the equilateral triangle and the arc length of two semicircles. You can immediately eliminate choices (A), (D), and (E) because the length of one side of the equilateral triangle is 6 inches. Both semicircles have a diameter of 6 and given $C = d\pi = 6\pi$, each semicircle has an arc length of 3π. With the exposed side of the triangle, the perimeter of the figure should be $P = 6 + 3\pi + 3\pi = 6 + 6\pi$. If you selected choice (C), you may have found the circumferences of two full circles rather than two semicircles.

38. **H** Because *DEFG* is a rhombus, which has equal sides and equal angles, all 8 triangles formed by drawing the diagonals in the figure are equivalent. *HEFM* encloses the area of 3 triangles and the shaded region the area of 5 triangles, thus the ratio is 3:5. Choice (J) is the ratio of the unshaded area to the total area.

39. **C** The midpoint is the average of the endpoints, so the y-coordinate of the midpoint is $\frac{y_1 + y_2}{2} = \frac{10 + (-2)}{2} = 4$. Choice (A) is the x-coordinate of the midpoint. Choices (B) and (E) only find the sum of the endpoint coordinates. Choice (D) confuses the negative sign and finds the average of 10 and 2.

40. **F** The volume of a cube is s^3, so this cube is $9^3 = 729$ cubic feet. Choice (G) gives the surface area of the cube. Choice (J) the area of 3 faces of the cube, choice (H) gives the area of 1 face, and choice (J) confuses the side as 3 feet rather than 9.

41. **D** Rearrange both equations into $y = mx + b$ form to compare their slopes and y-intercepts. The first equation $rx + sy = t$ becomes $y = -\frac{r}{s}x + \frac{t}{s}$. The second equation, $rx + sy = v$, becomes $y = -\frac{r}{s}x + \frac{v}{s}$. Both functions have the slope of $-\frac{r}{s}$ so they cannot intersect at only 1 point, eliminating Roman numeral I, thus choices (A), (C), and (E). A system of two linear functions can give a single line graph if the equations have the same slope and y-intercept, which occurs if $t = v$. Lines with same slope and different y-intercepts are parallel and never intersect so when t and v are not equal, you'll get two parallel lines, thus the answer must be choice (D).

42. **F** Because you are finding the side *O*pposite the 34° angle and are given the *H*ypotenuse, use SOHcahtoa or the *sine* function, eliminating choices (G), (H), and (K). Since $\sin 34° = \frac{\text{opposite}}{40}$, you solve for the distance by multiplying 40, not dividing and thus eliminating choice (J).

43. **D** Because 6th graders comprise 22% of the total number of students, $100 - 22 = 78\%$ of the students are not in 6th grade. The odds is the ratio of 22:78, which reduces to 11:39. Choice (E) incorrectly calculates the ratio of 6th graders to the total number of students. Choices (A), (B), and (C) are approximations of 22%; however, not as accurate as choice (D).

44. **H** Lines of symmetry cut the figure into two mirror images.

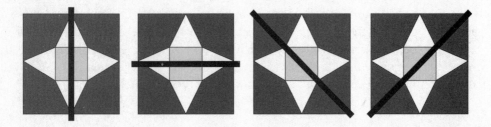

Since each of the divisions above creates two mirror images, the figure has four lines of symmetry.

45. **D** Because a square has right angles, you can determine the diagonal length using the Pythagorean theorem: $3^2 + 3^2 = d^2$. The diagonal is $3\sqrt{2}$ meters ≈ 4.2 meters. Choices (A) and (C) take the square root of 6 and 12, rather than 18. Choices (B) and (E) incorrectly calculate the diagonal without the Pythagorean theorem.

46. **G** Because the office wall is shorter, you can eliminate choices (J) and (K) immediately. Calculate 20% of the length of the current mosaic: 0.20×3 meters = 0.6 meters. Since the length is 20% shorter, subtract 0.6 meters from the original 3 meters. Choice (F) is a partial answer, but does not give the actual length of the office wall. Choice (G) subtracts 0.2 rather than 20%.

47. **B** Because $\overline{DG}$ bisects $\angle HDE$, $\angle HDG = \angle EDG = 68$. Since $\overline{DE} \parallel \overline{FG}$, $\angle FGD = \angle EDG = 68$. Since $\overline{HG}$ bisects $\angle FGD$, $\angle DGH = 34°$ $\angle DHG + \angle HDG + \angle DGH = 180'$, thus $\angle DHG = 78°$.

48. **H** Given the area of the circle is 16π square meters, the radius is 4 meters. $\overline{AC}$ is the longest chord in the circle, which is the diameter of the circle, so O can be labeled as the midpoint. $\overline{OA}$ and $\overline{OB}$ are each 4 meters, so ΔOAB is an equilateral triangle whose angles measure 60°. $\angle AOB + \angle BOC = 180$, so $\angle BOC$ measures 120°, making the arc degree also 120°. Choice (F) gives the measure of arc AB rather than BC. Choices (G) and (J) use an incorrect triangle.

49. **A** A system of equations has no solutions if the equations have the same slope and different y-intercepts. Two linear equations have the same slope if they have the same ratio of coefficients for x and y. Set up a proportion of the coefficients: $\dfrac{12}{8} = \dfrac{3}{b}$. $12b = 24$ so $b = 2$. Choices (B), (C), (D), and (E) do not give slopes equal to that of the first equation.

50. **F** The shading above the horizontal line segment means that the y-values, which represent the number of pies Rebecca and Scott make, are never less than 1. In other words, they always make at least 1 pie, which is choice (F).

51. **B** The best way to approach this question, since it asks about the *maximum*, is check the endpoints or extremes of the graph: (7,1) and (0,4). Using the provided expression for weekly profit, $12(7) + 25(1) = \$109$, which is choice (B). Alternatively, if you started with (0,4), $12(0) + 25(4) = \$100$, choice (A). This doesn't tell you much, but moving from there on to testing (7,1) will catch you up pretty quickly. After that, if you picked choice (E), be careful! You may have reversed d and p: $12(1) + 25(7) = \$87$.

52. **K**   If Rebecca and Scott made 5 pies at 3 hours each and 3 dozen cookies at 1 hour each, then they spent 18 hours baking that week. They donated $2 for every hour they spent baking, so they donated $36. The question asks what percent of that week's profit they donated, so calculate that week's profit. According to the provided expression for weekly profit, $12(3) + 25(5) = \$161$. The $36 donated, out of $161 earned, is approximately 22%, which is choice (K).

53. **A**   Following the formula provided, $(w)(10) - (w)(w) = 25$. Rearranging, $10w - w^2 = 25$ becomes $w^2 - 10w + 25 = 0$. Factoring the quadratic into $(w - 5)(w - 5) = 0$, the only possible value for w is 5, choice (A).

54. **K**   This formula may look complicated, but be careful with the pieces and this will be basic golden-rule algebra. If $x = B(1 + .2g)^n$, then divide both sides by $(1 + .2g)^n$ to get $\dfrac{x}{\left(1 + .2g\right)^n} = B$, which is choice (K). If you find the algebra daunting, you can also plug in simple numbers and find a target value for B.

55. **C**   The main things you know for sure about m and n are that m is negative and n is positive. The least complicated option is to plug in values for m and n that adhere to the rules you're given, making m negative and n positive. Testing each answer choice using those values allows you to eliminate any that don't work out to be true. Even if you have several answer choices remaining after crossing out the ones that don't work with those numbers, picking a second set of numbers—still playing by the rules!—and testing each of your *remaining* answer choices with your new values should help you narrow it down to one. Alternatively, consider your answer choices. For choice (A), a positive number divided by a negative number will produce a negative number, not something greater than 1. Cross this answer out. For choice (B), remember that absolute value makes the inside result positive, and this will happen to both n and m. Then $|n|$ is squared, which will still be positive. A positive number, $|n|^2$, may or may not be bigger than another positive number, $|m|$, so cross this answer out. In choice (C), subtract 2 from both sides and then multiply both sides by seven, so the expression becomes simply $n > m$, which you know to be true. Keep this answer. In choice (D), squaring both m and n make both values positive, without any sense of how large or small these newly positive numbers are. Thus, even after adding 1, there's still no way to say for sure which side is larger or smaller. As for choice (E), n^{-2} and m^{-2}, which are $\dfrac{1}{n^2}$ and $\dfrac{1}{m^2}$, are both positive numbers, but again you're given no sense of which is larger or smaller. The only answer that *must* be true is choice (C).

56. **J**

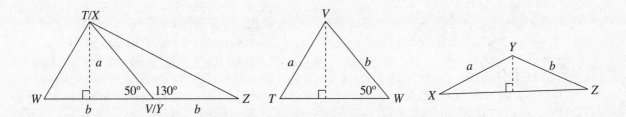

There are several ways to think about this question. There's not a lot of information to go on, so it becomes really important to pay very careful attention to what you do know and, since you're being asked to compare two things, any relationships you can discern. Noticing that the 50° angle and the 130° angle were supplementary might lead you to match up the a-sides to make the big triangle pictured above on the left. If Area $= \frac{1}{2} bh$, then for $\triangle TVW$, $\frac{1}{2}bh = 45$, so $bh = 90$. Looking at $\triangle TZW$, Area $= \frac{1}{2}(2b)(h) = bh = 90$. If the area of $\triangle TZW$ is 90, and the area of $\triangle TVW$ is 45, then $90 - 45 = 45$, so the area of $\triangle XYZ$ is also 45, choice (J). Alternatively, consider the two triangles side by side, as pictured above on the right. Given that a and b are the legs of both triangles, to go from the 50° angle to the 130° angle requires dropping the height and lengthening the base proportionally. Because the base and height are inversely related this way, the area will stay constant even as the height and base shift.

57. **E**

The first decision you have to make is which one (or both) of these laws is useful to you. You're trying to solve for a side where you have the opposite angle, but you don't have angles to match up with either of the other two sides you know. The sides are not equivalent, so you can't assume that the angles are equivalent. Consequently, you may not have enough information to use the law of sines. The law of cosines, on the other hand, would let you solve for the missing side, c, knowing only the other sides and the opposite angle. Line up each piece of the formula to find that $LJ^2 = 9^2 + 6^2 - 2(9)(6) \cos 50$. Before you start calculating this value, glance at your answer choices—they aren't asking you to solve completely, just to match up the filled-in formula. Take the square root of both sides to find $LJ = \sqrt{9^2 + 6^2 - 2(9)(6)\cos 50}$, or choice (E).

58. **G** Break this problem up into little pieces. An arithmetic sequence has a common difference between terms, so the same number is being added to get from one term to the next. If the 7th is 13.5 and the 11th term is 18.3, the 9th term must be exactly halfway between them at 15.9. Halfway between the 7th term and the 9th term is the 8th term, which would be at 14.7. If the 7th term is 13.5 and the 8th term is 14.7, then the common difference between terms is 1.2. Working backward from the 7th term, the 6th term is 12.3, the 5th term is 11.1, the 4th term is 9.9, the 3rd term is 8.7, the 2nd term is 7.5, and the 1st term is 6.3. Adding up the first three terms, $6.3 + 7.5 + 8.7 = 22.5$, which is choice (G). There is a formula for arithmetic sequences, but when you're dealing with relatively small numbers in relatively small quantities, often the most reliable thing to do is simply write it out.

59. **C** If the *only* possible value for w is 8, then the quadratic in factored form is $(w - 8)(w - 8) = 0$. Expanding this by FOILing gives you $w^2 - 16w + 64 = 0$. Line this up with the original equation to find that p must be 16, and q must be 64. With your answer choices, make sure you know what you're looking for—if you picked choice (E), you may have solved for q instead of p.

60. **F** The simplest thing to do is to start by determining which values the problem is describing. Since it wants the numbers that are 4 units from –1, only two points satisfy that: –5 and 3. If you're having trouble thinking about that, simply draw a number line and count it out.

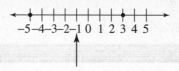

If the answer choices describe the solution set of –5 and 3, then you can test these values in each of the answer choices to eliminate ones that don't work. In choice (F), $|3 + 1| = 4$ and $|-5 + 1| = 4$. Both values work, so this will be your answer. In choice (G), $|3 - 1| \neq 4$, so eliminate that. In choice (H), $|3 + 4| \neq 1$, so eliminate that. In choice (J), $|-5 - 4| \neq 1$, so eliminate that, too. In choice (K), $|3 + 4| \neq 1$, so eliminate that.

Math for the SAT

Now that you've mastered the math and science sections for the ACT, it's time to switch gears.

Your preparation for the ACT math sections won't hurt your chances of getting a high SAT math score, but learning the test-specific strategies will only help you score higher.

Much of this chapter will be review, but study it well. Even though the SAT tests very basic mathematical concepts, these concepts are tested in very particular ways. To do well on the SAT requires that you know these definitions backward and forward.

After each section of review is a Quick Quiz with a variety of questions: easy, medium, and hard. If you get all of them right, you're in very good shape. And keep in mind: You could leave *all* the hard questions blank and still get a good score. So make sure you're getting the easy and medium ones right first.

DEFINITIONS

consecutive	numbers in order (1, 2, 3, etc.)
denominator	the bottom number of a fraction
difference	what you get when you subtract one number from another
digit	a number from 0 to 9. For example, 376 is a three-digit number.
distinct	different (i.e., the distinct factors of 4 are 1, 4, and 2—not 1, 4, 2, and 2)
even	a number evenly divisible by 2 (0 is even)
factor	same meaning as "division": a smaller number that goes into your number (example: 2 is a factor of 8)
multiple	a bigger number that your number goes into (example: 8 is a multiple of 2)
numerator	the top number of a fraction
odd	a number not evenly divisible by 2
PEMDAS	you won't see that written on the test—it's a handy acronym for the order of operations: Parentheses, Exponents, Multiplication, Division, Addition, Subtraction. Learn it, live it.
places	in 234.167, 2 is the hundreds place, 3 is the tens place, 4 is the ones or units digit, 1 is the tenths place, 6 is the hundredths place, and 7 is the thousandths place.
prime	a number divisible evenly only by itself and 1. The first five primes are 2, 3, 5, 7, and 11. (Note: 1 is *not* prime.)
product	what you get when you multiply two numbers together
quotient	what you get after dividing one number into another
reciprocal	whatever you multiply a number by to get 1 (i.e., the reciprocal of $\frac{1}{2}$ is $\frac{2}{1}$. The reciprocal of 6 is $\frac{1}{6}$.)
remainder	what's left over if a division problem doesn't work out evenly
sum	what you get when you add together two numbers

QUICK QUIZ #1

Easy

1. What is the greatest common prime factor of 32 and 28 ?

   (A) 1
   (B) 2
   (C) 3
   (D) 4
   (E) 7

Medium

9. If x is a positive integer greater than 1, and
   $x(x + 4)$ is odd, then x must be

   (A) even
   (B) odd
   (C) prime
   (D) a factor of 8
   (E) divisible by 8

Hard

20. Each of prime numbers p and q is greater than 12, their
    difference is two, and there is no prime number between
    p and q. Which of the following is the least possible
    value of $p + q$?

    (A) 18
    (B) 24
    (C) 28
    (D) 36
    (E) 42

Answers and Explanations: Quick Quiz #1

1. **B** Plug in the answer choices. Why bother thinking up the answer yourself when they give you five choices? Since the question asks for the greatest common *prime* factor, you can cross out anything that isn't prime—get rid of (A) and (D). Now start with (E), because it's the greatest answer choice. Does 7 go into 32? No. Cross out (E). (C): Does 3 go into 28? No, cross out (C). That leaves us with (B). Does 2 go into 32 and 28? Yep.

9. **B** Plug in your own number for x. If x has to be a positive integer greater than 1, try $x = 2$. But $2(2 + 4)$ isn't odd. So try $x = 3$. $3(3 + 4) = 21$, which works. Now you can cross out everything but (B) and (C). Try an odd number that isn't prime, say $x = 9$. $9(9 + 4) = 117$, which is odd. So cross off (C).

20. **D** This question requires careful reading and a bit of trial by error. Both p and q must be greater than 12 and prime. The first prime numbers greater than 12 are 13 and 17, but they do not differ by two. The next two prime numbers are 17 and 19; these work. Their sum is 36.

DIVISIBILITY

On the SAT, **divisible** means divisible *evenly*, with no remainder. This means that 16 is divisible by 4, but 18 is *not* divisible by 4. To figure out whether one number is divisible by another, use your calculator.

Factoring shows up on the SAT all over the place. That's okay, it's easy.

To find all of the factors of a number, factor in pairs. Start with 1 and make a list of all the pairs that multiply together to equal the original number:

What are the factors of 36?

1, 36

2, 18

3, 12

4, 9

6, 6

To find the **prime factors** of a number, simply find all the factors as shown above, and then select only those that are also prime numbers.

QUICK QUIZ #2

Easy

2. Which of the following could be a factor of
   $n(n + 1)$, if n is a positive integer less than 3 ?

   (A) 3
   (B) 4
   (C) 5
   (D) 8
   (E) 9

Medium

10. If Darlene divided 210 chocolate kisses into bags
    containing the same number of kisses, each of the
    following could be the number of kisses per bag
    EXCEPT

    (A) 35
    (B) 21
    (C) 20
    (D) 15
    (E) 14

Answers and Explanations: Quick Quiz #2

2. **A** Plug in. If $n = 1$, $1(1 + 1) = 2$. None of the answers are factors of 2. If $n = 2$, $2(2+1) = 6$. 3 is a factor of 6, so the answer is (A).

10. **C** You could use your calculator and divide each answer into 210, then pick the one that doesn't go evenly. Or you could factor 210 as $7 \times 5 \times 3 \times 2$. Now factor the answers. (A): 7×5, which goes in, so cross it out. (B): 7×3. Cross it out. (C): $2 \times 2 \times 5$. That doesn't go in because there's only one factor of 2 in 210.

FRACTIONS

To add fractions, get a common denominator and then add across the top:

$$\frac{1}{2} + \frac{2}{3} = \frac{3}{6} + \frac{4}{6} = \frac{7}{6}$$

To subtract fractions, it's the same deal, but subtract across the top:

$$\frac{3}{4} - \frac{1}{3} = \frac{9}{12} - \frac{4}{12} = \frac{5}{12}$$

To multiply fractions, cancel if you can, then multiply across, top and bottom:

$$\frac{1}{2} \cdot \frac{3}{5} = \frac{3}{10} \qquad\qquad \frac{2}{7} \cdot \frac{\overset{2}{\cancel{14}}}{9} = \frac{4}{9}$$

To divide fractions, flip the second one, then multiply across, top and bottom:

$$\frac{2}{3} \div \frac{1}{2} = \frac{2}{3} \cdot \frac{2}{1} = \frac{4}{3}$$

To see which of the two fractions is bigger, cross-multiply from bottom to top. The side with the bigger product is the bigger fraction.

$$55 \leftarrow \frac{5}{7} \times \frac{8}{11} \rightarrow 56$$

56 is bigger than 55, so $\dfrac{8}{11}$ is bigger.

QUICK QUIZ #3

Easy

3. Which of the following is greatest?

   (A) $\dfrac{3}{5} \times \dfrac{5}{3} =$

   (B) $\dfrac{3}{5} \div \dfrac{5}{3} =$

   (C) $\dfrac{3}{5} + \dfrac{3}{5} =$

   (D) $\dfrac{5}{3} - \dfrac{3}{5} =$

   (E) $\dfrac{5}{3} \div \dfrac{3}{5} =$

Medium

13. In a jar of cookies, there is $\dfrac{1}{6}$ probability of randomly selecting an oatmeal-raisin cookie and a $\dfrac{1}{8}$ probability of selecting a sugar cookie. If the remaining cookies are all chocolate chip cookies, then which one of the following could be the number of cookies in the jar?

    (A) 14
    (B) 16
    (C) 20
    (D) 24
    (E) 32

Hard

20. At a track meet, $\frac{2}{5}$ of the first-place finishers attended Southport High School, and $\frac{1}{2}$ of them were girls. If $\frac{2}{9}$ of the first-place finishers who did NOT attend Southport High School were girls, what fractional part of the total number of first-place finishers were boys?

(A) $\frac{1}{9}$

(B) $\frac{2}{15}$

(C) $\frac{7}{18}$

(D) $\frac{3}{5}$

(E) $\frac{2}{3}$

Answers and Explanations: Quick Quiz #3

3. **E** You can do some estimating here, but be careful—remember that when you divide by a fraction, you're really multiplying by the reciprocal. (E) is $\frac{5}{3} \div \frac{3}{5}$, which is $\frac{5}{3} \times \frac{5}{3} = \frac{25}{9}$. (A): 1. (B): $\frac{9}{25}$. (C): $\frac{6}{5}$. (D): $\frac{16}{25}$. If you had trouble figuring out any of those, go back to the fraction review.

13. **D** Plug in the answers. Start with (C). If there are 20 cookies in the jar, how many oatmeal-raisin cookies are there? Not a whole number, so this can't be correct. While it is not clear whether you need a bigger or smaller number, you now see that you need a number that is divisible by both six and eight, so both fractions will yield a whole number. Only (D) works.

20. **E** Plug in. The total number of first-place finishers was 30. You can find the number who were from Southport by taking $\frac{2}{5}$ of 30 = 12. That leaves 18 who did not go to Southport High School. If half the 12 Southport runners were girls, that means 6 were girls and 6 were boys. If $\frac{2}{9}$ of the non-Southport runners were girls, then $\frac{2}{9}$ of 18 = 4 girls, which leaves 14 boys. That means a total of 14 + 6 = 20 boys, out of a total of 30, or $\frac{20}{30} = \frac{2}{3}$. You will be happier if you make a tree chart:

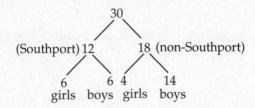

DECIMALS

To add, subtract, multiply, or divide decimals, use your calculator. Remember to check each number as you punch it in, and be extra careful with the decimal point.

To convert a fraction to a decimal, use your calculator to divide the numerator by the denominator:

$$\frac{1}{2} = 1 \div 2 = .5 \qquad \frac{5}{8} = 5 \div 8 = .625 \qquad \frac{4}{3} = 1.333$$

To convert a decimal to a fraction, count up the number of digits to the right of the decimal point and put that many zeros in your denominator:

$$0.2 = \frac{2}{10} \qquad .314 = \frac{314}{1000} \qquad 2.23 = \frac{223}{100}$$

QUICK QUIZ #4

Easy

1. If $0.2p = 4$, then $4p =$

   (A) 0.2
   (B) 2
   (C) 8
   (D) 40
   (E) 80

Medium

10. For positive integers y and z, if $z^2 = y^3$ and $y^2 = 16$, then $\dfrac{y}{z} =$

    (A) 0.8
    (B) 0.5
    (C) 0.4
    (D) 0.2
    (E) 2

Hard

19. $\dfrac{\frac{ad}{bc}}{\frac{ac}{bd}} =$

    (A) 1

    (B) a^2c^2

    (C) $\dfrac{a^2}{b^2}$

    (D) $\dfrac{d^2}{c^2}$

    (E) b^2d^2

Answers and Explanations: Quick Quiz #4

1. **E** If $0.2p = 4$, then $p = 20$, and $4p = 80$.

10. **B** If $y^2 = 16$, then $y = 4$. If $z^2 = y^3$, then $z^2 = 64$ and $z = 8$.

So $\dfrac{y}{z} = \dfrac{4}{8} = \dfrac{1}{2} = 0.5$.

19. **D** Remember that to divide fractions you flip the denominator and multiply. (Dividing is the same as multiplying by the reciprocal.)

So $\dfrac{\dfrac{ad}{bc}}{\dfrac{ac}{bd}} = \dfrac{ad}{bc} \cdot \dfrac{bd}{ac} = \dfrac{adbd^2}{abc^2} = \dfrac{d^2}{c^2}$.

PERCENTAGES

For some reason, many people get hung up on percents, probably because they are trying to remember a series of operations rather than using their common sense.

A percentage is simply a fractional part—50% of something is one-half of something, and 47% is a little less than half. It is very helpful to approximate percents in this way, and not to think of them as abstract, meaningless numbers. 3.34% is very little of something, 0.0012% a tiny part of something, and 105% a little more than the whole.

Keep in mind that since percents are an expression of the fractional part, they do not represent actual numbers. If, for example, you're a salesperson, and you earn a 15% commission on what you sell, you'll get a lot richer selling Rolls-Royces than you will selling doughnuts. Even thousands of doughnuts. All examples of 15% are not created equal, unless they are 15% of the same number.

Now for the nitty-gritty:

To convert a percent to a decimal, move the decimal point two spaces to the left:

50% = .5   4% = .04   .03% = .0003   112% = 1.12

To convert a decimal to a percent, move the decimal point two spaces to the right:

.5 = 50%   .66 = 66%   .01 = 1%   4 = 400%

To convert a percent to a fraction, put the number over 100:

$$50\% = \frac{50}{100} \qquad 4\% = \frac{4}{100} \qquad 106\% = \frac{106}{100} \qquad x = \frac{x}{100}$$

To get a percent of a number, multiply by the decimal. So to get 22% of 50, first change the percentage to a decimal by moving the decimal point two places to the left = .22. Then multiply on your calculator.

The second way to get a percent of a number is to translate your sentence into an equation. This is easier than it sounds. Convert the percent to a fraction and substitute × for *of*, = for *is*, and *x* for *what*.

What is 50% of 16?

This question translates to $x = \frac{50}{100} \times 16$.

This method is particularly useful for complicated percents:

What is 10% of 40% of 22?

This question translates to $x = \frac{10}{100} \times \frac{40}{100} \times 22$.

To calculate what percent one number is of another number, use the translation method, substituting $\frac{x}{100}$ for *what percent*.

What percent of 16 is 8?

This question translates to $\frac{x}{100} \times 16 = 8$.

8 is what percent of 16?

This question translates to $8 = \frac{x}{100} \times 16$.

Notice that even though these equations look a little different, they will produce the same answer.

QUICK QUIZ #5

Easy

3. If 20% of p is 10, then 10% of p is

(A)   2
(B)   4
(C)   5
(D)   8
(E)   14

Medium

11. Mabel agreed to pay the tax and tip for dinner at a restaurant with her four friends. Each of the friends paid an equal part of the cost of the dinner, which was $96. If the tax and tip together were 20% of the cost of the meal, Mabel paid how much less than any one of her friends?

(A) $2.40
(B) $4.80
(C) $9.20
(D) $19.20
(E) $24.00

Hard

18. If 200% of 40% of x is equal to 40% of y, then x is what percent of y?

(A)   10%
(B)   20%
(C)   30%
(D)   50%
(E)   80%

Answers and Explanations: Quick Quiz #5

3. **C** 10% is half of 20%, and half of 10 is 5. That way you don't have to worry about p. To figure p, translate the sentence: $\frac{20}{100} \times p = 10$.

$\frac{p}{5} = 10$, and $p = 50$. Now do the next step: $0.1 \times 50 = 5$.

11. **B** First calculate what each friend paid: $96 \div 4 = \$24$. Now do the percentage: $0.20 \times 96 = \$19.20$. Subtract the second number from the first. If you noticed that each of the four friends paid 25%, and Mabel paid 20%, you could take a fast shortcut by taking the difference, or 5% of 96. [If you picked (D) or (E), you should reread the question before picking your final answer.]

18. **D** Plug in $100 = x$. 40% of 100 is 40, and 200% of 40 is $2 \times 40 = 80$.

Now our question says that 80 is 40% of y, so $y = 200$, and $(80 = 0.4y)$.

The question asks "x is what percent of y?", which you can write out as $100 = \frac{p}{100} \times 200$. Or you can simply realize that 100 is half of 200, which is 50%.

More on Percentages

To calculate percent increase or decrease, use the following formula:

$$\text{percent increase or decrease} = \frac{\text{difference}}{\text{original amount}} \times 100$$

For instance, if a $40 book was reduced to $35, the difference in price is $5. Therefore, the percent decrease is equal to $\frac{5}{40} \times 100$, which is the same as $\frac{1}{8} \times 100$ or 12.5%.

QUICK QUIZ #6

Medium

14. A store owner buys a pound of grapes for 80 cents and sells it for a dollar. What percent of the selling price of grapes is the store owner's profit?

   (A) 10%
   (B) 20%
   (C) 25%
   (D) 40%
   (E) 80%

Hard

17. On the first test of the semester, Barbara scored a 60. On the last test of the semester, Barbara scored a 75. By what percent did Barbara's score improve?

   (A) 12%
   (B) 15%
   (C) 18%
   (D) 20%
   (E) 25%

Answers and Explanations: Quick Quiz #6

14. **B** First determine the store owner's profit. Change everything to cents so that you're only working with one unit: $100 - 80 = 20$. Now translate the question into math terms: $\dfrac{x}{100} \cdot 100 = 20$.

17. **E** Find the difference: $75 - 60 = 15$. Put this difference (15) over the lower number: $\dfrac{15}{60}$. Reduce the fraction to $\dfrac{1}{4}$, which is 25%. Or divide it on your calculator, which will give you 0.25. Convert it to a percentage by moving the decimal two places to the right.

> Estimating is always a good idea when you're doing a percentage question—a lot of the time there are silly answers that you can cross out before you do any math at all.

RATIOS

A ratio is like a percentage—it tells you how much you have of one thing compared to how much you have of another thing. For example, if you have hats and T-shirts in a ratio of 2:3, then for every two hats, you have three T-shirts. What we don't know is the actual number of each. It could be two hats and three T-shirts. Or it could be four hats and six T-shirts. Or 20 hats and 30 T-shirts.

A ratio describes a relationship, not a total number.

Whenever you need to convert from a ratio in its most reduced form to real-life numbers, there are two key steps:

- Always add the ratio numbers to get a whole.

- Find the factor that connects a ratio number to its real-life counterpart. All of the ratio numbers get multiplied by this factor to convert to real-life numbers.

A great way to see those two steps in action is to use a Ratio Box.

2. In Mr. Peterson's class of 48 students, the ratio of boys to girls is 3:5.

Boys	Girls	Whole
3 +	5 =	8	← Ratio
×	×	×
=	=	6	← Multiply by
=	=	=
+	=	48	← Actual number

i. How many girls are in the class? _____

ii. How many boys are in the class? _____

iii. Boys make up what fractional part of the class? __

iv. If you answered $\dfrac{18}{48}$ above, what does that reduce to?

Don't get the order of the ratio mixed up—if the problem says red marbles and blue marbles in a ratio of 1:2, the first number represents the red marbles and the second number represents the blue marbles.

Medium

12. If $\dfrac{x}{y} = \dfrac{4}{3}$ and $\dfrac{x}{k} = \dfrac{1}{2}$, then $\dfrac{k}{y} =$

    (A) $\dfrac{1}{6}$

    (B) $\dfrac{3}{8}$

    (C) $\dfrac{2}{3}$

    (D) $\dfrac{3}{2}$

    (E) $\dfrac{8}{3}$

16. The junior class at Mooreland High is composed of boys and girls in a ratio of 5:1. All of the following could be the number of students in the junior class EXCEPT

    (A) 12
    (B) 24
    (C) 42
    (D) 54
    (E) 62

Hard

20. In a certain ocean region, the ratio of sharks to tuna to damselfish to guppies is 1 to 3 to 5 to 6. If there are 1,500 total fish in that region, how many of the fish are sharks?

    (A)　　15
    (B)　　100
    (C)　　150
    (D)　　300
    (E)　　450

Answers and Explanations: Quick Quiz #7

12. **E** Since $x = 4$ in one ratio and $x = 1$ in the other, you can't compare them. First make them equal. If you multiply the second ratio by $\frac{4}{4}$, you get $\frac{4}{4}$. (Notice that if you multiply all parts of the ratio by the same number, it doesn't change. It just takes an unreduced form.) Now the x's are the same in both ratios, so you can compare them, and $\frac{k}{y} = \frac{8}{3}$. You could also plug in, which would work at least as well.

16. **E** If the ratio is 5:1, you can add the parts and get 6 students. Therefore, the number of students in the class must be a multiple of 6. All of the choices are multiples of 6 except (E).

20. **B** Make the ratio box. There are always three rows: ratio, multiply by, and actual. Here, the columns are: sharks, tuna, damselfish, guppies, and Total. In the first row, enter the ratio numbers: 1, 3, 5, and 6. Add them up, and put the sum (15) under Total. As the actual total is 1,500, enter that number in the lower, right cell. What times 15 is 1,500? 100. So, enter 100 in all of the multiply by cells. You can solve for all four fish types by multiplying the ratio number by 100, or just solve for sharks, as that is the question.

PROPORTIONS

To set up a **proportion**, match categories on top and bottom. For example:

If 10 nails cost 4 cents, how much do 50 nails cost?

$$\text{(nails)} \quad \frac{10}{4} = \frac{50}{x} \quad \text{(cents)}$$

$10x = 200$, so $x = 20$ cents

The great thing about proportions is that it doesn't matter which is on top—if you match nails to nails and cents to cents (or whatever), you'll get the right answer. Be consistent.

To solve an **inverse variation** problem, use the following set-up.

$$x_1 y_1 = x_2 y_2$$

If the value of x is inversely proportional to the value of y and $y = 4$ when $x = 15$, what is the value of x when y is 12?

$$x(12) = (15)(4)$$

$$x = 5$$

To solve rate problems, set up a proportion:

If Bonzo rode his unicycle 30 miles in 5 hours, how long would it take him to ride 12 miles at the same rate?

$$\text{(miles)} \quad \frac{30}{5} = \frac{12}{x} \quad \text{(hours)}$$

$$30x = 60$$
$$x = 2 \text{ hours}$$

QUICK QUIZ #8

Easy

2. Laura can solve 6 math questions in 12 minutes. Working at the same rate, how many minutes would it take Laura to solve 5 math questions?

   (A) 6
   (B) 8
   (C) 9
   (D) 10
   (E) 11

Medium

8. The length of time in hours that a certain battery will last is inversely proportional to the length of time in years that the battery spends in storage. If the battery spends 3 years in storage, it will last 25 hours, so how long must the battery have been in storage if it will last 15 hours?

   (A) 1.75 years

   (B) 5 years

   (C) 7.5 years

   (D) $41\dfrac{2}{3}$ years

   (E) 75 years

Hard

16. A factory produced 15 trucks of the same model. If the trucks had a combined weight of $34\dfrac{1}{2}$ tons, how much, in pounds, did one of the trucks weigh?

   (One ton = 2000 pounds)

   (A)   460
   (B) 2200
   (C) 4500
   (D) 4600
   (E) 5400

Answers and Explanations: Quick Quiz #8

2. **D** $\frac{6}{12} = \frac{5}{x}$. Cross-multiply to get $6x = 60$ and $x = 10$.

8. **B** To do this problem, it is important to know the formula for inverse variation: $x_1 y_1 = x_2 y_2$. In this case, the x_1 is 3 years, y_1 is 25 hours, and y_2 is 15 hours. So set up the equation as follows: $3 \times 25 = x_2 \times 15$. $\frac{75}{15} = x_2 = 5$ years.

16. **D** You can do this two ways: You can convert from tons to pounds first or do it later. If you do it first, multiply 34.5×2000. That gives you 69,000. Your proportion should look like this: $\frac{15}{69,000} = \frac{1}{x}$. So $15x = 69,000$, and $x = 4600$. Or you can divide 15 into 34.5, which gives you 2.3 tons per truck. Then multiply 2.3 times 2000.

AVERAGES

You already know how to figure out an average. You can figure out your GPA, right?

To get the average (arithmetic mean) of a set of numbers, add them up, then divide by the number of things in the set:

What's the average of 3, 5, and 10? $3 + 5 + 10 = 18$ and $18 \div 3 = 6$.

Most of the time on the SAT you are not given a set of numbers and asked for the average—they want to make their questions a little harder than that. There are three elements at work here: the sum of the numbers, the number of things in the set, and the average. To get any of these elements, you need to know the other two.

The easy way to remember these relationships is by memorizing the "Average Pie."

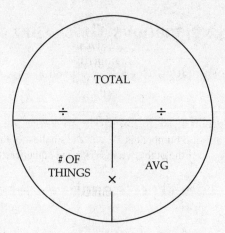

If you want to find any one element, cover it up, and what remains is the formula for finding it.

- The sum divided by the number of things = the average.

- The sum divided by the average = the number of things.

- The average multiplied by the number of things = the sum.

To solve an average problem, put whatever elements you are given into the average pie, and solve for the remaining element. The problem will always give you two parts out of the three, which will enable you to solve for the third.

QUICK QUIZ #9

Easy

6. The average of 3 numbers is 22, and the smallest of these numbers is 2. If the other two numbers are equal, each of them is

    (A) 22
    (B) 30
    (C) 32
    (D) 40
    (E) 64

Medium

12. Caroline scored 85, 88, and 89 on three of her four history tests. If her average score for all tests was 90, what did she score on her fourth test?

    (A) 89
    (B) 90
    (C) 93
    (D) 96
    (E) 98

Hard

14. The average of 8, 13, x, and y is 6. The average of 15, 9, x, and x is 8. What is the value of y ?

    (A) −1
    (B) 0
    (C) 4
    (D) 6
    (E) 8

Answers and Explanations: Quick Quiz #9

6. **C** If the average of 3 numbers is 22, then their sum is 3 × 22 or 66. Take away the 2 and you've got 64 left. If the other two numbers are equal, divide 64 by 2 = 32.

12. **E** Caroline's final average was 90 on 4 tests. Therefore you can use the average pie to figure out the total number of points she had on those four tests, by multiplying 90 × 4 = 360. You also know her scores on the first three tests, so if you subtract 360 − 85 − 88 − 89, you get 98 points, which is the total score she must have gotten on her fourth test.

14. **A** Since the average of 8, 13, x, and y is 6, you know that their total must be equal to 6 × 4 or 24. This means that 8 + 13 + x + y = 24. If you subtract the 8 and the 13, you find that $x + y = 3$. You also know that the average of 15, 9, x, and x is 8, so their total must be equal to 32. 15 + 9 + x + x = 32, so $x + x$ must equal 8, and $x = 4$. Since you know from earlier that $x + y = 3$, $y = -1$.

MEDIAN, MODE, SET, INTERSECTION, UNION, AND RANGE

Each of these terms involves finding a value or values in **sets** of numbers. A **set** is just a fancy term for a list of numbers.

The most common type of set question involves median.

To find the median, first put the group of numbers in ascending order. If the group has an odd number of elements, the median is the middle number.

set: 1, 4, 9, 18, 54	median: 9
set: 2, 4, 4, 4, 5	median: 4

If the group has an even number of elements, the median is *the average (arithmetic mean) of* the two middle numbers.

set: 3, 15, 17, 74	median: 16
set: 1, 6, 7, 8	median: 6.5

The remaining types of set questions are quite rare:

To find the mode, just look to see which number in the group appears the most often.

        set: 1, 1, 3, 5, 3, 4, 22, 3, 6   mode: 3

        set: 2, 5, 9, 11, 11, 15, 22   mode: 11

To find the intersection, list all the elements common to both sets.

        set: 2, 5, 8, 9, 12, 17

        set: 5, 9, 17, 25, 43   intersection: 5, 9, 17

To find the union, list all of the elements in each set.

        set: 2, 11, 13, 19, 33, 41

        set: 4, 8, 18, 19, 39, 75   union: 2, 4, 8, 11, 13, 18, 19, 33, 39, 41, 75

Note that even though the number 19 appears in both sets, it is only listed once for purposes of finding the union.

To find the range, subtract the smallest number from the largest.

        set: 3, 15, 28, 33, 33, 33, 42   range: 39

QUICK QUIZ #10

Easy

Set Q: {10, 2, 3, 5, 1, 7, 5, 2}

6. If the smallest and largest numbers in Set Q are removed, what is the median of Set Q?

   (A) 3.5
   (B) 4
   (C) 5
   (D) 6
   (E) 7

Medium

High Temperatures

Temperature	Number of days
22	2
25	2
28	3
31	0
34	4
37	1
40	2

12. Janet recorded the number of days certain high temperatures were reached over a 14-day period. She later decided to add data for one more day. If the high temperature on that day was 37, what is the median temperature for the set of days?

    (A) 26.5
    (B) 28
    (C) 31
    (D) 34
    (E) 35.5

Hard

18. If a set of 9 randomly selected numbers is generated, which one of the following changes CANNOT affect the value of the median?

(A) Subtracting 2 from each number
(B) Taking the square of each number
(C) Decreasing the largest number only
(D) Decreasing the smallest number only
(E) Increasing the largest and smallest numbers only

Answers and Explanations: Quick Quiz #10

6. **B** Take out 10 and 1. Now write down the numbers in order: 2, 2, 3, 5, 5, 7. The middle of the list falls between 3 and 5, so the median is 4.

12. **D** On a median question, it is essential to list out all of the numbers, including all of the repeated numbers. The original list of numbers, in order, is:

22, 22, 25, 25, 28, 28, 28, 34, 34, 34, 34, 37, 40, 40

Once the new number is added the set of numbers is:

22, 22, 25, 25, 28, 28, 28, 34, 34, 34, 34, 37, 37, 40, 40

The middle number of the new list is 34. If you picked (C), you chose the original median.

18. **D** Write out any set of nine numbers, such as 1 through 9. The median is 5. If you subtract 2 from each number, the median changes to 3, so (A) is wrong. If you square each number, the median changes to 25, so (B) is wrong. If you decrease the largest number to 4 or less, the median will change to 4, so (C) is wrong. On the other hand, no matter how much you decrease the smallest number, the median will remain the same, so (D) is correct. (E) is wrong because increasing the smallest number to 6 or more will change the median.

EXPONENTS AND ROOTS

An exponent tells you how many times to multiply a number by itself. So x^3 is really shorthand for $x \cdot x \cdot x$. If you have a momentary lapse and can't remember the following rules, it may help to write out your problem the long way and work from there.

For exponents with the same base, remember MADSPM:

To Multiply, Add the exponents: $x^2 \cdot x^5 = x^{2+5} = x^7$

To Divide, Subtract the exponents: $x^6 \div x^3 = x^{6-3} = x^3$

To raise the Power, Multiply: $(x^4)^3 = x^{4 \times 3} = x^{12}$

You cannot add or subtract different exponents, so $x^6 + x^3$ is just $x^6 + x^3$. You can't reduce it.

For exponents with different bases:

The trick is to try to rewrite the numbers in terms of the same base. For example:

$$6^2 \times 12^4$$

becomes

$$6^2 \times (6 \times 2)^4 \times = 6^2 \times 6^4 \times 2^4$$

Now you can combine terms with the same base as above.

To deal with exponents and parentheses, remember that the exponent carries over to all parts within the parentheses:

$$2(3a^3)^2 = 2[(3^2)(a^6)] = 2(9a^6) = 18a^6$$

Keep in mind that 1 raised to any power is still just 1. ($1^{357} = 1$.)

Negative numbers with even exponents are positive; negative numbers with odd exponents are negative. Fractions with exponents get smaller, not bigger.

A **square root** is just a backward exponent; in other words, the number under the $\sqrt{}$ is what you get when you raise a number to a power of 2.

$$\sqrt{4} = 2 \qquad\qquad \sqrt{36} = 6 \qquad\qquad \sqrt{1} = 1$$

To multiply or divide square roots, just multiply or divide as usual.

$$\sqrt{7} \cdot \sqrt{3} = \sqrt{21} \qquad\qquad \sqrt{15} \div \sqrt{3} = \sqrt{5}$$

To add or subtract square roots, first make sure you have the same number under the $\sqrt{}$. Then add or subtract the number outside of the $\sqrt{}$.

$$5\sqrt{3} + 2\sqrt{3} = 7\sqrt{3} \qquad 6\sqrt{2} - \sqrt{2} = 5\sqrt{2}$$

Note that:

- A square root multiplied by itself is just that number without the $\sqrt{}$. $\left(\sqrt{3} \cdot \sqrt{3} = 3\right)$

- The square root of a fraction gets bigger. For example, $\sqrt{\dfrac{1}{4}} = \dfrac{1}{2}$.

- The square root of a number is always positive (on the SAT, anyway).

- The square root of 1 is 1.

Rational exponents combine powers with roots. To simplify the following expression:

$$8^{\frac{2}{3}}$$

First we raise the base to the power of the numerator of the fraction. In this case, the numerator is two, so we'll square the base and get the following:

$$8^2 = 64$$

Now we'll deal with the denominator of the fraction. The denominator tells us what root to take the number to. In this case, the denominator is three, so we'll find the third root and end up with the following:

$$\sqrt[3]{64} = 4$$

QUICK QUIZ #12

Easy

1. If $(3x)^2 = 81$, then $x =$

   (A) 2
   (B) 3
   (C) 6
   (D) 9
   (E) 12

Medium

16. If $a > 0$, $b < 1$, and $c < 0$, assuming $b \neq 0$, which of the following must be true?

    (A) abc is positive.

    (B) abc is negative.

    (C) a^2b^2c is positive.

    (D) ab^2c^2 is positive.

    (E) $a^3b^3c^3$ is negative.

Hard

18. Which one of the following must be greater than x, if x is a real number?

    (A) $\dfrac{x}{4}$

    (B) $4x$

    (C) $x^2 + 1$

    (D) $x^3 + 1$

    (E) $\sqrt{x}$

Answers and Explanations: Quick Quiz #12

1. **B** Square everything within the parentheses, so you get $3^2 x^2 = 81$, or $9x^2 = 81$. Divide by 9 and you get $x^2 = 9$, and x could equal 3.

16. **D** Your life will be easier if you make a little chart showing the signs of each variable:

   $a +$

   $b \,?$

   $c -$

   Now go to the answers. If you don't know the sign of b, you don't know the sign of (A), (B), or (E). In (C), a^2 is positive, b^2 will have to be positive no matter what the sign of b is, and c is negative. So the whole thing is negative. The answer is (D).

18. **C** Because there are variables in the answer choices, plug in. Start with an easy number, such as $x = 2$. (A) is less than x, so eliminate it. (B) is greater than x, so keep it. (C) is greater than x, so keep it as well. So is (D). (E) is less than x, so eliminate it. Now try a different type of number. If you try 0 or a fraction, you'll get rid of (B), but not (C) or (D). Try a negative number, such as −3. While (C) is still greater than x, (D) is not.

PROBABILITY AND ARRANGEMENTS

Probability measures the likelihood something will happen:

$$\text{Probability} = \frac{\text{What You Want}}{\text{What You Have}}$$

Here's an example:

In a small garden of flowers, 3 are daisies, 4 are sunflowers, 2 are gardenias, and 3 are carnations. If a flower is selected at random, what is the probability that it will be a gardenia?

Solution: As there are 2 gardenias, the numerator of the fraction is 2. As there are 12 flowers in all, the denominator of the fraction is 12. Thus, the probability of selecting a gardenia is $\frac{2}{12}$ or $\frac{1}{6}$.

Questions about **arrangements** ask such questions as how many ways there are to order something or how many outfits are possible. These are easy to solve if you follow the steps shown for this example:

A restaurant offers a three-course dinner menu from which a person can select 1 of 4 appetizers, 1 of 5 main courses, and 1 of 3 desserts. How many different combinations of appetizer, main course, and dessert are possible?

As we are selecting three different items, first draw three slots as place-holders:

_____ _____ _____

Let's use the first slot for appetizers. How many appetizers are there, any one of which might be selected? 4, so write 4 above the slot. The next slot is for main course. How many main courses are there, any one of which can be selected? 5, so write 5 above the slot. The final slot is for dessert. As there are 3 desserts from which the selection can be made, write 3 in that slot. Your slots now look like this:

<u>4</u> <u>5</u> <u>3</u>

The final step is to multiply. $4 \times 5 \times 3 = 60$. That's it!

QUICK QUIZ #14

Easy

5. What is the probability of randomly choosing a white marble from a bag that contains 4 white marbles, 2 blue marbles, and 3 green marbles?

(A) $\dfrac{1}{4}$

(B) $\dfrac{2}{5}$

(C) $\dfrac{2}{7}$

(D) $\dfrac{4}{9}$

(E) $\dfrac{4}{5}$

Medium

11. In a drawer of socks, the probability of selecting a black pair of socks is $\dfrac{3}{8}$, and there are $\dfrac{1}{3}$ as many blue pairs of socks as there are black pairs of socks. If there are 12 brown pairs of socks, how many socks are there in the drawer?

(A) 16
(B) 24
(C) 32
(D) 40
(E) 48

Hard

18. Janice has 3 belts (one blue, one red, and one green), 3 bracelets (one blue, one red, and one green), and 3 scarves (one blue, one red, and one green). If Janice wants to create an outfit containing a belt, a bracelet, and a scarf such that each item is a different color, how many possible outfits can she create?

(A) 6
(B) 9
(C) 15
(D) 21
(E) 27

5. **D** The total number of marbles is 9, and 4 of them are white. That means there's a 4-in-9 chance of picking a white marble. Keep in mind that the total goes on the bottom and the part goes on the top, which gives you $\frac{4}{9}$. $\frac{9}{4}$ isn't one of the choices here, but a lot of people might have wanted to pick it. Be careful.

11. **B** You can plug in the answers. Start with (C). If $\frac{3}{8}$ of the pairs of socks are black, there are 12 pairs of black socks ($\frac{3}{8} \times 32$). As there are $\frac{1}{3}$ as many pairs of blue socks as pairs of black socks, there are 4 pairs of blue socks ($\frac{1}{3} \times 12$). Add the 12 pairs of brown socks to the pairs of black and blue socks to get 28 socks—not 32. At this point, it may not be clear whether to pick a bigger number or a smaller number, so just pick a direction. If the answer is even further off, then switch directions. Try a smaller number. If $\frac{3}{8}$ of the pairs of socks are black, there are 9 pairs of black socks ($\frac{3}{8} \times 24$). As there are $\frac{1}{3}$ as many pairs of blue socks as pairs of black socks, there are 3 pairs of blue socks ($\frac{1}{3} \times 9$). Add the 12 pairs of brown socks to the pairs of black and blue socks to get 24 socks—exactly what you wanted.

18. **A** Set up a slot for each of the three items. Start with the belt. How many belts are there, any one of which Janice might select? 3, so write 3 in the first slot. Move on to the bracelet. This time, there are only 2 bracelets she might choose, as she has already chosen a belt in a particular color—that color cannot be repeated. So, write 2 in the second slot. From the scarves, Janice may select only 1, as the other two colors are already chosen, so write 1 in the last slot. Multiply to get 6. If you picked (E), you did not account for the restriction on colors; there are 27 possible combinations, but only 6 involving all three colors.

SEQUENCES

Most **sequence** problems ask you to find a repeating pattern in a set of numbers.

To attack sequence problems, write out the pattern until it repeats itself. Then extend the pattern out until you can answer the question.

> A rainbow bracelet has a repeating sequence of beads that repeat in the following order: red, orange, yellow, green, blue, violet. What is the color of the 602nd bead?

First write out the pattern:

Red, orange, yellow, green, blue, violet, red, orange, yellow, green, blue, violet

Notice that the pattern repeats itself after every six beads. That means that every multiple of six will be violet, the sixth bead in the pattern. What multiple of six is closest to 602? 600 is a good choice. Thus…

600	601	602
Violet	Red	Orange

The 602nd bead is orange.

QUICK QUIZ #15

Easy

4. A certain list contains 11 consecutive multiples of 3. The first number is 21. What is the middle number?

   (A) 26
   (B) 27
   (C) 36
   (D) 39
   (E) 51

Medium

11. The first three numbers of a sequence are 1, 3, and 5, respectively. Every number in the sequence beyond the first three numbers can be found by taking the three preceding numbers, subtracting the second from the first, and adding the third. Which of the following is the sum of the first 40 numbers of the above sequence?

    (A) 6
    (B) 12
    (C) 24
    (D) 120
    (E) 480

Answers and Explanations: Quick Quiz #15

4. **C** The middle number in the list is the sixth term. Don't write out all the terms; just list them up to the sixth one: 21, 24, 27, 30, 33, **36**.

11. **D** If you follow the sequence out, the next number is 3, and then if you keep following the instructions, the sequence repeats itself (1,3,5,3 1,3,5,3 1,3,5,3 1,3,5,3) in sets of 4. So, take the first four numbers and find the sum (12) and multiply by 10 since you actually want the first 40 numbers.

Algebra on the SAT

In the section on strategy, we gave you some ways to avoid algebra altogether—but you still need to be able to work with simple equations and review some other algebraic principles that don't exactly crop up in everyday life.

SIMPLE EQUATIONS

Sometimes you can plug in with these, sometimes not. You will definitely need to be comfortable manipulating equations to do well on the SAT.

To solve a simple equation, get the variable on one side of the equals sign and the numbers on the other.

$$9x - 4 = 12 + x$$
$$8x - 4 = 12$$
$$8x = 16$$
$$x = 2$$

We just added 4 to both sides and subtracted x from both sides. Then we divided both sides by 8. You can add, subtract, multiply, or divide either side of an equation, but remember that what you do to one side you have to do to the other.

Polynomial equations look tricky but follow all the same rules of simple equations. You can add and subtract like terms—terms that have the same variables raised to the same powers.

What is the value of z if $3z + 4z + 7z = 42$?

In this case, the terms all have the same variable and are all to the same power. Thus, we can combine them to get $14z = -42$.

Now we'll divide each side by 14 and get $z = -3$.

To solve a proportion, cross-multiply:

$$\frac{3}{x} = \frac{1}{2}$$
$$x = 6$$

Remember that you can't cancel across an equals sign!

QUICK QUIZ #1

Easy

3. If $\dfrac{3x}{5} = \dfrac{x+2}{3}$, what is the value of x ?

(A) $\dfrac{1}{2}$

(B) 1

(C) 2

(D) $2\dfrac{1}{2}$

(E) 3

Medium

6. If $\dfrac{5}{x} = \dfrac{y}{10}$ and $x - y = y$, then $y + x =$

(A) 5
(B) 10
(C) 15
(D) 25
(E) 50

Hard

15. If 40 percent of x is equal to 160 percent of y, what is the value of $\dfrac{x}{y}$?

(A) $\dfrac{1}{12}$

(B) $\dfrac{1}{4}$

(C) 4

(D) 12

(E) 20

Answers and Explanations: Quick Quiz #1

3. **D** Cross-multiply, and you get $9x = 5(x + 2)$

$$9x = 5x + 10$$

$$4x = 10$$

$$x = 2\frac{1}{2}$$

6. **C** Plug in 10 for x and 5 for y. Both equations are satisfied by those numbers. So $y + x = 15$.

   Just to show you the kind of algebra that you'd be forced to do if you didn't plug in—first, cross-multiply to get $xy = 50$. Your other equation is $x - y = y$, so $x = 2y$. Substitute that x into the first equation, and you get $2y^2 = 50$, or $y^2 = 25$. So $y = 5$. Substitute $y = 5$ into either equation and solve for x. You get $x = 10$. Now add them up and you get $x + y = 15$. A lot more work, huh? If you don't plug in when you can, it's really going to slow you down. And that's the least of it. You're also more likely to get the question wrong because the algebra takes so many steps.

15. **C** Although you can plug in for one of the variables and solve for the other, you may find it easier to translate English into Math, and then isolate the two variables. As *percent* means "over 100," *of* means "times," and *is equal to* means "equals," the expression can be rewritten as follows:

$$\frac{40}{100} \times x = \frac{160}{100} \times y$$

Reduce the two fractions:

$$\frac{2}{5} \cdot x = \frac{8}{5} \cdot y$$

Now, isolate the variables on one side of the equation and the numbers on the other side. So, divide both sides by y, and multiply both side by $\frac{5}{2}$:

$$\frac{x}{y} = \frac{8}{5} \times \frac{5}{2} = \frac{8}{2} = 4$$

QUADRATIC EQUATIONS

Even the name is scary. What does it mean, anyway? No matter. All you need to know are a few simple things: factoring and recognizing perfect squares.

To factor, first draw a pair of empty parentheses. Deal with the first term, then the signs, then the last term. For example:

$$x^2 + x - 12 \qquad (\quad)(\quad)$$
$$(x \quad)(x \quad) \ldots \text{first term}$$
$$(x + \quad)(x - \quad) \ldots \text{signs}$$
$$(x + 4 \quad)(x - 3 \quad) \ldots \text{last term}$$

Check your factoring by multiplying the terms:

first term $= x \bullet x = x^2$

inner term $= 4x$

outer term $= -3x$

last term $= 4 \times -3 = -12$

Then add them up:

$$x^2 + 4x + -3x + -12 = x^2 + x - 12$$

Some guidelines:

If the last term is positive, your signs will be either +, + or −, −.

If the last term is negative, your signs will be +, −.

Your first try may not be right—don't be afraid to mess around with it a little.

To recognize the difference of two squares, memorize the following:

$$(x + y)(x - y) = x^2 - y^2$$

This format works whether you have variables, as above, or numbers:

$$57^2 - 43^2 = (57 + 43)(57 - 43) = 100 \times 14 = 1400$$

One more thing—memorize the following:

$$(x + y)^2 = (x + y)(x + y) = x^2 + 2xy + y^2$$

$$(x - y)^2 = (x - y)(x - y) = x^2 - 2xy + y^2$$

> When you see anything that looks like one form of these expressions, try converting to its other form. That should lead you straight to the correct answer.

QUICK QUIZ #2

Easy

7. If $\dfrac{x^2 + 5x + 6}{x + 2} = 12$, then $x =$

(A) −2
(B) 2
(C) 3
(D) 6
(E) 9

Medium

15. If $a - b = 3$ and $a^2 - b^2 = 21$, then $a =$

(A) −3
(B) −2
(C) 2
(D) 5
(E) 7

Hard

20. If $x < 0$ and $(2x - 1)^2 = 25$, then $x^2 =$

(A) −4
(B) −2
(C) 3
(D) 4
(E) 9

Answers and Explanations: Quick Quiz #2

7. **E** First, factor the expression to $(x + 3)(x + 2)$. Now you have $\dfrac{(x+3)(x+2)}{x+2} = 12$. The $(x + 2)$ cancels, and you have $x + 3 = 12$, so $x = 9$. Or you could plug in: If $x = 9$, $\dfrac{9^2 + 5(9) + 6}{9 + 2} = 12$, or $\dfrac{132}{11} = 12$.

It looks funny, but it works.

15. **D** Factor $a^2 - b^2$ to equal $(a + b)(a - b) = 21$. If $a - b = 3$, then $a + b = 7$. Here you could do one of two things. You can try some different numbers and see what satisfies both simple equations, or you could add the two equations together and get $2a = 10$, $a = 5$.

20. **D** Lots of algebra:

$$(2x - 1)^2 = 25$$

$$(2x - 1)(2x - 1) = 25$$

$$4x^2 - 4x + 1 = 25$$

$$4x^2 - 4x - 24 = 0$$

$$x^2 - x - 6 = 0$$

$$(x - 3)(x + 2) = 0$$

So x can be 3 or -2. If x is negative, it has to be -2, and $-2^2 = 4$. You could also Plug in, but you have to remember that the question asks for x^2, not x. That means (D) and (E) are good answers to try, since they're squares.

Don't forget that one of your main jobs on the SAT is following directions. If you picked (B) or (C), we suspect you did most of the problem correctly but forgot that x is negative, or failed to square x. Don't let carelessness rob you of your hard-earned points!

SIMULTANEOUS EQUATIONS

Two different equations, two different variables. You will not usually have to solve for both variables.

To solve simultaneous equations, stack 'em up, and either add or subtract:

If $2x + 3y = 12$ and $3x - 3y = -2$, what is the value of x?

$$\begin{array}{r} 2x + 3y = 12 \\ + \ 3x - 3y = -2 \\ \hline 5x = 10 \\ x = 2 \end{array}$$

If we had subtracted, we'd have gotten $-x + 6y = 14$, which wouldn't get us anywhere. If you choose the wrong operation, no big deal, just try the other one.

> Don't automatically start solving for x and y—you may not need to. Focus on what the question is specifically asking.

QUICK QUIZ #3

Medium

9. If $3x + 3y = 4$ and $2x - 3y = 1$, what is the value of x ?

   (A) $\dfrac{1}{3}$

   (B) 1

   (C) 3

   (D) 5

   (E) 6

11. If $3x + 5y = 15$ and $x - 2y = 10$, then $2x + 7y =$

    (A) 5
    (B) 10
    (C) 15
    (D) 25
    (E) 50

9. **B** Stack 'em and add:

$$3x + 3y = 4$$
$$+ \ 2x - 3y = 1$$
$$\overline{5x = 5}$$
$$x = 1$$

11. **A** Stack 'em and subtract: $\dfrac{-(x - 2y = 10)}{}$ $\quad$ $3x + 5y = 15$
$$3x + 5y = 15$$
$$- \ x - 2y = -10$$
$$\overline{2x + 7y = 5}$$

That's it. You don't have to solve for x or y individually. Less work is good. (Be careful with the signs when you subtract one equation from another.)

INEQUALITIES

Treat these just like equations, but remember one rule: **If you multiply or divide by a negative number, the sign changes direction.**

$$x + 6 > 10 \qquad\qquad 2x > 16 \qquad\qquad -2x > 16$$

$$x > 4 \qquad\qquad\quad x > 8 \qquad\qquad\quad x < -8$$

It's very easy to mix up the direction of the > or < sign.
Be extra careful.

QUICK QUIZ #4

Easy

3. If $3x + 7 < 5x - 4$, then

    (A) $\dfrac{11}{2} < x$

    (B) $x < \dfrac{3}{2}$

    (C) $x < \dfrac{11}{8}$

    (D) $x > \dfrac{2}{3}$

    (E) $\dfrac{11}{2} > x$

Medium

11. If $3b + 8 > 6 + 2b$, and b is a negative integer, then $b =$

    (A) 1
    (B) 0
    (C) −1
    (D) −2
    (E) −3

Hard

20. A "Prime Two Set" is defined as two prime numbers whose difference is 2. For example, 27 and 29 comprise a Prime Two Set, because the difference between them is 2. If p and q comprise a Prime Two Set, which one of the following must be true about p and q ?

    I.   The product of the two numbers is an odd number.
    II. $3p$ and $3q$ comprise a Prime Two Set.
    III. The difference between the squares of p and q is 2.

    (A) None
    (B) I only
    (C) I and II only
    (D) II and III only
    (E) I and III only

Answers and Explanations: Quick Quiz #4

3. **A** Treat the inequality just like an equation—subtract $3x$ from both sides, and you get $7 < 2x - 4$. Add 4 to both sides, and you get $11 < 2x$. Divide through by 2, which leaves you with $\frac{11}{2} < x$.

11. **C** Move the bs to one side and the integers to the other, and you get $b > -2$. If b is a negative integer, the only possibility is -1.

20. **B** As there are variables in the answer choices, plug in. Pick an easier Prime Two Set, such as 3 and 5. Roman I is true. While that does not prove it must be true, hang on to it for now. Roman II is false, as 9 and 15 are not prime, nor is their difference 2. Eliminate (C) and (D). Roman III is also false, as the difference between 9 and 25 is not 2. Eliminate (E). Now try one more Prime Two Set to ensure that Roman I is always true. 11 and 13 will work. The product is still odd. It always will be, as a Prime Two Set contains two odd numbers. Eliminate (A).

FUNCTIONS

Functions come in many forms on the SAT, but all of them require you to follow directions.

ETS may make up a math term you've never heard before. Relax, you didn't miss anything exciting in algebra class. Just follow the directions given by the definition of the term.

> The "prime component" of an integer is defined as the sum of all the prime factors of that integer. What is the prime component of 39 ?

First, break down 39 into its prime factors, 3 and 13. Next, find the sum: $3 + 13 = 16$. That's all there is to it.

Alternately, ETS may designate a function by using a strange-looking symbol. For example:

> For any integer t, $[t] = t^2 + t$. What is the value of $[4] - [3]$?

Solution: Take $[4]$ first. The direction tells us to square the number, and then add the number, so $4^2 + 4 = 20$. Now do the same for $[3]$. $3^2 + 3 = 12$. So $[4] - [3] = 20 - 12 = 8$.

Finally, ETS may resort to using actual mathematical functions, indicated by the expression $f(x)$.

If $f(x) = 2x^2 + 4x + 12$, what is the value of $f(4)$?

Don't be distracted by the fancy symbols; just pop the number into the function and crank out the answer. We want the $f(4)$, so wherever there is an x in the function, we'll replace it with a 4.

$$f(4) = 2(4)^2 + 4(4) + 12$$

$$= 2(16) + 16 + 12$$

$$= 60$$

QUICK QUIZ # 5

Easy

4. If $f(x) = 2x^2 + 3$, for which of the following values of x does $f(x) = 21$?

(A) −9
(B) −3
(C) 0
(D) 1
(E) 9

Medium

16. If $[a + b] = a^2 - b^2$, then $\dfrac{[x + y]}{x + y} =$

(A) $x + y$
(B) $x - y$
(C) $2x - 2y$
(D) 1
(E) $(x + y)^2$

Hard

19. The height of the steam burst of a certain geyser varies with the length of time since the previous steam burst. The longer the time since the last burst, the greater the height of the steam burst. If t is the time in hours since the previous steam burst and H is the height in meters of the steam burst, which of the following could express the relationship of t and H?

(A) $H(t) = \dfrac{1}{2}(t - 7)$

(B) $H(t) = \dfrac{2}{t - 7}$

(C) $H(t) = 2 - (t - 7)$

(D) $H(t) = 7 - 2t$

(E) $H(t) = \dfrac{2}{7t}$

Answers and Explanations: Quick Quiz #5

4. **B** In this case, plug in answer choices for the value of x, starting with (C). Plugging in 0 for x gives you $f(0) = 2(0)^2 + 3 = 3$. But you want $f(x) = 21$, so eliminate (C). Now try (B): $f(-3) = 21$, so this is the right answer. Alternatively, set $f(x) = 21$, and solve $21 = 2x^2 + 3$.

16. **B** $[x + y] = x^2 - y^2$, which factors to $(x + y)(x - y)$. When you divide, the $(x + y)$ term cancels, and you're left with $x - y$.

19. **A** The relationship is the greater the time, the greater the height. So the correct function is one that yields a greater H as you increase t. Try plugging in for t in the functions to see which one increases as t increases. Try $t = 10$ and $t = 20$. Only (A) has a greater H for $t = 10$ than it does for $t = 20$. That is $\dfrac{1}{2}(10 - 7) > \dfrac{1}{2}(20 - 7)$. The answer is (A).

Geometry on
the SAT

You're not going to believe how simple this is—no proofs, no trig, no parabolas. Just a few rules, a couple of formulas, and your common sense. And don't forget about estimating.

DEFINITIONS

arc	part of a circumference
area	the space inside a two-dimensional figure
bisect	cut in two equal parts
chord	a line that goes through a circle, but does not go through the center; it will always be shorter than the diameter
circumference	the distance around a circle
diagonal	a line from one corner of a square to its opposite corner
diameter	a line directly through the center of a circle; the longest line you can draw in a circle
equidistant	exactly in the middle
equilateral	a triangle with three equal sides, therefore three equal angles (60 degrees each)
hypotenuse	the longest leg of a right triangle, opposite the right angle
isosceles	a triangle with two equal sides and two equal angles
parallel	lines that will never intersect (think railroad tracks)
perimeter	the distance around a figure
perpendicular	two lines that intersect to form 90-degree angles
quadrilateral	any four-sided figure
radius	a line from the center of a circle to the edge of the circle (half the diameter)
volume	the space inside a three-dimensional figure

LINES AND ANGLES

A line has 180°, so the angles formed by any cut to your line will add upto 180°:

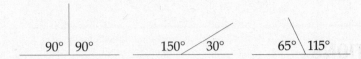

Two intersecting lines form a pair of **vertical angles**, that are equal:

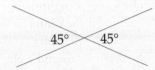

Parallel lines cut by a third line will form two kinds of angles: big ones and little ones. All the big ones are equal to each other; all the little ones are equal to each other. Any big angle plus any little angle will equal 180°:

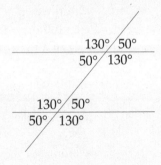

QUICK QUIZ #1

Easy

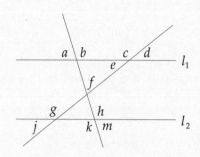

4. In the figure above, l_1 is parallel to l_2. Which of the following angles are NOT equal?

   (A) c and g
   (B) b and h
   (C) a and m
   (D) a and k
   (E) d and j

Medium

10. In the figure above, what is the value of $4a - b$?

   (A)   18°
   (B)   27°
   (C)   45°
   (D)   54°
   (E)   115°

Hard

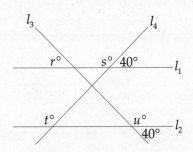

Note: Figure not drawn to scale.

18. Which of the following must be true?

(A) $l_1 \parallel l_2$
(B) l_3 bisects l_4
(C) $r = 40°$
(D) $s = t$
(E) $u = 140°$

Answers and Explanations: Quick Quiz #1

4. **D** Start with (A) and cross off as you go along. In (D), $a = m$, not k. Keep in mind that the two lines cutting through l_1 and l_2 aren't parallel, and so the angles made by one line have no relationship to the angles made by the other line.

10. **B** Estimate first. Outline the measurement of four of the a's. That's about 60. Now pretend you are subtracting b, about 45. How much is left? Not so much, right? Cross out (D) and (E). Now do the math: $2b = 90°$, so $b = 45°$. $5a = 90$, so $a = 18°$. Now plug those numbers into the equation: $4(18) - 45 = 27$.

18. **E** This question is actually very easy, as long as you don't pick the first answer that looks halfway decent and not even get to (E). Angle u has to be 140° because it's on a straight line with the angle marked 40°. All the other answers look like they're true, but you can't know for certain. The only thing you know for sure is that angles on the same line add up to 180°, and vertical angles are equal. None of these lines are necessarily parallel, so you can't assume anything else.

TRIANGLES

Triangles have 180°.

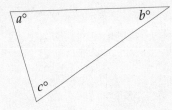 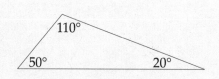

$a + b + c = 180°$ $50° + 20° + 110° = 180°$

Area = $\frac{1}{2} bh$.

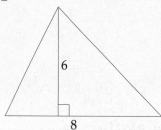 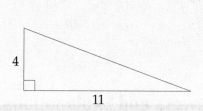

area = $\frac{1}{2}$ (8)(6) = 24   area = $\frac{1}{2}$ (11)(4) = 22

Perimeter: Add up the sides.

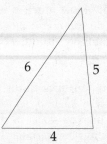

Perimeter = 15

Right triangles have a right, or 90°, angle:

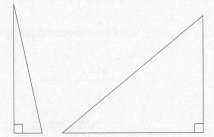

Isosceles triangles have two equal sides and two equal angles:

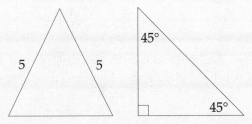

Equilateral triangles have three equal sides and three equal angles:

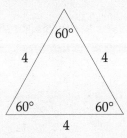

Similar triangles have equal angles and proportional sides:

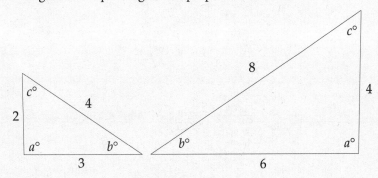

The Wonderful World of Right Triangles

For any right triangle, if you know the lengths of two of the sides, you can figure out the length of the third side by using the Pythagorean theorem:

$$a^2 + b^2 = c^2$$

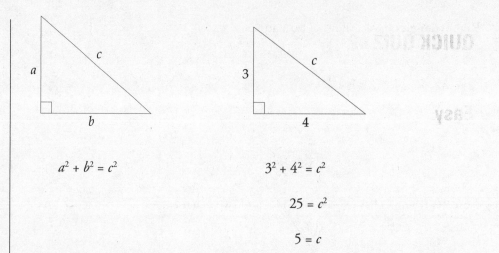

$$a^2 + b^2 = c^2$$

$$3^2 + 4^2 = c^2$$

$$25 = c^2$$

$$5 = c$$

However, you almost never need to use the theorem, because almost every right angle you will find will have lengths that fit one of these common Pythagorean triples.

3:4:5   6:8:10   5:12:13

In two special cases, you only have to know one side to figure out the other two, because the sides are in a constant ratio.

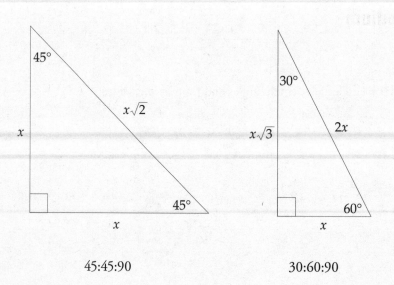

45:45:90   30:60:90

QUICK QUIZ #2

Easy

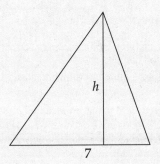

5. If the triangle above has an area of 21, then *h* equals

(A) 3
(B) 4
(C) 6
(D) 7
(E) 8

Medium

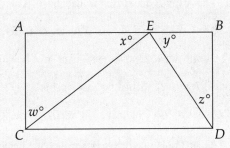

14. If *ABCD* is a rectangle, what is the value of
w + *x* + *y* + *z* ?

(A) 90
(B) 150
(C) 180
(D) 190
(E) 210

Hard

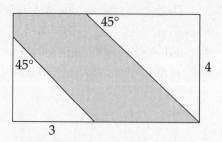

Note: Figure not drawn to scale.

20. If the rectangle above has an area of 32, and the unshaded triangles are isosceles, what is the perimeter of the shaded area?

(A) 16
(B) $10 + 7\sqrt{2}$
(C) $10 + 12\sqrt{2}$
(D) 32
(E) $70\sqrt{2}$

Answers and Explanations: Quick Quiz #2

5. **C** Estimate first—it's drawn to scale. If the base is 7, how long does the height look? About the same? Cross out at least (A) and (E), and (B) if you're feeling confident. Now do the math: area = $\frac{1}{2}$ bh, so $\frac{1}{2}$ $(7h) = 21$, and $h = 6$. It would be easy to pick (A) if you weren't paying attention, because $7 \times 3 = 21$, and so it seems appealing.

14. **C** If you picked (A) or (E), you didn't estimate. See how the rectangle is cut up into three triangles? Each of those triangles has 180°. Both of the triangles with marked angles also have right angles because they're corners of a rectangle. So $\Delta ACE + \Delta EBD = 360°$. Subtract the two right angles, and you're left with 180°.

20. **B** First write in everything you know: If the area is 32, the length is 8. That means the base is 3 + 5 and the left side is 1 + 3. The triangles in opposing corners are both 45:45:90 triangles: The one on the base has a hypotenuse of $3\sqrt{2}$, and the one with sides of 4 has a hypotenuse of $4\sqrt{2}$. Add up all the sides of the shaded part, and you get $10 + 7\sqrt{2}$.

Here's how it should look:

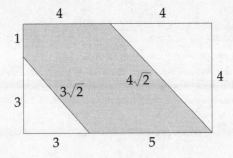

CIRCLES

Circles have 360°. Area = πr^2.

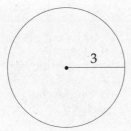

Circumference = $2\pi r$

$r = 3$

$C = 2\pi(3) = 6\pi$

$A = \pi(3)^2 = 9\pi$

> For any pie slice of a circle, the central angle, arc,
> and area are in proportion to the whole circle.

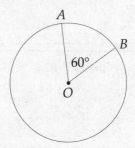

$\dfrac{60°}{360°} = \dfrac{1}{6}$, so arc AB is $\dfrac{1}{6}$ of the circumference, and pie slice AOB is $\dfrac{1}{6}$ of the total area.

QUICK QUIZ #4

Easy

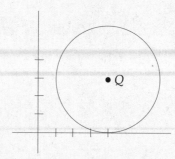

4. Center Q of the circle above has coordinates of $(4, 3)$.
   What is the circumference of the circle?

   (A) π
   (B) 2π
   (C) 6π
   (D) 8π
   (E) 9π

Medium

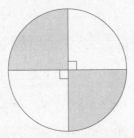

13. If the circumference of the circle above is 16π, what is the total area of the shaded regions?

    (A) 64π
    (B) 32π
    (C) 12π
    (D) 8π
    (E) 4π

Hard

20. One circle has a radius of r, and another circle has a radius of $2r$. The area of the larger circle is how many times the area of the smaller circle?

    (A) .5
    (B) 1.5
    (C) 2
    (D) 3
    (E) 4

Answers and Explanations: Quick Quiz #4

4. **C** The easiest way to solve this is simply to count the number of units in the radius, which is 3. Make sure you draw a radius on the diagram—if you draw it perpendicular to the y-axis you'll be able to count the units with no problem. If you picked (E), you found the area. Read the question carefully and give 'em what they ask for.

13. **B** The circumference is 16π, so use the circumference formula to get the radius: $2\pi r = 16\pi$, and $r = 8$. The area of the whole circle is $\pi r^2 = \pi(8)^2 = 64\pi$. Hold on—don't pick (A). At this point, you could happily estimate the shaded area as half the circle and pick (B). (Nothing else is close.) In fact, the shaded area is exactly half of the circle because each marked angle is 90°, which makes each of those pie slices $\dfrac{90°}{360°}$ or $\dfrac{1}{4}$ of the circle. So two of them make up $\dfrac{1}{2}$ of the circle, or 32π. Trust what your eyes tell you.

20. **E** Plug in. If $r = 2$, then the area of the small circle is 4π. The radius of the second circle is 2(2) or 4, so the area is 16π. The larger circle is 4 times as big as the smaller circle. (Don't you just love to plug in?)

> Notice how the hard question doesn't give you a picture or any real numbers to use. So draw the picture and make up your own numbers. Try to visualize the problem. Plugging In works just as well on geometry problems as it does on algebra problems.

Note: A very common careless error on circle problems is getting the area and circumference mixed up. Don't worry! The formulas are printed on the first page of each math section in case you forgot them.

QUADRILATERALS

Quadrilaterals have 360°.

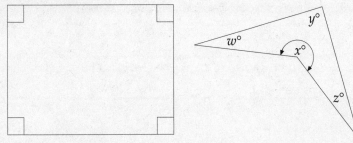

$$90° + 90° + 90° + 90° = 360° \qquad w + x + y + z = 360°$$

Perimeter: Add up the sides.

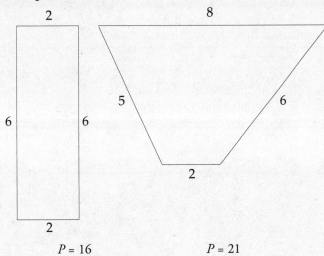

$$P = 16 \qquad\qquad P = 21$$

PARALLELOGRAMS

Parallelograms have two pairs of parallel lines, but no right angles.

Area = Base × Height

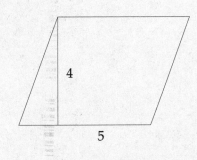

$$A = bh \qquad A = (5)(4) \qquad A = 20$$

Rectangles have four 90° angles and two pairs of parallel lines.

Area = $l \times w$

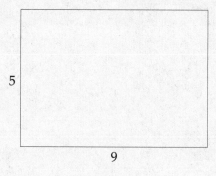

$A = lw$

$A = (9)(5)$

$A = 45$

Note that there's no relationship between the perimeter of a rectangle and its area.

$P = 36$	$P = 36$
$A = 17$	$A = 81$

Squares have four 90° angles and two pairs of parallel lines, all the same length.

Area = $l \times w$ or s^2

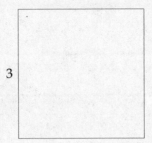

$A = s^2$
$A = 3^2$
$A = 9$

If you cut a square diagonally, you form two 45:45:90 triangles.

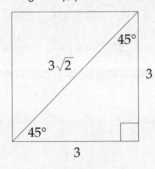

QUICK QUIZ #5

Easy

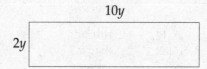

3. If $y = 3$, what is the perimeter of the figure above?

   (A) 12
   (B) 20
   (C) 50
   (D) 60
   (E) 72

Medium

9. What is the area of a square with a diagonal 5 ?

   (A) 10

   (B) 12.5

   (C) 25

   (D) $25\sqrt{2}$

   (E) $50\sqrt{2}$

Hard

B

A

Note: Figures not drawn to scale.

12. The length of Rectangle A is $\frac{1}{3}$ the length of Rectangle B, and the width of A is twice the width of B. What is the ratio of the area of A to the area of B ?

(A) $\frac{1}{3}$

(B) $\frac{2}{3}$

(C) 1

(D) $\frac{3}{2}$

(E) $\frac{3}{4}$

Answers and Explanations: Quick Quiz #5

3. **E** Figure out the dimensions of the rectangle if $y = 3$. That makes the length $10 \times 3 = 30$, and the width $2 \times 3 = 6$. Write those numbers on the diagram where they belong. To get the perimeter, add up all the sides. $30 + 30 + 6 + 6 = 72$.

9. **B** If the square has diagonal 5, then 5 is also the hypotenuse of the two 45:45:90 right triangles that are formed by the diagonal. Since you know the hypotenuse, you can find the other sides of the triangle, which are the sides of the square. As you know, in a 45:45:90 triangle, the ratio of the sides is $x:x:x\sqrt{2}$. Since the diagonal is 5, you know that $x\sqrt{2} = 5$, so the side $x = \dfrac{5}{\sqrt{2}}$. The area of the square is therefore $\dfrac{5}{\sqrt{2}} \times \dfrac{5}{\sqrt{2}} = 12.5$.

12. **B** Plug in. If the length of A is $\dfrac{1}{3}$ the length of B, make the length of $B = 6$ and the length of $A = 2$. If the width of A is twice the width of B, make the width of $B = 4$ and the width of $A = 8$. Now the area of $A = 2 \times 8 = 16$, and the area of B is $6 \times 4 = 24$. $\dfrac{A}{B}$ is $\dfrac{16}{24}$, or $\dfrac{2}{3}$.

BOXES AND CANS

Forget spheres, cones, and other complicated 3-D nightmares. Most often, you will be asked only to deal with rectangular solids (boxes), cubes (square boxes), and possibly cylinders (cans).

No matter what the shape is, the volume equals the area of one face × the third dimension (the depth or the height). Here are the formulas you need to know:

Rectangular Box

Volume = $l \times w \times h$

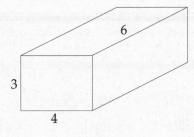

$$V = lwh$$

$$V = 6(3)(4)$$

$$V = 72$$

Cube

Volume = s^3

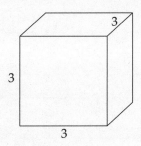

$$V = s^3$$

$$V = 3^3$$

$$V = 27$$

To find the diagonal of a box, draw in two right triangles: one on the end of the box and the other cutting through the box. The second triangle will have the hypotenuse of the first triangle as its base, the length of the box as its height, and the diagonal of the box as its hypotenuse. Here's how it will look:

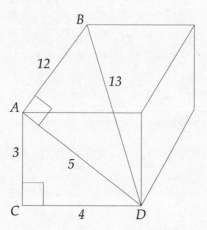

If *AC* is 3 and *DC* is 4, then *AD* is 5 (Pythagorean triple). If *AD* is 5 and *AB* is 12, then *BD* (the diagonal) is 13. (Another Pythagorean triple.) As you can probably guess, this only shows up on hard questions and not that often. You can also estimate the length of the diagonal—it will be a little longer than the longest edge of the box.

Surface Area

The surface area of a box is the sum of the areas of each of the faces.

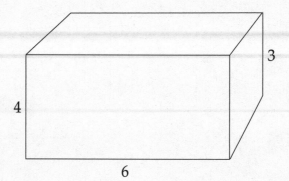

In the figure above, the front and back faces each measure 6 by 4; the side faces each measure 4 by 3; and the top and bottom faces each measure 6 by 3.

Front face (6 × 4) = 24

Back face (6 × 4) = 24

Left face (4 × 3) = 12

Right face (4 × 3) = 12

Top face (6 × 3) = 18

Bottom face (6 × 3) = 18

The surface area is the sum of these faces. 24 + 24 + 12 + 12 + 18 + 18 = 108.

Cylinder

Volume = $\pi r^2 h$

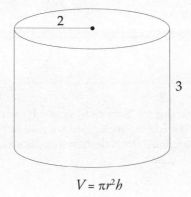

$$V = \pi r^2 h$$

$$V = \pi 2^2(3)$$

$$V = 12\pi$$

If the problem concerns a cone, pyramid, or any shape other than the ones described above, the necessary formula will be given in the question. If you aren't given a formula, you don't need one.

QUICK QUIZ #6

Easy

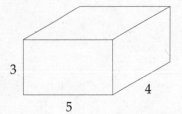 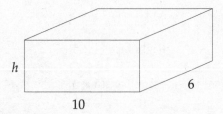

Note: Figures not drawn to scale.

6. If the volumes of the two boxes above are equal, then h equals

    (A)   1
    (B)   2
    (C)   4
    (D)   5
    (E)   20

Medium

9. Sam is packing toy blocks into a crate. If each block is a cube with a side of 6 inches, and the crate is 1 foot high, 2 feet long, and 2 feet wide, how many blocks can Sam fit into the crate?

    (A)   6
    (B)   12
    (C)   24
    (D)   32
    (E)   40

Hard

12. The surface area of a rectangular solid measuring $5 \times 6 \times 8$ is how much greater than the surface area of a rectangular solid measuring $3 \times 6 \times 8$?

    (A)   12
    (B)   24
    (C)   48
    (D)   56
    (E)   96

Answers and Explanations: Quick Quiz #6

6. **A** The box on the left has volume = $3 \times 4 \times 5 = 60$. The box on the right is then $10 \times 6 \times h = 60$. So $h = 1$. Don't forget to estimate!

9. **D** First draw the crate. It should look like this:

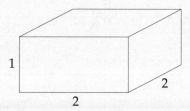

Now visualize putting blocks into the crate. If the blocks are 6 inches high, you'll be able to stack 2 rows in the crate since the crate is a foot high. Now mark off 6-inch intervals along the side of the crate. (You're dividing 2 feet, or 24 inches, by 6 inches.) You can fit 4 blocks along each side. Now multiply everything together and you get $2 \times 4 \times 4 = 32$ blocks.

You can also divide the volume of the crate by the volume of each block, as long as your units are consistent:

$$\frac{1 \text{ ft} \times 2 \text{ ft} \times 2 \text{ ft}}{\frac{1}{2} \text{ ft} \times \frac{1}{2} \text{ ft} \times \frac{1}{2} \text{ ft}} \quad \text{or} \quad \frac{12 \text{ in} \times 24 \text{ in} \times 24 \text{ in}}{6 \text{ in} \times 6 \text{ in} \times 6 \text{ in}}$$

12. **D** Find the surface area of the first figure. It has two sides 5×6, two sides 6×8, and two sides 5×8. Therefore its surface area is $30 + 30 + 48 + 48 + 40 + 40$, which makes 236. The second figure has two sides 3×6, two sides 6×8, and two sides 3×8. Its surface area is $18 + 18 + 48 + 48 + 24 + 24$, or 180. The difference between these two surface areas is 56.

COORDINATE GEOMETRY

Remember how to plot points? The first number is *x* and the second is *y*.

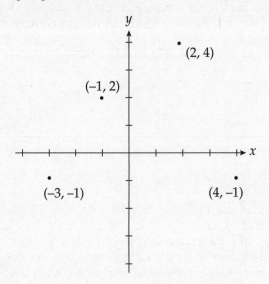

To find the length of a horizontal or vertical line, count the units:

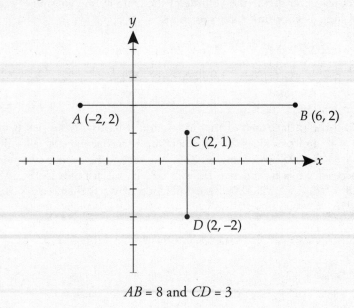

$AB = 8$ and $CD = 3$

To find the length of any other line, draw in a right triangle and use the Pythagorean theorem:

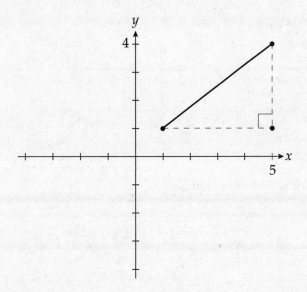

The triangle has legs of 3 and 4, so $3^2 + 4^2 = c^2$, and $c = 5$. (It's a Pythagorean triple again.)

To find the slope, put the rise over the run. The formula is

$$\text{slope} = \frac{y_1 - y_2}{x_1 - x_2}$$

It doesn't matter which point you begin with, just be consistent.

What is the slope of the line containing points (2, –3) and (4, 3)?

$$\text{slope} = \frac{-3 - 3}{2 - 4} = \frac{-6}{-2} = 3 \text{ or } \frac{3 - (-3)}{4 - 2} = \frac{6}{2} = 3$$

A slope that goes from low to high is positive.

A slope that goes from high to low is negative.

A slope that goes straight across is 0.

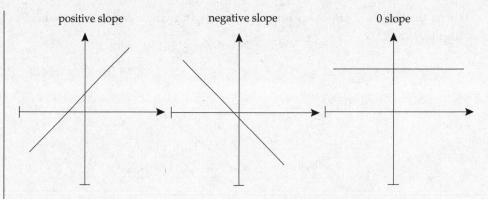

positive slope   negative slope   0 slope

Parallel lines have equal slopes. **Perpendicular lines** have slopes that are negative reciprocals of each other. For example:

> Which of the following sets of points lies on the line that is parallel to the line that passes through the points (1, 3) and (5, 8) ?
>
> (A) (−5, −8), (1, 3)
> (B) (12, 2), (8, −3)
> (C) (5, 3), (1,8)
> (D) (15, 3), (6, 2)
> (E) (−7, −5), (2, 3)

First, find the slope of the first set of points.

$$\text{slope} = \frac{3-8}{1-5} = \frac{-5}{-4} = \frac{5}{4}$$

Then check the answer choices and look for the set of points that has an equal slope. The correct answer is (B).

Try the same thing with perpendicular lines.

> Which of the following sets of points lies on the line that is perpendicular to the line that passes through the points (1, 3) and (5, 8) ?
>
> (A) (16, 7), (11, 11)
> (B) (8, 5), (3, 1)
> (C) (2, 5), (3, 13)
> (D) (7, 8), (5, 11)
> (E) (3, 3), (8, 8)

We already found the slope. Now we need its negative reciprocal, which is $\frac{-4}{5}$. Check the answers. Answer choice (A) gives us:

$$\text{slope} = \frac{7-11}{16-11} = \frac{-4}{5}$$

Bingo!

QUICK QUIZ #7

Easy

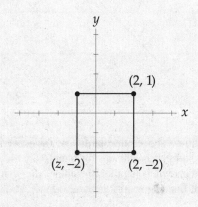

4. If the figure above is a square, what is the value of z ?

   (A)   –2
   (B)   –1
   (C)   1
   (D)   2
   (E)   4

Medium

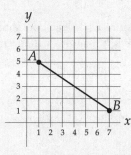

14. In the figure above, what is the length of AB ?

   (A) 4

   (B) $2\sqrt{6}$

   (C) 7

   (D) $\sqrt{52}$

   (E) $\sqrt{63}$

Hard

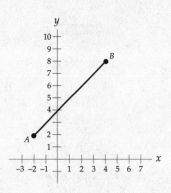

19. In the figure above, the coordinates for point *A* are (–2, 2) and the coordinates for point *B* are (4, 8). If line *CD,* not shown, is parallel to the line *AB,* what is the slope of line *CD* ?

(A) –1
(B) 0
(C) 1
(D) 2
(E) 4

Answers and Explanations: Quick Quiz #7

4. **B** Just count the units. Remember that coordinates in the lower left quadrant will always be negative.

14. **D** Use the units to measure each leg. You should get one leg = 4 and the other = 6. Now use the Pythagorean theorem: $4^2 + 6^2 = c^2$.

$$16 + 36 = c^2$$

$$52 = c^2$$

$$\sqrt{52} = c$$

19. **C** Write in the coordinates of *A* and *B*. *A* = (–2, 2) and *B* = (4, 8). So the slope of *AB* = $\dfrac{2-8}{-2-4} = \dfrac{-6}{-6}$ = 1. If *CD* is parallel to *AB*, it has the same slope. (You could draw in a parallel line and recalculate the slope, but you'd be doing extra work.)

CHARTS AND GRAPHS

The key to chart questions is to take a moment to size up the chart before you attack the question. Pay particular attention to what units are used.

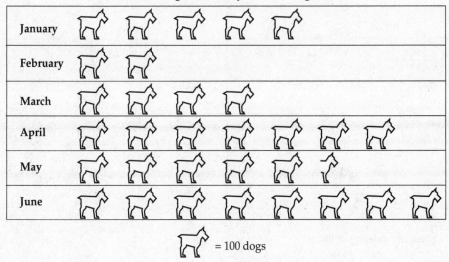

Number of Dogs Washed by Deidre's Dog Wash

= 100 dogs

Above is a chart representing how many dogs were washed by Deirdre's Dog Wash in the first half of 2004. Which month features the greatest percent increase of the number of dogs washed over the previous month?

(A) February
(B) March
(C) April
(D) May
(E) June

First, note the units. Each dog shape represents 100 dogs. Now, attack the question. You need to find the percent increase, which you'll recall is the difference between two numbers divided by the original number. (A) and (D) both show a decrease in the number of dogs, so eliminate them. In March, 400 dogs were washed, while 200 dogs were washed in the previous month. Using our percent increase formula, we get

$$\frac{\text{difference}}{\text{original}} = \frac{400 - 200}{200} = \frac{200}{200} = 100\%$$

None of the other choices is even close, so (B) is our answer.

For graphs involving functions, you will sometimes be asked to provide info on a portion of a function or how one function was translated into another function.

Consider the following function *f(x)*, with *x* values of *a* and *b*, as indicated:

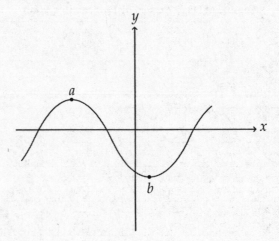

At $x < a$, *f(x)* is rising

At $a < x < b$, *f(x)* is falling

At $b < x$, *f(x)* is rising again

If a new function, *g(x)*, is formed by moving our original function *f(x)*, *g(x)* would be defined as follows:

If *f(x)* is moved 4 units up the *y* axis, then $g(x) = f(x) + 4$

If *f(x)* is moved 5 units down the *y* axis, then $g(x) = f(x) - 5$

If *f(x)* is moved 2 units to the right along the *x* axis, then $g(x) = f(x - 2)$

If *f(x)* is moved 3 units up the *y* axis, then $g(x) = f(x + 3)$

QUICK QUIZ #8

Easy

Adore-a-Bubble Soda Company's Sales

Flavor	1980	2000
Snappy Apple	50%	50%
Raspberry Rush	25%	5%
Fresh Fizz	10%	12%
Cranberry Crackle	12%	10%
Purple Pop	3%	3%
Total	100%	100%

6. The table above shows the Adore-a-Bubble Soda
   Company's sales for 1980 and 2000. The company sold
   200 trillion cans of soda in 1980. If the company sold
   40 trillion more cans of soda in 2000 than it did in 1980,
   then for which flavor did the <u>number</u> of cans of soda sold
   increase by 20% from 1980 to 2000 ?

   (A) Snappy Apple
   (B) Raspberry Rush
   (C) Fresh Fizz
   (D) Cranberry Crackle
   (E) Purple Pop

Medium

t	−1	0	1	2
$g(t)$	0	−2	0	6

11. The table above provides values for the function g for selected values of t. Which of the following defines the function g ?

(A) $g(t) = t^2 - 2$
(B) $g(t) = t^2 + 2$
(C) $g(t) = 2t^2 - 2$
(D) $g(t) = 2t^2 + 2$
(E) $g(t) = t^2 + 6$

Hard

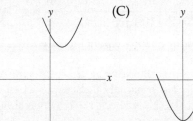

18. The quadratic function $y = f(x)$ is shown above. Which of the following graphs represents the function $y = f(x + 3) - 4$?

(A)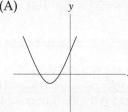

(B)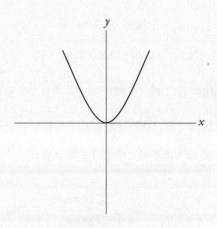

(C)

(D)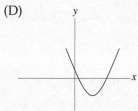

(E)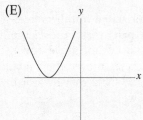

Answers and Explanations: Quick Quiz #8

6. **A** Use percent translation and the percent increase/decrease formula. For example, the number of cans of Snappy Apple sold in 1980 is 50% of 200 trillion. Using translation, you get $\frac{50}{100} \times 200$ trillion = $\frac{1}{2} \times 200$ trillion = 100 trillion. In 2000, the company sold 50% of 240 trillion. Using translation again gives you 120 trillion. Now you need to find the percent increase using the formula:

$$\text{Percent increase} = \frac{\textit{Difference}}{\textit{Original}} \times 100$$

Plugging in the values you found above gives you $\frac{120 \text{ trillion} - 100 \text{ trillion}}{100 \text{ trillion}} \times 100 = \frac{1}{5} \times 100 = 20$. This means that sales of Snappy Apple increased by 20%, so (A) is the correct answer.

11. **C** Plug the values in the chart into the answer choices. Start with the easiest value for t, namely 0. Because when t is 0, $g(t)$ is –2, eliminate (B), (D), and (E). Now check $t = 1$, which should yield $g(t) = 0$. Eliminate (A). (C) is the answer.

18. **A** Don't worry about actual numbers here—just how the graph moves. The – 4 outside of the parentheses moves the function down, so eliminate any answer choices that do not move down. (B) and (E) are wrong. The + 3 inside the parentheses moves the function to the left, so eliminate any remaining answer choices that do not move to the left. (C) and (D) are wrong. Only (A) works.

Geometry: Final Tips and Reminders

- Always estimate first when the figure is drawn to scale.

- Always write the information given on the diagram, including any information you figure out along the way.

- If you don't know how to start, just look and see what shapes are involved. The solution to the problem will come through using the information we've gone over that pertains to that shape.

QUICK QUIZ #9

Easy

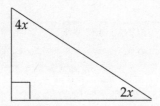

6. In the figure above, $x =$

(A) 15
(B) 45
(C) 85
(D) 105
(E) 125

Medium

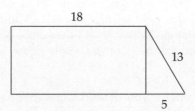

Note: Figure not drawn to scale.

11. The figure above is composed of a rectangle and a triangle. What is the perimeter of the figure above?

(A) 49
(B) 66
(C) 70
(D) 93
(E) 111

Hard

14. What is the slope of a line that is perpendicular to the line that passes through points (1, 2) and (2, 4) ?

    (A) −2

    (B) $-\dfrac{1}{2}$

    (C) 1

    (D) $\dfrac{1}{2}$

    (E) 2

Answers and Explanations: Quick Quiz #9

6. **A** Since the angles in a triangle always add up to 180, and you have a right angle, you know that the other two angles must have a sum of 90. You can write the equation: $4x + 2x = 90$. Now you can solve $6x = 90$, so x must be equal to 15.

11. **B** If you remember the ratios that work for the Pythagorean theorem, you'll remember that 5:12:13 is one common set of sides for right triangles on the SAT. Since this right triangle has sides 5 and 13, you know that the height of the triangle (which is also the height of the rectangle) is 12. So to figure out the perimeter of the whole figure, you need to add up the sides: 18 + 12 + 18 + 5 + 13 = 66.

14. **B** Start by estimating. If you draw the line that passes through (1, 2) and (2, 4), you see that it goes up and to the right, so it has a positive slope. If you draw a line perpendicular to it, the new line will go down and to the right, so it must have negative slope. This means that the answer has to be either (A) or (B). Further, if you drew your diagram accurately, you'll notice that the second line is at a very shallow angle, so its slope must be between −1 and 0, leaving only (B) as the possible answer choice.

Grid-In Questions
on the SAT

GRID-INS

Grid-in questions have no answer choices. You must solve the question, write your answer on a grid, and bubble it in. This isn't as bad as it sounds. The order of difficulty applies, so the first three questions (11–13) are easy, the middle four questions (14–17) are medium, and the final three questions (18–20) are hard. Take your time on the easy and medium questions, as always.

Tips for Grid-In Happiness

- Don't bother to reduce fractions: $\frac{3}{6}$ is as good as $\frac{1}{2}$.

- Don't round off decimals. If your answer has more than four digits, just start to the left of the decimal point and fit in as many as you can.

- Don't grid in mixed fractions. Either convert to one fraction or a decimal. (Use 4.25 or $\frac{17}{4}$, not $4\frac{1}{4}$.)

- If the question asks for "one possible value," any answer that works is okay.

- Forget about negatives, variables, and π. You can't grid them.

- You can still plug in if the question has an implied variable.

QUICK QUIZ #1

Easy

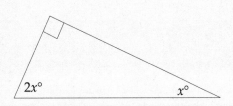

11. What is the value of *x* ?

Medium

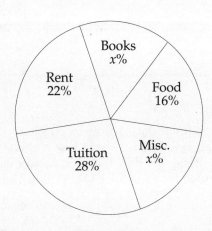

14. The chart above shows Orwell's projected expenditures for his freshman year at River State University. If he plans to spend a total of $10,000 for the year, how many dollars will Orwell spend on books?

Hard

17. If the function *r*(*s*) is defined as 2*s* + 3 for all values of *s*, and *r*(4) = *x*, what is the value of *r*(*x*) ?

Answers and Explanations: Quick Quiz #1

11. **30**

Since this is a right triangle, the other 2 angles add up to 90. So $3x = 90$ and $x = 30$.

14. **1700**

Two steps: First figure out the percentage of the budget spent on books, and then calculate the actual amount. All the pie slices add up to 100%, so $28 + 16 + 22 + 2x = 100$. $2x = 34$ and $x = 17\%$. Take 17% of 10,000, which is 1,700.

17. **25**

When a number is inside the parentheses, plug it into the equation. Thus, $r(4) = 2(4) + 3 = 11$. Thus $x = 11$. The question is not asking for $r(4)$, but $r(x)$. As you know $x = 11$, the question is asking for $r(11)$, so plug 11 into the formula. $r(11) = 2(11) + 3 = 25$.

SAT Problem Sets

The following groups of questions were designed for quick, concentrated study. The problems come in groups of ten (three easy, four medium, three hard). Answers and explanations follow immediately. The idea is for you to check your answers right after working the problems so that you can learn from your mistakes before you continue.

Don't simply count up how many you got wrong and then breeze on to the next thing—take a careful look at *how* you got the question wrong. Did you use the wrong strategy? Not remember the necessary basic math? Make a goofy computation error? Write an equation and plug in at the same time?

> You need to know the cause of your mistakes
> before you can stop making them.

Here are sets of plugging in, geometry, exponent, and other typical problem types to help you learn how to recognize those types of questions when they come up—so pay attention to the look and feel of them.

One last thing—the question numbers correspond to the difficulty level. For the 20-question multiple-choice section, the easy questions are number 1 to 8, the mediums are number 7 to 14, and the hard ones are number 15 to 20. You must always be aware of the difficulty level of the question you're working on.

PROBLEM SET 1: PLUGGING IN

Easy

1. Sinéad has 4 more than three times the number of hats that Maria has. If Maria has x hats, then in terms of x, how many hats does Sinéad have?

   (A) $3x + 4$
   (B) $3(x + 4)$
   (C) $4(x + 3)$
   (D) $4(3x)$
   (E) $7x$

2. When 6 is subtracted from $10p$, the result is t. Which of the following equations represents the statement above?

   (A) $t = 6(p - 10)$
   (B) $t = 6p - 10$
   (C) $t = 10(6 - p)$
   (D) $10p - 6 = t$
   (E) $10 - 6p = t$

3. Sally scored a total of $4b + 12$ points in a certain basketball game. She scored the same number of points in each of the game's 4 periods. In terms of b, how many points did she score in each period?

   (A) $b - 8$
   (B) $b + 3$
   (C) $b + 12$
   (D) $4b + 3$
   (E) $16b + 48$

Medium

4. If t is a prime number, and x is a factor of 12, then $\dfrac{t}{x}$ could be all of the following EXCEPT

   (A) $\dfrac{1}{12}$

   (B) $\dfrac{1}{4}$

   (C) $\dfrac{1}{2}$

   (D) 1

   (E) 2

5. Roseanne is 6 years younger than Tom will be in 2 years. Roseanne is now x years old. In terms of x, how old was Tom 3 years ago?

   (A) $x - 7$
   (B) $x - 1$
   (C) $x + 1$
   (D) $x + 3$
   (E) $x + 5$

6. A phone company charges 10 cents per minute for the first 3 minutes of a call and $10 - c$ cents for each minute thereafter. What is the cost, in cents, of a 10-minute phone call?

   (A) $200 - 20c$
   (B) $100c + 70$
   (C) $30 + 7c$
   (D) $100 - 7c$
   (E) $100 - 70c$

7. If $0 < pt < 1$, and p is a negative integer, which of the following must be less than -1 ?

   (A) p

   (B) $p - t$

   (C) $t + p$

   (D) $2t$

   (E) $t \times \dfrac{1}{2}$

Hard

8. If x and y are positive integers, and
$\sqrt{x} = y + 3$, then $y^2 =$

(A) $x - 9$

(B) $x + 9$

(C) $x^2 - 9$

(D) $x - 6\sqrt{x} + 9$

(E) $x^2 - 6\sqrt{x} + 9$

9. If cupcakes are on sale at 8 for c cents, and gingerbread squares are on sale at 6 for g cents, what is the cost, in cents, of 2 cupcakes and 1 gingerbread square?

(A) $8c + 3g$

(B) $\dfrac{cg}{3}$

(C) $\dfrac{8c + 6g}{3}$

(D) $\dfrac{8c + 3g}{14}$

(E) $\dfrac{3c + 2g}{12}$

10. If the side of a square is $x + 1$, then the diagonal of the square is

(A) $x^2 + 1$

(B) $2x + 2$

(C) $x\sqrt{2} + \sqrt{2}$

(D) $x^2 + 2$

(E) $\sqrt{2x} + \sqrt{2}$

Answers and Explanations: Problem Set 1

Easy

1. **A** Forget the algebra. Plug in 2 for x, so Maria has 2 hats. Triple that number is 6. Sinéad has 4 more than triple, so Sinéad has $4 + 6 = 10$. You should put a circle around 10, so you can remember it's the answer to the question, the magic number. Now plug 2 into the answer choices. (A) gives us $3(2) + 4 = 10$, which is just what you're looking for.

2. **D** Plug in 2 for p. $2 \times 10 = 20$; $20 - 6 = 14$. So $t = 14$. (Since this is an equation, when you pick one number, the other number is auto-matically produced by the equation.) If $p = 2$ and $t = 14$, (A) is $14 = 6(2 - 10)$. Does $14 = 12 - 60$? Not on this planet. (D) is $10(2) - 6 = 14$, or $20 - 6 = 14$. The equation works, so that's your answer.

3. **B** Make $b = 2$. That means she scored $4(2) + 12 = 20$ points total. If she scored the same number of points in each of the 4 periods, you have to divide the total by 4, so she scored $20 \div 4 = 5$ points per period. Put a circle around 5. Now on to the answer choices. (A) is $2 - 8$. (B) is $2 + 3 = 5$, which is our magic number.

Notice how we keep plugging in 2? That's because we're trying to make things as easy as possible. To get these questions right, you didn't have to pick 2; on some questions, 2 might not work so well. You can pick whatever you want. Just make sure your number doesn't require you to make ugly, unpleasant calculations. *Avoiding hard work* is the name of the game. If the number you pick turns bad on you, pick another one.

Always check all five answers when you plug in, just in case you get two correct answers. In that case, quickly plug in with a new number to find out which one was wrong.

Medium

4. **A** This question is tricky to spot as a plugging in question because the answer choices don't have variables. It does, however, ask how variables relate, so you can still plug in. Make a short list of possibilities for t, starting with the first prime number. Then do the same for x, listing the factors of 12 in pairs.

$$t = 2, 3, 5, 7 \qquad\qquad x = 1, 12, 2, 6, 3, 4$$

The question asks for $\dfrac{t}{x}$, which you can make by putting any number in your t column over any number from your x column. (B) is $\dfrac{3}{12}$. (C) is $\dfrac{3}{6}$. (D) is $\dfrac{2}{2}$. (E) is $\dfrac{2}{1}$. No matter what you do, you can't make $\dfrac{1}{12}$, so (A) is your answer. If you didn't remember that 1 is not prime, you were probably banging your head against a wall. When that happens, go on to the next question.

5. **C** Let $x = 10$, so Roseanne is now 10 years old. That's 6 years younger than 16, so Tom must be 16 in 2 years, which makes him 14 now. The question asks for Tom's age 3 years ago; if he's 14 now, 3 years ago he was 11. Circle 11. In the answer choices, plug 10 in for x. (A) is $10 - 3$. Nope. (B) is $10 - 1$. Nope. (C) is $10 + 1$. Yeah!

6. **D** Let $c = 8$. The first 3 minutes of the call would be $3(10)$, or 30 cents. The remaining minutes would be charged at $10 - 8$ cents, or 2 cents a minute. There are 7 minutes remaining, so $2 \times 7 = 14$. The total cost is $30 + 14 = 44$ cents. On to the answer choices: (A) and (B) are way too big. (C) is $30 + 7(8) = 86$. (D) is $100 - 56 = 44$.

7. **C** First take a good look at $0 < pt < 1$. You know that pt is a positive fraction. If p is a negative integer, then t must be a negative fraction. Now plug in. (Or you can just try numbers until you find some that satisfy the inequality.) Let $p = -1$ and $t = -\dfrac{1}{2}$. Try them in the answer choices, crossing out any answer that's -1 or higher. (A) is -1, cross it out. (B) is $-\dfrac{1}{2}$, cross it out. (C) is $-1\dfrac{1}{2}$, leave it in. (D) is -1, cross it out. (E) is -1, cross it out. The trouble with *must be* questions is that you can only *eliminate* answers by plugging in, you can't simply choose the first answer that works. That's because the answer may work with certain numbers but not with others— and you're looking for an answer that *must be true*, no matter what numbers you pick. These questions can be time-consuming, so if you're running low on time, you may want to skip them.

Hard

8. **D** Let $x = 25$. That makes $y = 2$. The question asks for y^2, and $2^2 = 4$. Circle it. Now try the answer choices. (A) is $25 - 9$. (B) is $25 + 9$. (C) is huge. (D) is $25 - 30 + 9 = 4$. Not so bad, huh?

9. **E** Let $c = 16$ and $g = 12$. That means the cupcakes and the gingerbread squares sell for 2 cents apiece. One gingerbread square and two cupcakes will cost 6 cents. Circle 6. On to the answer choices, plugging in 16 for c and 12 for g. (E) gives you $\dfrac{3(16) + 2(12)}{12} = 6$. Use your calculator for that last part. Get it right? Then go to a bakery and celebrate.

10. **C** Draw yourself a little square and label the sides $x + 1$. Draw in a diagonal. Let $x = 2$. The side of the square is then 3, and the diagonal is $3\sqrt{2}$. (The diagonal is the hypotenuse of a 45:45:90 triangle.) Plug 2 into the answer choices. (C) gives you $2\sqrt{2} + \sqrt{2} = 3\sqrt{2}$.

PROBLEM SET 2: MORE PLUGGING IN

Easy

1. Jim and Pam bought x quarts of ice cream for a party. If 10 people attended the party, including Jim and Pam, and if each person ate the same amount of ice cream, which of the following represents the amount of ice cream, in quarts, eaten by each person at the party?

   (A) $10x$

   (B) $5x$

   (C) x

   (D) $\dfrac{x}{5}$

   (E) $\dfrac{x}{10}$

2. If x and y are integers and $\dfrac{x}{y} = 1$, then $x + y$ must be

   (A) positive
   (B) negative
   (C) odd
   (D) even
   (E) greater than 1

3. If $3x - y = 12$, then $\dfrac{y}{3} =$

   (A) $x - 3$
   (B) $x - 4$
   (C) $3x - 4$
   (D) $9x - 12$
   (E) $3x + 4$

Medium

4. When x is divided by 3, the remainder is z. In terms of z, which of the following could be equal to x ?

   (A) $z - 3$
   (B) $3 - z$
   (C) $3z$
   (D) $6 + z$
   (E) $9 + 2z$

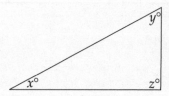

5. In the figure above, $2x = y$. In terms of x, $z =$

   (A) $180 + 2x$
   (B) $180 + x$
   (C) $180 - x$
   (D) $180 - 3x$
   (E) $180 - 4x$

6. If w, x, y, and z are consecutive positive integers, and $w > x > y > z$, which of the following CANNOT be true?

   (A) $x + z = w$
   (B) $y + z = x$
   (C) $x - y = z$
   (D) $w - x = y$
   (E) $w - z = y$

7. The volume of a certain rectangular solid is $12x$. If the dimensions of the solid are the integers x, y, and z, what is the greatest possible value of z ?

   (A) 36
   (B) 24
   (C) 12
   (D) 6
   (E) 4

Hard

8. If $x^3 < 0 < xy^2z$, which of the following must be true?

    I. xyz is positive
    II. $x^2y^2z^3$ is positive
    III. $x^3y^2z^3$ is positive

    (A) I only
    (B) III only
    (C) I and II only
    (D) II and III only
    (E) I, II, and III

9. When a is divided by 7, the remainder is 4. When b is divided by 3, the remainder is 2. If $0 < a < 24$ and $2 < b < 8$, which of the following could have a remainder of 0 when divided by 8 ?

    (A) $\dfrac{a}{b}$

    (B) $\dfrac{b}{a}$

    (C) $a - b$

    (D) $a + b$

    (E) ab

10. If $3x$, $\dfrac{3}{x}$, and $\dfrac{15}{x}$ are integers, which of the following must also be an integer?

    I. $\dfrac{x}{3}$

    II. x

    III. $6x$

    (A) I only
    (B) II only
    (C) III only
    (D) I and III only
    (E) II and III only

Answers and Explanations: Problem Set 2

Easy

1. **E** Plug in 20 for x. If 10 people eat 20 quarts, and they all eat the same amount, then each person eats 2 quarts. Put a circle around 2. Go to the answers and remember that $x = 20$. (A) $= 10 \times 10 = 100$. Nope. (E) $= \dfrac{20}{10} = 2$. Yep.

2. **D** Plug in 2 for x and 2 for y. That satisfies the equation $\dfrac{x}{y} = 1$, and makes $x + y = 4$. Eliminate (B) and (C). How about $-2 = x$ and $-2 = y$? That makes $x + y = -4$. Eliminate (A) and (E).

3. **B** Plug in 5 for x, which makes $y = 3$. So $\dfrac{y}{3} = \dfrac{3}{3} = 1$. Circle 1. On to the answers, and plug in $x = 5$. (A) $= 5 - 3 = 2$. No good. (B) $= 5 - 4 = 1$. There you go.

> Why do we keep saying "circle it" in the explanations? Because that's the arithmetic answer to the question. All that's left to do is plug in for the variables in the answer choices, and look for your circled number. We tell you to circle that number so it won't get lost in the shuffle, and you can keep track of what you're doing.
>
> Notice how sometimes, as in question 2, you may have to plug in more than one set of numbers. That doesn't mean you're doing anything wrong, it's just the nature of the question—and it tends to happen on must be questions.
>
> Also remember that you are trying to find numbers to plug in that make getting an answer to the question easy—so in question 3, if we'd plugged in x = 2, that would've made y negative. Who wants to deal with negatives if they don't have to? If some kind of nastiness happens, bail out and *pick new numbers*.

Medium

4. **D**   Let $x = 7$ so $z = 1$. Try the answers. (D) is $6 + z$, or $6 + 1 = 7$. No sweat.

5. **D**   Plug in 10 for x, which makes $y = 20$. Remember that a triangle has $180°$, so the third angle, z, must equal $180 - 30 = 150$. Circle 150. Try the answers, with $x = 10$. (D) gives us $180 - 30 = 150$.

6. **D**   First put the inequalities in order: $w > x > y > z$. Plug in consecutive positive numbers for the variables: $w = 5$, $x = 4$, $y = 3$, $z = 2$. Now try the answers.

        (A) $4 + 2 = 5$. No, so leave it in.

        (B) $3 + 2 = 4$. No, so leave it in.

        (C) $4 - 3 = 2$. No, so leave it in.

        (D) $5 - 4 = 3$. No, so leave it in.

        (E) $5 - 2 = 3$. Yes, so cross it out.

Try a new set of numbers. $w = 4$, $x = 3$, $y = 2$, and $z = 1$. This time (A), (B), and (C) all work, so get rid of them—that leaves (D) as our answer. Watch out when the question says CANNOT; it's all too easy to get mixed up and start thinking in the wrong direction. Look for answers that *work* and cross them out, rather than looking for the answer that *doesn't* work.

7. **C**   First, draw yourself a picture. (Think shoebox.) Plug in 2 for x. The formula for volume of a rectangular solid is length × width × height—in this case, xyz. Our volume is $12x = 12(2) = 24$. Let's come up with 3 different numbers—2 is one of them—that give us 24 when multiplied together.

A chart is never a bad idea. It keeps you organized.

x	y	z
2	1	12

Since y is as low as possible, z is as big as possible. Go with it. If you're not convinced, try other combinations—but don't forget, the question asks for the greatest possible value of z.

Hard

8. **B** Since there are a lot of exponents, plug in the smallest numbers you can. Positive/negative is what this question is about. Let's take it part by part. If $x^3 < 0$, you know x must be negative: Let $x = -1$. If $-1(y^2z)$ is positive, let $z = -2$. Beware! You don't know whether y is positive or negative, so you can't plug in anything for it. Look at I, II, and III, and remember you're looking for something that *must be* true:

> I. $xyz = -1(y)(-2)$. Maybe it's positive and maybe it isn't. It depends on the sign of y, and you don't know the sign of y.
>
> II. $x^2y^2z = 1(y^2)(-2)$. Sorry. It's negative.
>
> III. $x^3y^2z^3 = -1(y^2)(-2^3)$. Well, well, well. Since y is squared, it has to be positive. And the product of the other two negatives equals positive. It works.

9. **D** Plug in 11 for a and 5 for b. Those two choices satisfy all the conditions of the problem. Check the answers: (A) and (B) are fractions, forget about 'em. (C) is $11 - 5 = 6$, which isn't divisible by 8. (D) gives you $11 + 5 = 16$. If you divide 16 by 8, you get a quotient of 2 and a remainder of 0. End of story.

10. **C** How about plugging in 3 for x? Try the answers—you're looking for integers, so if the answer isn't an integer, you can cross it out.

> I. $\dfrac{x}{3} = \dfrac{3}{3} = 1$ OK so far.
>
> II. $x = 3$ OK so far.
>
> III. $6x = 6 \cdot 3 = 18.$ OK so far.

At this point, your average test taker figures the question is pretty easy and picks (E). Not you, my friend. *This is a hard question.* You must go an extra step. Plug in a new number. Since the question concerns integers, what if you plug in something that isn't an integer? Like $x = \dfrac{1}{3}$?

> I. $\dfrac{\frac{1}{3}}{3} = \dfrac{1}{9}$. That's no integer. Cross it out.
>
> II. $\dfrac{1}{3}$. No good either.
>
> III. $6\left(\dfrac{1}{3}\right) = 2$. Okay.

Since you have eliminated I and II, only III remains.

PROBLEM SET 3: PLUGGING IN THE ANSWER CHOICES

Easy

1. If x is a positive integer, and $x + 12 = x^2$, what is the value of x ?

    (A) 2
    (B) 4
    (C) 6
    (D) 8
    (E) 12

2. If twice the sum of three consecutive numbers is 12, and the two lowest numbers add up to 3, what is the highest number?

    (A) 2
    (B) 3
    (C) 6
    (D) 9
    (E) 12

3. If $2x = 8^{(x-4)}$, then $x =$

    (A) 4
    (B) 6
    (C) 8
    (D) 9
    (E) 64

Medium

4. If Jane bought 3 equally priced shirts on sale, she would have 2 dollars left over. If instead she bought 10 equally priced pairs of socks, she would have 7 dollars left over. If the prices of both shirts and socks are integers, which of the following, in dollars, could be the amount that Jane has to spend?

    (A) 28
    (B) 32
    (C) 47
    (D) 57
    (E) 60

5. During a vacation together, Bob spent twice as much as Josh, who spent four times as much as Ralph. If Bob and Ralph together spent $180, how much did Josh spend?

   (A) $20
   (B) $80
   (C) $120
   (D) $160
   (E) $180

6. Tina has half as many marbles as Louise. If Louise gave away 3 of her marbles and lost 2 more, she would have 1 more marble than Tina. How many marbles does Tina have?

   (A) 2
   (B) 3
   (C) 5
   (D) 6
   (E) 7

7. In a bag of jellybeans, $\frac{1}{3}$ are cherry and $\frac{1}{4}$ are licorice.

   If the remaining 20 jellybeans are orange, how many

   jellybeans are in the bag?

   (A) 12
   (B) 16
   (C) 32
   (D) 36
   (E) 48

Hard

8. If the circumference of a circle is equal to twice its area, then the area of the circle equals

   (A)   2
   (B) π
   (C) 2π
   (D) 4π
   (E) 16π

9. If $r = \dfrac{6}{3s+2}$ and $tr = \dfrac{2}{3s+2}$, then $t =$

   (A) $\dfrac{1}{4}$

   (B) $\dfrac{1}{3}$

   (C) 2

   (D) 3

   (E) 4

10. If x^2 is added to $\dfrac{5}{4y}$, the sum is $\dfrac{5+y}{4y}$. If y is a positive integer, which of the following is the value of x ?

   (A) $\dfrac{1}{4}$

   (B) $\dfrac{1}{2}$

   (C) $\dfrac{4}{5}$

   (D) 1

   (E) 5

Answers and Explanations: Problem Set 3

Easy

1. **B** Start with (C), 6 = x. That gives you 6 + 12 = 36. No good. At this point, don't stare at the other choices, waiting for divine inspiration—just pick another one and try it. It's okay if the next answer you try isn't right either. If you plug in 4 for x, you get 4 + 12 = 16. The equation works, so that's that.

2. **B** Start with (C). If the highest number is 6, the other two are 5 and 4. 5 and 4 don't add up to 3—cross out (C). Try (B). If the highest number is 3, the other two numbers are 1 and 2. (They have to be consecutive.) The sum of 3 + 2 + 1= 6, and twice the sum of 6 = 12. If you picked (A), you didn't pay attention to what the question asked for. Be sure to reread the question so you know which number they want.

3. **B** Try (C) first. Does $2^8 = 8^4$? Nope. (Use your calculator.) Try something lower, like (B). Does $2^6 = 8^2$? Yes.

Medium

4. **C** Try (C) first. If Jane has $47 to spend, 47 ÷ 3 = 15 with 2 left over. (The shirts cost $15 apiece.) Now try 47 ÷ 10 = 4, with 7 left over. (Socks are $4 a pair.) It works.

5. **B** Try (C) first. If Josh spent $120, Bob spent $240 and Ralph spent $40. That means Bob and Ralph together spent $280, not $180 as the problem tells us. (C) is no good. Since your number is way too big, try something smaller. If Josh spent $80, Bob spent $160 and Ralph spent $20. So Bob and Ralph together spent $180. That's more like it.

6. **D** Start with (C). If Tina has 5 marbles, then Louise has 10. If Louise gives away 3, then she has 7. If she loses 2 more, she's down to 5. You're supposed to end up with Louise having 1 more than Tina, but they both have 5. Cross out (C)—and you know you're close to the right answer. Try (D) If Tina has 6, Louise has 12. If Louise gives away and loses 5, she's got 7, which is 1 more than Tina has.

7. **E** Try (C) first. Oops— $\frac{1}{3}$ of 32 is a fraction. Forget (C). Try (D): $\frac{1}{3}$ of 36 = 12. $\frac{1}{4}$ of 36 = 9. Does 12 + 9 + 20 = 36? No. Try (E). $\frac{1}{3}$ of 48 = 16. $\frac{1}{4}$ of 48 = 12. Does 16 + 12 + 20 = 48? Yes!

Making a simple chart will help you keep track of your work:

	D	E
cherry	12	16
licorice	9	12
orange	20	20
TOTAL	41	48

Hard

8. **B** Try (C) first. If the area is 2π, then the radius becomes a fraction. That's probably not going to be the answer, so you should move on. Try (B). If the area is π, then the radius is 1. ($\pi r^2 = \pi$, $r^2 = 1$, $r = 1$.) If $r = 1$, the circumference is $2\pi(1) = 2\pi$. So the circumference is twice the area. Beautiful.

9. **B** Try (C) first. If $t = 2$, then look at the second equation:

$$2r = \frac{2}{3s+2}$$
$$r = \frac{2}{3s+2} \cdot \frac{1}{2}$$
$$r = \frac{1}{3s+2}$$

Compare that to the first equation. No good. Try (B). If $t = \frac{1}{3}$, then

$$\frac{r}{3} = 2(3s+2)$$
$$r = \frac{2}{3s+2} \cdot 3$$
$$r = \frac{6}{3s+2}$$

Same as the first equation. You're done.

10. **B** Choice (C) is particularly nasty here, so ignore it. Try Choice (D), plugging in 1 for x. You get $1 + \dfrac{5}{4y} = \dfrac{4y+5}{4y}$ or $1 = \dfrac{1}{4}$. (The y drops out.) (B) gives you $\dfrac{1}{4} + \dfrac{5}{4y} = \dfrac{5+y}{4y}$ or $\dfrac{1}{4} = \dfrac{1}{4}$. You could also solve by plugging in—choose a positive integer for y, plug it into the equation, and see what happens. You end up with $x = \dfrac{1}{2}$.

When you're plugging in, start with (C) unless (C) is hard to work with, as in question 10. In that case, try the integers, since they'll be easier to do anyway. And don't worry if you have to try a couple of answer choices before you hit the right one—the first one you do is always the slowest, because you're still finding your way. Subsequent tries should be easier. And plugging in is always easier than writing equations.

PROBLEM SET 4: MORE PLUGGING IN THE ANSWER CHOICES

Easy

1. If $\dfrac{a-4}{28} = \dfrac{1}{4}$, then $a =$

    (A) 11

    (B) 10

    (C) 7

    (D) 6

    (E) $\dfrac{3}{28}$

2. If the area of $\triangle ABC$ is 21, and the length of the height minus the length of the base equals 1, then the base of the triangle is equal to

    (A) 1
    (B) 2
    (C) 4
    (D) 6
    (E) 7

3. If $d^2 = \sqrt{4} + d + 10$, then $d =$

    (A) –2
    (B) 2
    (C) 3
    (D) 4
    (E) 16

Medium

4. If $\dfrac{4}{x-1} = \dfrac{x+1}{2}$, which of the following is a possible

   value of x ?

   (A) −1
   (B)   0
   (C)   1
   (D)   2
   (E)   3

5. The product of the digits of a two-digit number is 6. If the tens digit is subtracted from the units digit, the result is 5. What is the two-digit number?

   (A) 61
   (B) 32
   (C) 27
   (D) 23
   (E) 16

6. If $16{,}000 = 400(x + 9)$, what is the value of x ?

   (A) 391
   (B) 310
   (C)   40
   (D)   31
   (E)   4

7. What is the radius of a circle with an area of $\dfrac{\pi}{4}$?

   (A)   0.2
   (B)   0.4
   (C)   0.5
   (D)   2
   (E)   4

Hard

8. If 20 percent of x is 36 less than x percent of $x - 70$, what is the value of x ?

   (A) 140
   (B) 120
   (C) 110
   (D) 100
   (E) 50

9. If $x^2 = y^3$ and $(x - y)^2 = 2x$, then y could equal

   (A) 64
   (B) 16
   (C) 8
   (D) 4
   (E) 2

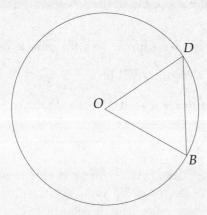

10. In the figure above, $OD = DB$ and arc $DB = 2$. What is the area of the circle?

   (A) 64π
   (B) 36π
   (C) 16π
   (D) 12π
   (E) 4π

Answers and Explanations: Problem Set 4

Easy

1. **A** Try (C) first. Does $\dfrac{3}{28} = \dfrac{1}{4}$? Nope. Look for a bigger number—(B) gives you $\dfrac{6}{28}$, which is closer, but still no cigar. (A) gives you $\dfrac{7}{28} = \dfrac{1}{4}$.

2. **D** Try (C) first. If the base = 4, then $h - 4 = 1$ and $h = 5$. The formula for area of a triangle is $\dfrac{1}{2}\,bh$, so the area would be 10. Too small. Try (D). If the base is 6, then $h - 6 = 1$ and $h = 7$. The area is $\dfrac{42}{2} = 21$.

3. **D** Yes, it looks nasty, but it's a breeze with the miracle of plugging in the answer choices. As always, try (C) first: $3^2 = \sqrt{4} + 3 + 10$; $9 = 2 + 13$. Forget it. Try (D). $4^2 = 2 + 4 + 10$; $16 = 16$. That's it.

> If you try (C) and it doesn't work, take a second to see if you need a higher or lower number. But if you can't tell *quickly*, don't spend too much time thinking about it— just try (B) or (D) and keep going.

Medium

4. **E** Try (C) first. If $x = 1$, does $\dfrac{4}{0}$ . . . forget it. You can't divide by 0. Try (D). If $x = 2$, does $\dfrac{4}{1} = \dfrac{3}{2}$? No way. Try (E). If $x = 3$, $\dfrac{4}{2} = \dfrac{4}{2}$. Yes. Remember to avoid trying negatives [like choice (A)] unless they're all you have left or you have some reason to think they'll be right.

5. **E** Take the directions of the problem one at a time. The product of the digits = 6, so cross out (C). Now for step two. Subtract the tens digit from the units digit, and look for 5. (E) does it. If you picked (A), you subtracted the units digit from the tens digit, which means you don't know the definitions (see the definitions review at the beginning of the Arithmetic section) or you didn't reread the question to see what your next direction was. Always reread the question before continuing on to the next step.

6. **D** Try (C) first. Does $400 \cdot 49 = 16,000$? No, and hopefully you just estimate that and don't bother doing it, with or without your calculator. How about (D)? $400(40) = 16,000$. Yep. If you picked (A), you miscounted the zeros. Try checking your answers on your calculator.

7. **C** Fabulous plugging in question. Try (C) first. Convert 0.5 to a fraction, because fractions are better than decimals and because the question has a fraction in it. If the radius is $\frac{1}{2}$, the area is $\pi\left(\frac{1}{2}\right)^2 = \pi\left(\frac{1}{4}\right) = \frac{\pi}{4}$.

Why do we like fractions better than decimals?

Mostly because that irritating little decimal point is so easily misplaced. Also because decimals can get very tiny and hard to estimate. You don't want to convert decimals to fractions automatically—only when the question would be easier to do that way. If the question is in decimals and the answers are in decimals, then don't bother converting.

Hard

8. **B** Try (D) first because the question is about percents and 100 is easy to do. 20% of 100 is 20. 100% of $100 - 70$ is 30. Does $30 - 20 = 46$? Nah. Try (B). 20% of 120 is 24. 120% of 50 is 60. Does $60 - 24 = 36$? Yes.

9. **D** Try (C) first. If $y = 8$, then $x^2 = 8^3$. $8^3 = 512$. If $x^2 = 512$, x isn't an integer. Forget (C). Try (D). If $y = 4$, then $x^2 = 4^3$. $x^2 = 64$; $x = 8$. Now try them in the second equation: $(8 - 4)^2 = 2(8)$. $4^2 = 16$. It works. Notice that when (C) didn't work, you went with a smaller number because it was easier.

10. **B** First, write in 2π beside arc DB. Now try (C). If the area is 16π, the radius is 4. Write in 4 beside the two radii, and also DB, because $OD = DB$. Aha! That makes triangle DOB equilateral! Since angle DOB is $60°$, and $\dfrac{60}{360} = \dfrac{1}{6}$, that makes arc DB $\dfrac{1}{6}$ of the circumference. Remember our radius is 4, so the circumference is 8π. Uh oh— 2π is not $\dfrac{1}{6}$ of 8π. So cross off (C). But at least now you know what to do. Try (B). If the area is 36π, the radius is 6 and the circumference is 12π. $\dfrac{1}{6}$ of 12π is 2π. Yeah! Did that seem really painful? It was a lot of work, but then, it was a hard question. The reason plugging in is a good technique for this problem is that if you plug in the answer choices, you get to move through the question like a robot, one step after the other, and you don't have to depend on a flash of insight.

PROBLEM SET 5: ESTIMATING

Easy

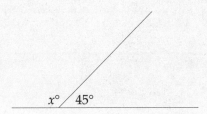

1. What is the value of $2x$?

   (A) 360
   (B) 270
   (C) 135
   (D)   90
   (E)   67.5

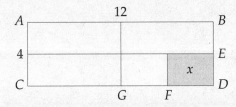

2. If F is equidistant from G and D, and E is equidistant from B and D, what fractional part of rectangle $ABDC$ is area x ?

   (A) $\dfrac{1}{16}$

   (B) $\dfrac{1}{8}$

   (C) $\dfrac{1}{4}$

   (D) $\dfrac{1}{3}$

   (E) $\dfrac{1}{2}$

3. If Sarah bought 12 pies for $30, how many pies could she have bought for $37.50 at the same rate?

   (A)   3
   (B)   9
   (C) 12
   (D) 15
   (E) 21

4. If a runner completes one lap of a track in 64 seconds, approximately how many minutes will it take her to run 40 laps at the same speed?

   (A)   25
   (B)   30
   (C)   43
   (D)   52
   (E)   128

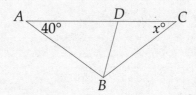

5. In the figure above, $BD = DC$ and $AB = AD$. What is the value of x ?

   (A)   110
   (B)   70
   (C)   55
   (D)   35
   (E)   15

6. Martina wants to buy as many felt-tip pens as possible for $10. If the pens cost between $1.75 and $2.30, what is the greatest number of pens Martina can buy?

   (A)   4
   (B)   5
   (C)   6
   (D)   7
   (E)   8

7. 1.2 is what percent of 600 ?

   (A)   0.002%
   (B)   0.2%
   (C)   5%
   (D)   20%
   (E)   500%

Hard

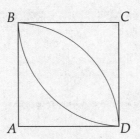

8. In the figure above, *ABCD* is a square with sides of 4.
   What is the length of arc *BD* ?

   (A) 8π
   (B) 4π
   (C) 3π
   (D) 2π
   (E) π

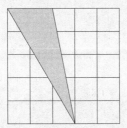

9. Each of the small squares in the figure above has an
   area of 4. If the shortest side of the triangle is equal in
   length to 2 sides of a small square, what is the area of the
   shaded triangle?

   (A) 160
   (B) 40
   (C) 24
   (D) 20
   (E) 16

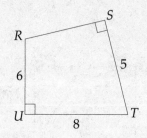

Note: Figure not drawn to scale.

10. In the figure above, what is the length of *RS* ?

(A)   10

(B) $5\sqrt{3}$

(C)   8

(D) $\sqrt{5}$

(E) $2\sqrt{3}$

Answers and Explanations: Problem Set 5

Easy

1. **B** Estimate first: x looks pretty big, doesn't it? Bigger than 90? Yes. So $2x$ will be bigger than 180. Cross out (C), (D), and (E). Is x a line of 180? Of course not. So $2x$ is less than 360. Cross out (A).

2. **B** Use your eyeballs and compare against the answer choices. Does x look like $\frac{1}{2}$ of the rectangle? No? Cross out (E). What about $\frac{1}{3}$? Cross out (D). $\frac{1}{4}$? Cross out (C). Could you fit 16 xs in the rectangle? No—cross out (A). It's also helpful to draw more boxes in the figure, and then you could count them up:

3. **D** $37.50 is going to buy more pies than $30, right? So cross out anything less than or equal to 12. Say goodbye to (A), (B), and (C). Now, any chance an extra 7.50 will buy nearly another 12 pies? No. Eliminate (E).

Medium

4. **C** This is a great question for estimating. Don't like 64 seconds? Call it 60, or 1 minute. If the runner completes a lap in just over a minute, she'll complete 40 laps in just over 40 minutes. Only (C) is close.

5. **D** First just eyeball the angle. It's smaller than 90°. It's close to angle *BAD*, which is marked 40. You're down to (C) and (D). Is it a little smaller than *BAD* or 15° bigger than *BAD*? Go for it! You can always come back and check your answer the long way if you have time.

   The long way: *BAD* is isosceles, since $AB = AD$. The two base angles of $BAD = 140$, so each is 70°. If $\angle BDA = 70°$, then $\angle BDC$ is 110°. Triangle *BDC* is isosceles too, with $\angle DCB$ and $\angle CBD = x°$. $2x = 70$, so $x = 35°$. Now admit it—isn't estimating easier?

6. **B** If Martina wants to buy as many pens as possible, she wants to buy the cheapest ones she can. Try plugging in the answer choices. Start with (C). If she buys 6 for $1.75, that equals $10.50. A bit more than $10, so pick the next lowest answer choice.

7. **B** 600 is pretty big, and 1.2 is pretty tiny. So you should be looking for a pretty small percentage. Cross out (D) and (E), and maybe even (C). Then use your calculator. The easiest way to figure out your next step would be to set up a proportion:

$$\frac{1.2}{600} = \frac{x}{100}$$

Or transform the sentence:

$$1.2 = \frac{x}{100} \cdot 600$$

Only 0.2, (B), fits the proportion.

Hard

8. **D** First mark the sides of the square with 4. Now estimate the length of *BD*, based on the side of the square. Think of the side of the square as a piece of spaghetti that you are going to drape over *BD*. So *BD* is longer than 4. Maybe around 6? Now go to the answers, and substitute 3 for π. (You know, π = 3.14, but you don't have to be so exact. You're just estimating.) Choice (A) is around 24. Way too big. (B) is around 12, (C) is around 9, and (D) is around 6. (E) is too small. Pick (D) and move on.

9. **D** When you estimate, remember that each shaded square has an area of 4. It's tricky to do this exactly, because mostly only slivers of squares are shaded. So fake it. Almost 2 full squares at the top, another square on the next row (that's 3 so far) and then slivers on the next 3 rows that make up about 2 full squares. So you've got 5 squares each with area 4; the area of the triangle is around 20, so pick (D).

So you want to cross out (A) and (B) and then get the answer exactly? You can do that. If each square has an area of 4, then the side of a little square is 2. Write that on the figure, in a couple of places. Now use the top of the triangle as the base. It equals 4. The other thing you need is the height, or altitude, of the triangle—and in this case, the height is equal to a side of the big square, or 10. Using the formula for the area of a triangle, plug 4 in for the base and 10 in for the height and you get 20 for the area.

10. **B** Hey, wake up! You can't estimate anything if the figure isn't drawn to scale! But you may want to re-draw the figure to make it look more like it's supposed to look. Now for the solution: Draw a line from *R* to *T*, slicing the figure into 2 triangles. Now all you have to do is use the Pythagorean theorem to calculate the lengths. Triangle *RUT* is a 6:8:10 triangle, a Pythagorean triple. Now for *RST*: $a^2 + 5^2 = 10^2$. So $a^2 = 75$ and $a = 5\sqrt{3}$.

PROBLEM SET 6: FACTORS, MULTIPLES, AND PRIMES

Easy

1. If t is even, which of the following expressions must be odd?

   (A) $t - 2$

   (B) t^2

   (C) $2(t + 1)$

   (D) $t(t + 1)$

   (E) $t + 3$

2. If m is a multiple of 5, and n is a factor of 3, which of the following could equal 13 ?

   (A) mn

   (B) $m + n$

   (C) $\dfrac{m}{n}$

   (D) $\dfrac{n}{m}$

   (E) $m - n$

   Set A: {0, 1, 2, 3, 4, 5}

   Set B: {1, 2, 7, 9, 10}

3. How many members of *Set A* are factors of any member of *Set B* ?

   (A) 2
   (B) 3
   (C) 4
   (D) 5
   (E) 6

Medium

4. Which of the following equations is equal to
   $6y + 6x = 66$?

   (A) $33 = x + y$
   (B) $33 = 2y + 2x$
   (C) $11 - x = y$
   (D) $11 - 2x = y$
   (E) $4y - 4x = 44$

5. If the greatest prime factor of 32 is a, and the least prime factor of 77 is b, then ab is divisible by which of the following numbers?

   (A) 3
   (B) 4
   (C) 8
   (D) 11
   (E) 14

6. If $[x]$ is defined as the greatest prime factor of x minus the least prime factor of x, then what is the value of $\dfrac{[20]}{[10]}$?

   (A) 10

   (B) 5

   (C) 2

   (D) 1

   (E) $\dfrac{1}{2}$

7. If p is the number of prime numbers between 65 and 75, then $p =$

   (A) 0
   (B) 1
   (C) 2
   (D) 3
   (E) 4

Hard

8. If *r, s,* and *t* are positive integers, and *rs = t*, then which of the following must be true?

    I. $r < t$
    II. $r \le t$
    III. $s \ge t$

    (A) I only
    (B) II only
    (C) III only
    (D) I and III only
    (E) II and III only

9. If $12y = x^3$, and *x* and *y* are positive integers, what is the least possible value for *y* ?

    (A) 3
    (B) 9
    (C) 18
    (D) 27
    (E) 64

10. The alarm of Clock *A* rings every 4 minutes, the alarm of Clock *B* rings every 6 minutes, and the alarm of Clock *C* rings every 7 minutes. If the alarms of all three clocks ring at 12:00 noon, the next time at which all the alarms will ring at exactly the same time is

    (A) 12:28 P.M.
    (B) 12:56 P.M.
    (C) 1:24 P.M.
    (D) 1:36 P.M.
    (E) 2:48 P.M.

Answers and Explanations: Problem Set 6

Easy

1. **E** Plug in an even number for t. How about $t = 2$? Now go to the answers, looking for something to be odd. (A) 0, (B) 4, (C) 6, (D) 10, and (E) 5. And remember that anything multiplied by an even number will be even, so you can eliminate (B), (C), and (D).

2. **B** Plug in again. Make $m = 10$ and $n = 3$. Run those through the answer choices, looking for 13. Choice (B) is $m + n$, or $10 + 3$ or 13. If you picked other numbers and didn't get an answer, don't get frustrated or think you're doing something wrong. Just pick another set of numbers, and make sure your numbers fit the directions of the problem (i.e., the number you pick for m has to be a multiple of 5, and the number you pick for n has to be either 1 or 3).

3. **C** Be methodical about this. Take each number in Set A, one at a time, and see if it divides evenly into anything in Set B. 0 isn't a factor of anything but 0. 1 is a factor of everything in Set B. Put a check by 1. 2 is a factor of 2, so put a check by 2. 3 is a factor of 9, so put a check by 3. 4 isn't a factor of anything in Set B. 5 is a factor of 10, so put a check by 5. How many checks do you have? Four of them.

Medium

4. **C** Try reducing the equation in the question first, by dividing the whole thing by 6. That leaves you with $x + y = 11$. That's the same as (C), if you just move the x to the other side.

5. **E** There's only one prime factor of 32, and it's 2. The prime factors of 77 are 7 and 11, so the smallest is 7. That makes $ab = 14$, which is certainly divisible by 14.

6. **D** This is a function question, as we're sure you noticed. First deal with [20]. The greatest prime factor of 20 is 5, and the least prime factor is 2. $5 - 2 = 3$, so [20] = 3. Now for [10]. The greatest prime factor of 10 is 5, and the least prime factor is 2. So [10] = $5 - 2 = 3$. $\frac{3}{3} = 1$.

7. **D** First write out the numbers: 66, 67, 68, 69, 70, 71, 72, 73, 74. Be methodical—cross out anything that's even: 66, 68, 70, 72, 74. Now cross out anything left that's divisible by 3: 69. Any number divisible by 4, 6, or 8 is even, and you've already crossed those out. Any number divisible by 9 is also divisible by 3, and you've crossed that out. All you have left is 7—you're left with 67, 71, and 73. None of them is divisible by 7, so they're all prime.

Hard

8. **B** Plug in. Make a chart:

r	s	t
1	2	2
1	1	1
2	3	6

That should do it. Now check our numbers against I, II, and III. I isn't true if r, s, and t all equal 1. III isn't true if $r = 2$, $s = 3$, and $t = 6$. That leaves you with II.

Why bother with a chart? On *must be* questions, picking one set of numbers probably isn't going to be enough. This question is pretty tricky for a medium, because I is true except when all the variables equal 1. But then I and II only isn't a choice, so you have to disprove one of them.

9. **C** Solve this problem with a combination of factoring and plugging in. The question looks like this: $2 \times 2 \times 3y = x^3$. Now factor the answer choices. Choice (A) is $3 \cdot 1$. If you plug that in for y, does it give you a cube? Nope. (B) is $3 \cdot 3$. No good either. (C) is $2 \times 3 \times 3$—now you have $(2 \times 3)(2 \times 3)(2 \times 3) = x^3$. It works.

Another way to do this problem is more straightforward plugging in: Plug in the answers for y, and use your calculator to see if that product is a cube root. If your calculator doesn't have the x^y function, then make a list of cubes to see if the product is on it.

10. **C** Ouch—this one is ugly. You can't simply multiply $4 \times 6 \times 7$ and add 168 minutes to 12:00. You'll get (E), and while it's true that all 3 alarms would ring at 2:48, that's not the *earliest* time they would ring at the same time. (And that solution is too easy for a hard question.) Instead, factor the ringing rates, so you get (2×2), (2×3), and (7). The lowest common multiple will be $2 \times 2 \times 3 \times 7$. Four goes in evenly, and so do 6 and 7. Now multiply it, and you get 84, which is 1 hour and 24 minutes. Add that to 12:00, and you're done.

When you're plugging in the answer choices, remember that if the question asks for the *least possible value*, start with the smallest answer choice. For *greatest possible value*, start with the biggest answer choice. That way you won't get caught picking an answer that works, but isn't the *least* or *greatest* answer that works.

PROBLEM SET 7: FRACTIONS, DECIMALS, AND PERCENTS

Easy

1. A big-screen TV is on sale at 15% off the regular price. If the regular price of the TV is $420, what is the sale price?

   (A) $63
   (B) $126
   (C) $357
   (D) $405
   (E) $435

2. Which of the following is the decimal form of
   $$70 + \frac{7}{10} + \frac{3}{1000} ?$$

   (A) 70.0703
   (B) 70.7003
   (C) 70.703
   (D) 70.73
   (E) 77.003

3. Six more than two-thirds of twelve is

   (A) 10
   (B) 12
   (C) 14
   (D) 18
   (E) 22

Medium

4. Walking at a constant rate, Stuart takes 24 minutes to walk to the nearest bus stop, and $\frac{1}{3}$ of that time to walk to the movie theater. It takes him half the time to walk to school than it does for him to walk to the movie theater.

   How many minutes does it take Stuart to walk to school?

   (A) 36
   (B) 24
   (C) 16
   (D)   8
   (E)   4

5. What is the value of x if $\dfrac{\frac{1}{2}}{x} = 4$?

   (A) 8

   (B) 2

   (C) $\dfrac{1}{2}$

   (D) $\dfrac{1}{4}$

   (E) $\dfrac{1}{8}$

6. If $x\%$ of y is 10, then $y\%$ of x is

   (A)   1
   (B)   5
   (C)   10
   (D)   50
   (E)   90

7. A certain drink is made by adding 4 parts water to 1 part drink mix. If the amount of water is doubled, and the amount of drink mix is quadrupled, what percent of the new mixture is drink mix?

   (A) 30%

   (B) $33\frac{1}{3}\%$

   (C) 50%

   (D) $66\frac{2}{3}\%$

   (E) 80%

Hard

8. Set *A* consists of distinct fractions, each of which has a numerator of 1 and a denominator *d* such that $1 < d < 8$, where *d* is an integer. If Set *B* consists of the reciprocals of the fractions with odd denominators in Set *A*, then the product of Set *A* and Set *B* =

   (A) $\dfrac{1}{96}$

   (B) $\dfrac{1}{48}$

   (C) $\dfrac{1}{24}$

   (D) 1

   (E) 8

9. For all values *x*, if *x* is even, *x** is defined as 0.5*x*; if *x* is odd, *x** is defined as $\dfrac{x}{3}$. What is the value of $\dfrac{(6a)^*}{9^*}$?

   (A) 2*a*
   (B) 3*a*
   (C) *a**
   (D) (2*a*)*
   (E) (4*a*)*

10. If *a*, *b*, and *c* are distinct positive integers, and 10% of *abc* is 5, then *a* + *b* could equal

   (A) 1
   (B) 3
   (C) 5
   (D) 8
   (E) 25

Answers and Explanations: Problem Set 7

Easy

1. **C** The numbers are too awkward to plug in, so do it the old-fashioned way: 15% of $420 is $0.15 \times 420 = 63$. $420 - 63 = 357$. Use your calculator.

2. **C** Take the pieces one at a time and eliminate. The first piece is 70: eliminate (E). The second piece is $\frac{7}{10}$, or 0.7. Eliminate (A). The last piece is $\frac{3}{1000}$, or 0.003. Eliminate (B) and (D). If you want to do the conversions on your calculator, that's cool. But adding the fractions together and then converting to a decimal would take more time, calculator or no calculator.

3. **C** Translate the problem into math language: $6 + \frac{2}{3} \times 12 = ?$. Then, don't forget PEMDAS: Multiply before you add. $6 + \frac{2}{3}(12) = 6 + 8 = 14$.

Medium

4. **E** Start working from the 24 minutes it takes poor Stuart to walk to the bus stop. (Won't anybody give the guy a ride?) If it takes $\frac{1}{3}$ of 24 to walk to the movies, that's 8 minutes. If it takes him half of that time to walk to school, $\frac{1}{2}$ of 8 is 4. This question requires close reading more than anything else.

5. **E** Plugging in the answer choices wouldn't be a bad idea here—you can eliminate (A) and (B) pretty quickly that way. (C) gives you $\frac{\frac{1}{2}}{\frac{1}{2}} = 1$. (D) is $\frac{\frac{1}{2}}{\frac{1}{4}} = 2$. (E) is $\frac{\frac{1}{2}}{\frac{1}{8}} = 4$.

6. **C** Plug in 10 for y, which makes $x = 100$. Plug those numbers into the second part: 100% of 10 = 10.

7. **B** First make a little chart: If you double the water and quadruple the mix, you get

water		mix
4	:	1
8	:	4

Reread the question. It asks for the percentage of the new mixture that's drink mix. You've got $\dfrac{4\,(\text{mix})}{12\,(\text{total})}$, which equals $\dfrac{1}{3}$, or $33\dfrac{1}{3}\%$.

If you made it almost to the end but picked (C), don't forget that you have to express the mix as a percentage of the total, not a percentage of the water.

Hard

8. **B** Read this carefully. Set A has different fractions, each with a numerator of 1. (You might as well write them down like that and fill in the denominators when you get there.) The denominators are between 1 and 8. That gives you Set A: $\dfrac{1}{2}, \dfrac{1}{3}, \dfrac{1}{4}, \dfrac{1}{5}, \dfrac{1}{6}, \dfrac{1}{7}$. Set B has the reciprocals of the members of Set A with odd denominators, so Set B: $\dfrac{3}{1}, \dfrac{5}{1}, \dfrac{7}{1}$. Now multiply the sets together—see how the fractions that have reciprocals cancel each other out? You're left with $\dfrac{1}{2} \times \dfrac{1}{4} \times \dfrac{1}{6}$, which is $\dfrac{1}{48}$.

9. **D** It's a function, so just follow the directions. Looking at the numerator, $6a$ has to be even because it has an even number as a factor. (Or plug in any low number for a.) Since $6a$ is even, follow the first direction: $6a \times 0.5 = 3a$. Now for the denominator: 9 is odd, so follow the second direction. $\dfrac{9}{3} = 3$. So $\dfrac{(6a)^*}{9^*} = \dfrac{3a}{3} = a$. Did you pick (C)? Well, sorry, you aren't getting off that easy. (C), (D), and (E) are functions, too, so you have to translate them, looking for your answer, a. Skip (A) and (B). For (D), $(2a)$ is even, so $(2a)^* = 2a \times 0.5 = a$.

10. **B** First translate the middle part of the problem into an equation. 10% of abc is 5 translates to $\frac{10}{100} \cdot abc = 5$. Now solve for abc, and you get $abc = 50$. Reread the question. Each variable is different, each is positive, and multiplied together they produce 50. Now plug in the answer choices, and remember that the answers represent $a + b$. Choice (A) is silly, because it would make a and b fractions, and they can't be fractions. In (B), $a + b$ would have to be 1 + 2. If $a = 1$ and $b = 2$ and $abc = 50$, what is c? $c = 25$, so it works.

A couple of reminders: If you are making mistakes on the easy and medium problems, don't spend a lot of time—if any—working on the hard problems. You need to hone your skills first; you may want to go back to the review section and do some work before continuing. And don't forget, you probably want to leave some questions blank on the real thing.

Speaking of leaving questions blank, question 9 would be a fine choice to avoid entirely. Long functions in the hard problems can be really nasty.

PROBLEM SET 8: AVERAGES, RATIOS, PROPORTIONS, AND PROBABILITIES

Easy

1. Three consecutive integers add up to 258. What is the smallest integer?

   (A) 58
   (B) 85
   (C) 86
   (D) 89
   (E) 94

2. A factory produces 6,000 plates per day. If one out of 15 plates is broken, how many unbroken plates does the factory produce each day?

   (A) 5800
   (B) 5600
   (C) 1500
   (D) 800
   (E) 400

3. It takes 4 friends 24 minutes to wash all the windows in Maria's house. The friends all work at the same rate. How long would it take 8 friends, working at the same rate, to wash all the windows in Maria's house?

   (A) 96
   (B) 32
   (C) 20
   (D) 12
   (E) 8

Medium

4. The value of *t* is inversely proportional to the value of *w*. If value of *w* increases by a factor of 5, what happens to the value of *t* ?

(A) *t* increases by a factor of 5.
(B) *t* increases by a factor of 2.
(C) *t* remains constant.
(D) *t* decreases by a factor of 2.
(E) *t* decreases by a factor of 5.

5. A drawer holds only blue socks and white socks. If the ratio of blue socks to white socks is 4:3, which of the following could be the total number of socks in the drawer?

(A) 4
(B) 7
(C) 8
(D) 12
(E) 24

6. The probability of choosing a caramel from a certain bag of candy is $\frac{1}{5}$, and the probability of choosing a butterscotch is $\frac{5}{8}$. If the bag contains 40 pieces of candy, and the only types of candy in the bag are caramel, butterscotch, and fudge, how many pieces of fudge are in the bag?

(A)   5
(B)   7
(C)   8
(D) 16
(E) 25

7. Dixie spent an average of *x* dollars on each of 5 shirts and an average of *y* dollars on each of 3 hats. In terms of *x* and *y*, how many dollars did she spend on shirts and hats?

(A) $5x + 3y$
(B) $3x + 5y$
(C) $15(x + y)$
(D) $8xy$
(E) $15xy$

8. The ratio of $\frac{1}{6}:\frac{1}{5}$ is equal to the ratio of 35 to

   (A)   24
   (B)   30
   (C)   36
   (D)   42
   (E)   45

9. An artist makes a certain shade of green paint by mixing blue and yellow in a ratio of 3:4. She makes orange by mixing red and yellow in a ratio of 2:3. If on one day she mixes both green and orange and uses equal amounts of blue and red paint, what fractional part of the paint that she uses is yellow?

   (A) $\frac{7}{12}$

   (B) $\frac{17}{29}$

   (C) $\frac{7}{5}$

   (D) $\frac{17}{12}$

   (E) $\frac{9}{6}$

10. The areas of two circles are in a ratio of 4:9. If both radii are integers, and $r_1 - r_2 = 2$, which of the following is the radius of the larger circle?

    (A)   4
    (B)   5
    (C)   6
    (D)   8
    (E)   9

Answers and Explanations: Problem Set 8

Easy

1. **B** If the three integers add up to 258, then their average is 258 ÷ 3, or 86. Since the integers are consecutive, they must be 85, 86, and 87. Check it on your calculator. If you picked (C), what did you do wrong? Forget what the question asked for? Divide 258 by 3 and then quit? Even easy problems may have more than one step. This would also be a good question to plug in the answer choices.

2. **B** First estimate. You're looking for the number of unbroken plates—if only one broke out of 15, there should be a lot of unbroken plates, right? Cross out (C), (D), and (E). Now set up a proportion:

$$\frac{\text{broken}}{\text{total}} = \frac{1}{15} = \frac{x}{6000}$$

   And cross-multiply. You get $6000 = 15x$, so using your calculator, $x = 400$. That's the number of broken plates, so subtract 400 from 6000 and you've got the answer. If you picked (E), you could have gotten the problem right if you had either estimated first or reread the question right before you answered it.

3. **D** There are twice as many people, so the work will go twice as fast. You can't set up a normal proportion because it's an inverse proportion—the more people you have, the less time the work takes. So if you multiply the number of people by 2, you divide the work time by 2. Don't forget to use your common sense.

Medium

4. **E** Since no values were given, try plugging in values of your own to test what happens. If t starts out as 10 and w starts out as 5, you can set up the formula for inverse variation as follows: $t_1 w_1 = t_2 w_2$. In this case, the t_1 is 10, w_1 is 5, and w_2 is 25 (since you multiply it by 5). So set up the equation as: $10 \times 5 = t_2 \times 25$. $\frac{50}{25} t = 2$. So what happened to the value of t? It decreased by a factor of 5.

5. **B** The total must be the sum of the numbers in a ratio, or a multiple of that sum. In this case, $4 + 3 = 7$, so the number of socks could be 7 or any multiple of 7. (You can have fractions in a ratio, it's true, but not when you're dealing with socks or people or anything that you can't chop into pieces. And probably not on a medium question, either.)

6. **B** Here's what to do: Take $\dfrac{1}{5}$ of 40, which is 8 caramels. Take $\dfrac{5}{8}$ of 40, which is 25 butterscotches. The caramels and the butterscotches are 8 + 25 = 33. Subtract that from 40 and you've got the fudge.

7. **A** Plug in. Let $x = 2$. If Dixie spent an average of $2 a shirt, then she spent a total of $10 on shirts. Let $y = 4$, and she spent an average of $4 a hat, for a total of $12. Our total is 10 + 12 = $22. Circle that. Now on to the answer choices, and $x = 2$ and $y = 4$. (A) is $5(2) + 3(4) = 22$.

Hard

8. **D** First multiply the ratio by something big to get rid of the fraction. Any multiple of 6 and 5 will do. So $30\left(\dfrac{1}{6}\right) : 30\left(\dfrac{1}{5}\right) = 5:6$. Now you've got $5:6 = 35:x$. Since 35 is 5×7, x is 6×7, or 42. The new ratio is 35:42, which is the same as 5:6.

9. **B** Write down your ratios and label them neatly. You have

$$\dfrac{b:y}{3:4} \qquad \dfrac{r:y}{2:3}$$

If the artist uses equal amounts of blue and red, you have to multiply each ratio so the numbers under b and r are the same:

$$\dfrac{b:y}{(2)(3:4)} \qquad \dfrac{r:y}{(2:3)(3)}$$

The result is

$$\dfrac{b:y}{6:8} \qquad \dfrac{r:y}{6:9}$$

The yellow is 8 parts + 9 parts = 17 parts, and the total is 6 + 8 + 6 + 9 = 29 parts. On complicated ratio problems, it's important, to organize the information legibly and label everything as you go along, or else you'll find yourself looking at a bunch of meaningless numbers.

10. **C** Plug in the answer choices! Start with (C) If the larger radius is 6, the smaller radius is 2 less than that, or 4. The area of the smaller circle = 16π, and the area of the larger circle is 36π. 16π : 36π is a ratio of 4:9. (Just divide the whole ratio by 4) If you picked (E), you must've had a momentary blackout—that answer is way too appealing to be right on a hard question. If you're going to guess, guess something that is not too good to be true.

A shortcut for averages: If the list of numbers is consecutive, consecutive odd, or consecutive even, then the average will be the middle number. (If the list has an even number of elements, you have to average the two middle numbers.) The average will also be the middle number (or average of the two middle numbers) of any list that goes up in consistent increments. For example, the average of 6, 15, 24, 33, and 42 is 24, since the numbers go up in increments of 9.

PROBLEM SET 9: EXPONENTS, ROOTS, AND EQUATIONS

Easy

1. If $t^3 = -8$, then $t^2 =$

   (A) -4
   (B) -2
   (C) 2
   (D) 4
   (E) 8

2. If $60 = (7 + 8)(x - 2)$, then $x =$

   (A) 15
   (B) 10
   (C) 9
   (D) 7
   (E) 6

3. If $4x - 2y = 10$, and $7x + 2y = 23$, what is the value of x ?

   (A) $\dfrac{1}{3}$

   (B) 1

   (C) 3

   (D) 13

   (E) 14

Medium

4. For all integers x and y, let

   $\bigstar (x + y) = \dfrac{x^2}{y^2}$. What is the value of

   $\bigstar (2 + y) \times \bigstar (y + 1)$?

   (A) 16
   (B) 9
   (C) 5
   (D) 4
   (E) 3

5. For their science homework, Brenda and Dylan calculated the volume of air that filled a basketball. If the formula for the volume of a sphere is $V = \dfrac{4}{3}\pi r^3$, and the diameter of the basketball was 6, what was the volume of the air inside the basketball?

   (A) 4π
   (B) 14π
   (C) 32π
   (D) 36π
   (E) 72π

6. $\dfrac{\sqrt{a} \cdot \sqrt{b}}{3\sqrt{a} - 2\sqrt{a}} =$

   (A) $\dfrac{\sqrt{b}}{\sqrt{a}}$

   (B) $\sqrt{b}$

   (C) $\dfrac{2\sqrt{a}}{b}$

   (D) $\sqrt{ab}$

   (E) $\sqrt{a^2 b}$

7. On a certain test, Radeesh earned 2 points for every correct answer and lost 1 point for every incorrect answer. If he answered all 30 questions on the test and received a score of 51, how many questions did Radeesh answer *incorrectly*?

   (A)   3
   (B)   7
   (C)   15
   (D)   21
   (E)   24

Hard

8. If $\frac{1}{2}(z-4)(z+4) = m$, then, in term of z, what is the value of $z^2 - 16$?

   (A) $\sqrt{m}$

   (B) $\frac{m}{2}$

   (C) m

   (D) $2m$

   (E) m^2

9. If $(y+5)^2 = 49$, then which one of the following could be the value of $(y+3)^2$?

   (A)   1
   (B)   49
   (C)   64
   (D)   81
   (E)   225

10. If $a-b = 4$, $b-6 = c$, $c-2 = d$, and $a+d = 4$, what is the value of a ?

    (A) 4
    (B) 8
    (C) 12
    (D) 16
    (E)   It cannot be determined from the information given.

Answers and Explanations: Problem Set 9

Easy

1. **D** $t = -2$, and $(-2)^2 = 4$.

2. **E** Plug in the answer choices. Try (C) first: $(15)(9-2) = (15)(7) = 105$. It should equal 60, so you need a much smaller number. Try (E): $(15)(6-2) = (15)(4) = 60$. It works. Or you could solve the equation algebraically:

   $60 = 15(x - 2)$
   $60 = 15x - 30$
   $90 = 15x$
   $6 = x$

3. **C** Stack 'em and add:

   $4x - 2y = 10$
   $7x + 2y = 23$
   $11x = 33$
   $x = 3$

Medium

4. **D** In this function, all you have to do is square the first thing in the parentheses and put it over the square of the second thing in the parentheses. So $(2 + y) = \dfrac{2^2}{y^2}$. And $(y + 1) = \dfrac{y^2}{1}$. Now multiply them. The y^2 cancels, so you get 2^2.

5. **D** Don't worry—you weren't supposed to know this formula. That's why they gave it to you, so don't get freaked out. Just use the information in the question to solve for V. If the diameter of the basketball was 6, the radius was 3:

   $$V = \frac{4}{3}\pi r^3, \text{ so } V = \frac{4}{3}\pi(3^3) = \frac{4}{3}\pi(27) = 36\pi.$$

   You may see some totally unfamiliar formula on the test—physics, for instance—but you don't have to understand the formula or know anything about it. All you have to do is substitute in any value they give you and solve for the variable they ask for.

6. **B** Remember that you can multiply or divide what's under a square root sign and add or subtract when what's under the square root sign is the same. Begin by simplifying the denominator. $\dfrac{\sqrt{a} \cdot \sqrt{b}}{3\sqrt{a} - 2\sqrt{a}} = \dfrac{\sqrt{a} \cdot \sqrt{b}}{\sqrt{a}} = \sqrt{b}$.

7. **A** Plug in the answer choices. If Radeesh got 2 points for every right answer, and the test had 30 questions, the top score was 60. If he got a 51, he did pretty well, so start with (A). (Remember, the answer choices represent the number of questions he answered incorrectly.) If he missed 3, then he got 27 right. $27 \times 2 = 54$. Subtract 3 for 3 wrong answers, and you get 51.

    [Don't worry if you didn't see which answer to start with. If you started with (C), it gave you way too many wrong answers, didn't it? So cross off (C), (D), and (E) and you've only got 2 left to try.]

Hard

8. **D** The easiest way to solve this question is to recognize that $(z - 4)(z + 4) = (z - 16)^2$. This, you can rewrite the initial equation as $\dfrac{1}{2}(z - 16)^2 = m$. Thus, $z - 16^2 = 2m$. Otherwise, plug in. Try $z = 6$, which means $m = 5$. The value of $z^2 - 16$ is 10.

9. **D** You need to do a bit of trial by error here. The easiest value of y is 2. However, 25 is not an answer choice. What other value of y would work? How about -12? That works, and 81 is an answer. If you picked anything else, you made a careless error involving positive and negative signs.

10. **B** Start off by eliminating (E), as that would be too easy for a complicated looking question towards the end. Before you start the lengthy process of substitution, try stack-and-add. You need to bring all of the variables to the left, and all of the numbers to the right, so your stack will look like this:

    $a - b = 4$
    $b - c = 6$
    $c - d = 2$
    $a + d = 4$

    Add everything up. It turns out that b, c, and d disappear, leaving $2a = 16$, or $a = 8$.

PROBLEM SET 10: LINES, ANGLES, AND COORDINATES

Easy

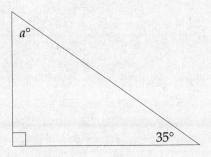

1. In the figure above, $3a - a =$

   (A) 40°
   (B) 55°
   (C) 90°
   (D) 110°
   (E) 165°

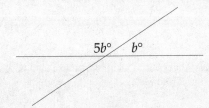

2. In the figure above, $b =$

   (A) 20°
   (B) 30°
   (C) 40°
   (D) 45°
   (E) 180°

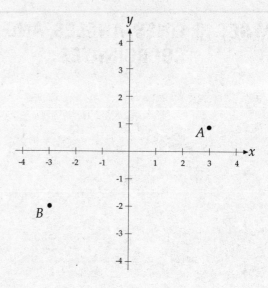

3. The *x*-coordinate of Point *A* minus the *y*-coordinate of Point *B* equals

(A) −2
(B) −1
(C)   0
(D)   3
(E)   5

Medium

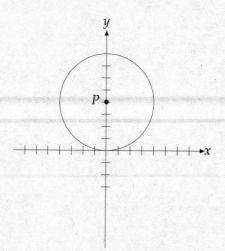

4. Point *P* is the center of circle *Q*, which has a radius of 4. Which of the following points lies on circle *Q* ?

(A) (4, 0)
(B) (0, 4)
(C) (−4, 4)
(D) (3, 1)
(E) (4, 3)

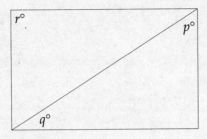

5. In the rectangle above, $p + q - r =$

   (A) 0°
   (B) 15°
   (C) 26°
   (D) 35°
   (E) 50°

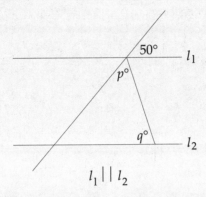

$$l_1 \mid\mid l_2$$

Note: Figure not drawn to scale.

6. In the figure above, $p + q =$

   (A) 180°
   (B) 150°
   (C) 130°
   (D)   90°
   (E)   70°

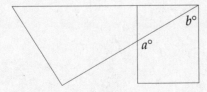

7. The figure above is formed by a triangle overlapping a rectangle. What does $a + b$ equal?

   (A)   80°
   (B)   90°
   (C) 150°
   (D) 180°
   (E) 270°

Hard

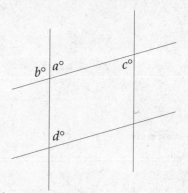

Note: Figure not drawn to scale.

8. Which of the following statements must be true?

   I. $a + b < 180$
   II. $a + d = 180$
   III. $a + d > 180$

   (A) None
   (B) I only
   (C) II only
   (D) I and II only
   (E) II and II only

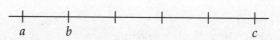

9. The tick marks on the number line above are equally spaced. If 2 is halfway between b and c, the value of $c - a$ is 10, what is the value of b ?

   (A) − 4
   (B) − 3
   (C) − 2
   (D) − 0
   (E) − 6

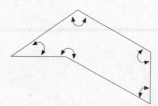

10. What is the total number of degrees of the marked angles?

   (A) 180
   (B) 270
   (C) 360
   (D) 540
   (E) 720

Answers and Explanations: Problem Set 10

Easy

1. **D** A triangle has 180°. So $90 + 35 + a = 180$, and $a = 55$. Plug that into the equation and get $3(55) - 55 = 110$.

2. **B** $5b$ and b lie on a straight line, so $5b + b = 180$ and $b = 30$.

3. **E** The x-coordinate of Point A is 3, and the y-coordinate of Point B is -2. So $3 - (-2) = 5$.

Medium

4. **C** Just plot the points and see which one falls on the circle.

5. **A** As always, mark whatever info you can on your diagram: $r = 90$, and the bottom angle is also 90, because this is a rectangle. $p + q = 90$, because they are the two remaining angles in a right triangle. That means $p + q - r = 0$.

6. **C** Again, mark info on the diagram. The unmarked angle of the triangle is 50° because l_1 and l_2 are parallel, so $50 + p + q = 180$ and $p + q = 130°$. (You can't figure out what p and q are individually, but the question doesn't ask you to.)

7. **D** Estimate first. a is around 130 and b is bigger than 45, so $a + b$ should be a little bigger than 175. Pick (D) and keep cruising. To figure the angles exactly, ignore the triangle and look at the quadrilateral in the bottom half of the rectangle. The angles are $a + b + 90 + 90$. Since a quadrilateral has 360°, $a + b = 180$.

Hard

8. **A** It's important to realize what you *don't* know: Are any of these lines parallel? *You don't know.* So you can't draw any conclusions at all other than the rule that a line contains 180°.

9. **C** The best way to approach this question is to plug in the answers. Suppose b is -2. Because the midpoint between b and c is 2, you can see that each tick mark represents a value of 2 more than the previous tick mark. Thus, a is -4, and c is 6. Now, you have to check this against the remaining information in the question. So $c - a$ must be 10. Is it? Yes, so (C) is our answer!

10. **D** Estimate first and see what you can cross out. Since you have two angles that are bigger than 90 and one angle that's bigger than 180, you should be able at least to cross out (A), (B), and (C). To figure out the exact number of degrees, divide the figure into three triangles:

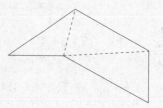

The total degrees will be $180 \times 3 = 540$.

PROBLEM SET 11: TRIANGLES

Easy

1. If the area of the triangle above is 6, what is its perimeter?

   (A)   8
   (B)   11
   (C)   12
   (D)   15
   (E)   16

2. If $x = 3$, what is the area of the triangle above?

   (A)   10
   (B)   12
   (C)   21
   (D)   30
   (E)   45

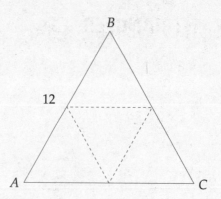

3. If equilateral triangle *ABC* is cut by three lines, as shown, to form four equilateral triangles of equal area, what is the length of a side of 1 of the smaller triangles?

(A) 3
(B) 4
(C) 5
(D) 6
(E) 8

Medium

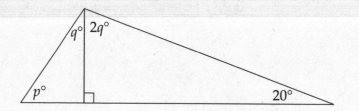

4. What is the value of *p* in the figure above?

(A) 50
(B) 55
(C) 60
(D) 65
(E) 70

5. A movie theater is 3 blocks due north of a supermarket, and a beauty parlor is 4 blocks due east of the movie theater. How many blocks long is the street that runs directly from the supermarket to the beauty parlor?

(A) 2.5
(B) 3
(C) 4
(D) 5
(E) 7

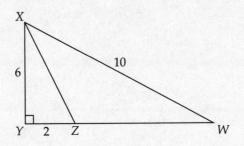

6. What is the area of triangle *WXZ* in the figure above?

(A)   6
(B)   12
(C)   18
(D)   24
(E)   36

Hard

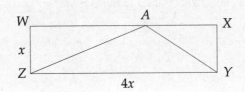

7. In the figure above, what is the area of triangle *YAZ* ?

(A) $3x$
(B) x^2
(C) $5x$
(D) $2x^2$
(E) $4x^2$

8. A square is inscribed in a circle with area 9π. What is the area of the square?

(A) $3\sqrt{2}$

(B) $9\sqrt{2}$

(C)   18

(D)   36

(E)   162

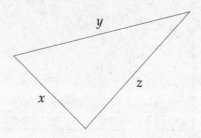

9. In the figure above, if $x = 7$ and $y = 11$, then the difference between the greatest and least possible integer values of z is

(A) 11
(B) 12
(C) 13
(D) 14
(E) 15

10. An equilateral triangle with a perimeter of 12 is inscribed in a circle. What is the area of the circle?

(A) $\dfrac{2\pi}{3}$

(B) $\dfrac{4\pi}{3}$

(C) 4π

(D) $\dfrac{16\pi}{3}$

(E) 16π

Answers and Explanations: Problem Set 11

Easy

1. **C** Several ways to get this question: You could recognize that it's a Pythagorean triple (3:4:5), which would give you the length of the unmarked leg. Or you could set up the following equation:

$$a = \frac{1}{2}bh$$

$\frac{1}{2}b(4) = 6$, so $2b = 6$ and $b = 3$. All you did was substitute the height and the area, both of which are given in the problem, into the formula for the area of a triangle.

2. **E** If $x = 3$, then the base of the triangle is 6 and the height is 15. That would mean the area is $\frac{1}{2}(6)(15) = 45$.

3. **D** Each vertex of the small triangles bisects a side of the big triangle, so each side is 6. (Don't forget to estimate.)

Medium

4. **B** Start with the triangle to the right of the height line. As the height forms an angle of 90 and the given angle is 20, the third angle is 70 (180 − 110). Thus, $2q = 70$, and $q = 35$. Now go to the triangle to the left of the height line. As the height forms an angle of 90 and q is 35, p is 55.

5. **D** Draw a little map, which should look like this:

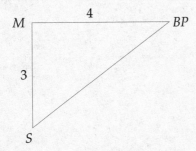

Now you have a 3:4:5 right triangle, so the street from the supermarket to the beauty parlor is 5 blocks long.

6. **C** Use the Pythagorean Theorem to find the base of triangle WYZ: $6^2 + b^2 = 10^2$. The base is 8. (This is the 6-8-10 triple, so you didn't really need to use the Pythagorean Theorem.) As $XY = 2$, the base of triangle WXZ is 6. The height of triangle WXZ is the same as the height of WYZ, also 6. Thus, the area ($\frac{1}{2}bh$) is 18.

Hard

7. **D** Plug in. If $x = 2$, then ZY is 8 and WZ is 2. (Write that on your diagram.) To get the area of YAZ, notice that WZ is the height of the triangle, so $\frac{1}{2}(8)(2) = 8$. Plug 2 back into the answer choices, and (D) is $2(2^2) = 8$.

8. **C** As there is no diagram, first draw a square in a circle. As the area of the circle is 9π, the radius is 3 as Area $= \pi r^2$. How does this help? Often on the SAT, questions involving squares are really about the diagonal of the square, so draw in the diagonal. The diagonal is the diameter of the circle, so the diagonal is 6. You can use the Pythagorean Theorem or your knowledge of 45-45-90 triangles to figure out the sides. Label the sides of the square x. If you use the Pythagorean Theorem, you will solve $x^2 + x^2 = 6^2$. $x = \sqrt{18}$. If you use the 45-45-90 relationships, you will get $x = \frac{6}{\sqrt{2}}$. Either way, the area of the square is 18.

9. **B** Here's the rule: The sum of any two sides of a triangle must be more than the third side. So if you already have sides of 7 and 11, the longest the third side could be is a little less than 18. Since the third side has to be an integer, the longest it could be is 17. Now for the shortest possible length of the third side: $11 - 7 = 4$, so the third side has to be an integer bigger than 4, which is 5. So the difference between the greatest possible and the least possible is $17 - 5 = 12$.

10. **D** As there is no diagram, first draw an equilateral triangle in a circle. As the perimeter of the triangle is 12, each side of the triangle is 4. The height of the equilateral triangle is perpendicular to the base and splits the base in half. Each of these halves serves as one side of a 30-60-90 triangle in which the radius of the circle is equal to half of the hypotenuse of each 30-60-90 triangle. Thus, because the side opposite the 60-degree in the small 30-60-90 triangle is 2, the other leg of the right triangle (opposite the 30-degree angle) is $2\sqrt{3}$. The hypotenuse of that 30-60-90 triangle is, therefore, $4\sqrt{3}$, which is also the radius of the circle. Know your 30-60-90 triangle rules! Since the formula for the area of a circle is Area = πr^2, you then get Area = $\dfrac{16\pi}{3}$. Answer choice (D) is correct.

PROBLEM SET 12: CIRCLES, QUADRILATERALS, BOXES, AND CANS

Easy

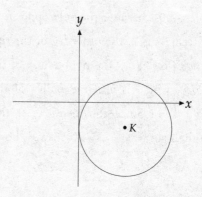

1. Point *K* is the center of the circle above, and the coordinates of Point *K* are (2, –1). What is the area of the circle?

   (A) π
   (B) 2π
   (C) 4π
   (D) 6π
   (E) 8π

2. Circle *P* has a radius of 7, and Circle *R* has a diameter of 8. The circumference of Circle *P* is how much greater than the circumference of Circle *R* ?

   (A)   π
   (B)   6π
   (C)   8π
   (D) 16π
   (E) 33π

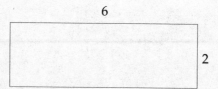

3. How many squares with sides of 1 could fit into the rectangle above?

   (A)   3
   (B)   4
   (C)   6
   (D)   9
   (E) 12

Medium

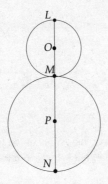

4. In the figure above, LM is $\dfrac{1}{3}$ of LN. If the radius of the circle with center P is 6, what is the area of the circle with center O ?

(A) 4π
(B) 9π
(C) 12π
(D) 18π
(E) 36π

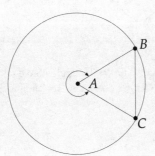

5. In the figure above, the circle has center A, and $BC = AB$. What is the degree measure of the marked angle?

(A) $60°$
(B) $180°$
(C) $270°$
(D) $300°$
(E) $340°$

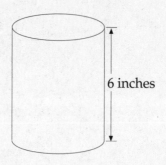

6 inches

6. In the figure above, the radius of the base of the cylinder is half its height. What is the volume of the cylinder in cubic inches?

(A) 9π
(B) 15π
(C) 18π
(D) 36π
(E) 54π

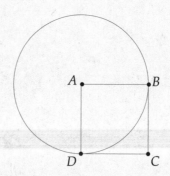

7. Points D and B lie on the circle above with center A. If square $ABCD$ has an area of 16, what is the length of arc BD ?

(A) 2π
(B) 4
(C) 8
(D) 4π
(E) 8π

Hard

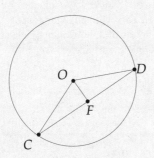

8. In the figure above, what is the circumference of the circle with center O, if COD is 120° and OF bisects CD and has a length of 1.5 ?

   (A) $\dfrac{2\pi}{3}$

   (B) $\dfrac{3\pi}{2}$

   (C) 3π

   (D) 6π

   (E) 9π

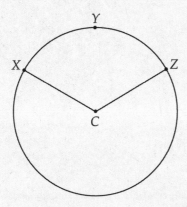

9. In the figure above, C is the center of a circle. If the length of the arc XYZ is 4π, what is the radius of the circle?

   (A)   4

   (B) $2\sqrt{3}$

   (C)   6

   (D) $2\sqrt{4}$

   (E)   12

10. Jeremy will fill a rectangular crate that has inside dimensions of 18 inches by 15 inches by 9 inches with cubical tiles, each with edge lengths of 3. If the tiles are packaged in sets of 8, how many packages will Jeremy need to completely fill the crate?

(A) 11
(B) 12
(C) 90
(D) 101
(E) 102

Answers and Explanations: Problem Set 12

Easy

1. **C** Count up the units of the radius—it's 2. Then use the formula for area of a circle: $\pi r^2 = \pi(2^2) = 4\pi$.

2. **B** The circumference of Circle P is $2\pi r = 2\pi(7) = 14\pi$. The circumference of Circle R is $2\pi r = 2\pi(4) = 8\pi$. Now just subtract. If you picked (E), you calculated area instead of circumference.

3. **E** Drawing on the diagram could help. How many sides of 1 can fit along the long edge of the rectangle? 6. And how many rows will fit along the short edge? 2. Now just multiply $6 \times 2 = 12$. Or draw them in and count them up.

Medium

4. **B** Write in 6 by the radius of the bigger circle. That makes the diameter of the bigger circle 12. If LM (the diameter of the smaller circle) is $\frac{1}{3}$ the length of LN, the equation is $\left(\frac{1}{3}\right)(12 + x) = x$. $4 = x - \frac{x}{3}$, and $x = 6$. (You don't have to write an equation. You could estimate and try some numbers. Doesn't LM look like it's about half of MN? It is.) If the diameter of the smaller circle is 6, then its radius is 3 and its area is 9π.

5. **D** Estimate first. The marked angle is way more than 180—in fact, it's not that far from 360. Cross out (A) and (B). You know $AC = AB$ because they're both radii. That means $BC = AB = AC$, and that triangle is equilateral. So angle BAC is 60°. Subtract that from 360 and you're in business. (Even if all you could do was estimate, go ahead and take a guess.)

6. **E** If the radius is half the height, then the radius is 3. To get the volume of a cylinder, multiply the area of the base times the height—in this case, $\pi(3^2) \times 6 = 54\pi$.

7. **A** If the square has an area of 16, then the side of the square is 4. Write that on your diagram. Now you know the radius of the circle is also 4, so the circumference is 8π. Angle BAD has 90°, since it's a corner of the square. And since 90 is $\frac{1}{4}$ of 360, arc BD is $\frac{1}{4}$ of the circumference. So arc BD is $\left(\frac{1}{4}\right)(8\pi)$, or 2π. If you estimated first, as we hope you did, you could have crossed out (D) and (E), and maybe even (C).

Hard

8. **D** Write the info on your diagram. If OF bisects CD, it also bisects angle COD, making two 60° angles. Now there are two 30:60:90 triangles. If the shortest leg of one of those triangles is 1.5, then the hypotenuse is 2×1.5, or 3. Aha! That distance is also the radius of the circle, so the circumference is 6π.

9. **C** The ratio of the length of an arc to the circumference of the circle is the same as the ratio of the degree measure of the arc to the 360 degrees of the circle. As 120 degrees is one-third of the circle, the length of the arc is one-third of the circumference. Thus, the circumference of the circle is 12π. As Circumference = $2\pi r$, the radius is 6.

10. **B** To find the number of tiles that will fit in the crate, you must divide the dimensions of the crate by all three dimensions of the tiles:

$$\frac{18 \times 15 \times 9}{3 \times 3 \times 3} = 90$$

But don't select 90 as your answer! The question asks how many packages of 8 tiles are needed. So, divide 90 by 8, which equals 11 plus a remainder. As 11 packages will contain only 88 of the 90 tiles needed, Jeremy must buy a 12th package.

One more thing: Circle questions tend to appear most of ten in the late-medium and hard questions.

PROBLEM SET 13: FUNCTIONS, CHARTS, AND GRAPHS

Easy

	Original Price	Sale Price
Store A	$25	$20
Store B	$20	$15
Store C	$30	$25
Store D	$35	$30

1. The chart above shows the original and sale prices of a certain item at each of four different stores. Which of the following stores provides a discount of 20% or more on this item?

    I.   Store A
   II.   Store B
  III.   Store C

(A) I only
(B) II only
(C) III only
(D) I and II only
(E) I and III only

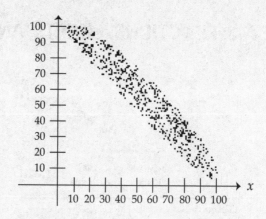

2. Which of the following is mostly likely the slope of the line of best fit for the scatterplot above?

(A) −10
(B) −1
(C) 0
(D) 1
(E) 10

3. If $f(x) = 2x + 1$ and $f(a) = 2$, what is the value of a ?

(A) −2

(B) $-\dfrac{1}{2}$

(C) $\dfrac{1}{2}$

(D) 2

(E) 5

Medium

4. If $f(x) = 4x + 2$, which of the following is the graph of $f(x)$?

(A)

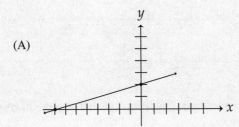

(B)

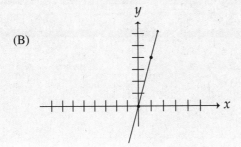

(C)

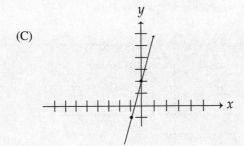

(D)

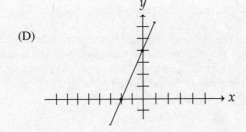

(E)

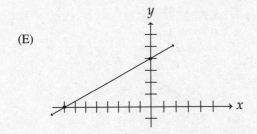

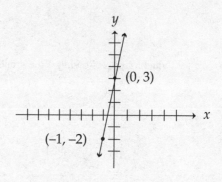

5. If the graph above is that of $f(x)$, which of the following could be $f(x)$?

(A) $f(x) = \dfrac{1}{5}x + \dfrac{1}{3}$

(B) $f(x) = \dfrac{1}{5}x + 3$

(C) $f(x) = \dfrac{1}{3}x + 5$

(D) $f(x) = 3x + 5$

(E) $f(x) = 5x + 3$

Bacteria Reproduction

Time (in seconds)	Population (in thousands)
t	p
1	2
2	6
3	18
4	54

6. The table above shows the population growth of a certain bacteria over four seconds. Which one of the following equations shows the relationship between t and p, according to the table?

(A) $p = 3t$
(B) $p = 2t^2$
(C) $p = 9(t + 2)$
(D) $p = 2 \times 3^t$
(E) $p = 2 \times 3^{(t-1)}$

Elevator Usage

Date	Number of uses
March 31	837
April 30	1,347
May 31	2,142
June 30	2,799
July 31	2,824
August 31	3,002

7. The table above shows the total number of times a certain elevator has been used by the end of the last day of each of six consecutive months. Local regulations require that the elevator undergo an inspection every 2,000 uses or every 4 calendar months, whichever occurs first. If an inspection took place on January 31, when was the next inspection required?

(A) April 30
(B) May 31
(C) June 30
(D) July 31
(E) August 31

Hard

$y = f(x)$

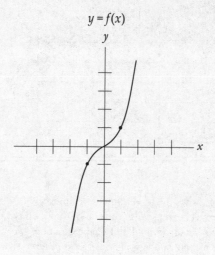

8. If the graph above shows the function $f(x) = x^3$, which one of the following graphs shows $f(x) = (x + 2)^3 - 3$?

(A)

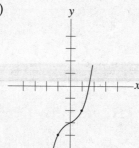

(B)

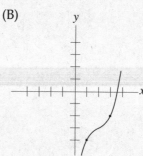

(C)

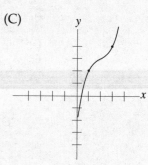

(D)

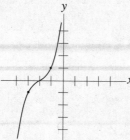

(E)

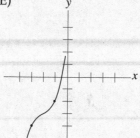

9. The function g is defined as $g(x) = \dfrac{x^2}{3 - |x - 4|}$. For which values of x is $g(x)$ NOT defined?

(A) $x = 1$ and $x = 3$
(B) $x = 4$ and $x = 7$
(C) $x = 3$ and $x = 4$
(D) $x = 3$ and $x = 7$
(E) $x = 1$ and $x = 7$

10. For all positive integers a and b, let $a \leftrightarrow b$ be defined by $a \leftrightarrow b = a^2 - b^a$. What is the value of $(2 \leftrightarrow 3) - (1 \leftrightarrow 2)$?

(A) -6
(B) -4
(C) 0
(D) 4
(E) 6

Answers and Explanations: Problem Set 13

Easy

1. **D** Remember that the formula for percent change is $\dfrac{difference}{original} \times 100$. The discount at Store A is $\dfrac{5}{25} \times 100 = 20\%$, and the discount at Store B is $\dfrac{5}{20} \times 100 = 25\%$. On the other hand, the discounts at Stores C and D, respectively, are $\dfrac{5}{30} \times 100 = 16.67\%$ and $\dfrac{5}{35} \times 100 = 14.29\%$. Thus, only Stores A and B have discounts of 20% or greater.

2. **B** Draw a line that connects most of the points. It is a straight line that goes down from right to left, which means it has a negative slope. Only (A) and (B) are negative slopes. Eyeball the line to see that it is not very steep. So, the slope is closer to 1 than 10. Alternatively, you could find points and ballpark the slope. The line roughly includes (50, 50), so the rise and run are the same. Therefore, the slope is −1.

3. **C** If $f(a) = 2a + 1$, and $f(a) = 2$, that means $2 = 2a + 1$. Subtract 1 from both sides to get $1 = 2a$. Divide both sides by 2 to find $a = \dfrac{1}{2}$.

Medium

4. **C** Don't do a lot of formula work. Think about how graphs work. In the equation, 2 represents the y-intercept, so eliminate any graphs that do not cross the y-axis at 2. You are down to (A) and (C). A slope of greater than 1 is relatively steep as compared to a 45-degree angle, while a fractional slope is relatively shallow. The slope here is 4, so you need a steep graph. Eliminate (A), and the answer is (C).

5. **E** Don't do a lot of formula work. Think about how graphs work. The y-intercept on the graph is 3, so you need a formula that ends in + 3. Eliminate (A), (C), and (D). A slope of greater than 1 is relatively steep as compared to a 45-degree angle, while a fractional slope is relatively shallow. The slope of the lines on the graph is relatively steep, so eliminate (B), and the answer is (E).

6. **E** Don't try to figure this one out by deriving an equation. Plug in by testing the numbers in the table against the functions in the answer choices. Only (E) is satisfied by all the data in the table.

7. **D** This question is a bit complicated to read, but once you understand what it is asking, the process is not difficult. To find out whether 2,000 uses or 4 months occurred first, check July (4 months after the previous inspection) first. If there have not yet been 2,000 uses, then that is your answer. If there have been more than 2,000 uses, you need to check June (and possibly earlier) to find out when 2,000 uses first occurred. As of July 31, there were 2,824 total uses. On March 31, there were 837 uses. The difference (1,987) is less than 2,000, so the 4-month period occurred first. If you picked (C), you didn't understand the table: the numbers are total uses, not the number of uses in that month.

Hard

8. **E** The easiest way to handle this is to understand how functions move. The − 3 outside the parentheses shifts the original graph down by 3 units. Eliminate (C) and (D) because they are not shifted down. The + 2 inside the parentheses shifts the original graph to the left by 2 units. Eliminate (A) and (B) because they are not shifted to the left. You can also plug in, testing one of the points indicated by a dot against the function you are looking for.

9. **E** The function will not be defined when the denominator is equal to 0. If you don't want to analyze the denominator to determine when it would equal 0, you can plug in the answers. Even though the answers are not in ascending or descending order, you can still start with (C). If you plug 3 into the denominator, you do not get zero, so eliminate (C) and anything else with 3: (A) and (D). Notice that both of the remaining answers have 7, so there's no need to test it. Try 1 in (E). You get 0, so that's your answer.

10. **B** When you see a weird symbol, it's really just a function question, so just follow the instructions. In this case, you are told that when you see numbers on either side of the arrow symbol, you square the first number and subtract from the value obtained when you raise the second number to the power of the first number. The tricky part here is making sure you follow PEMDAS and distribute your negative signs properly. Your work should look like this:

$$(2 \leftrightarrow 3) - (1 \leftrightarrow 2) = (2^2 - 3^2) - (1^2 - 2^1)$$
$$(4 - 9) - (1 - 2)$$
$$-5 - (-1) = -4$$

PROBLEM SET 14: MIXED BAG

Easy

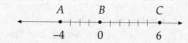

1. On the number line above, what is $BC - AB$?

   (A) 0
   (B) 2
   (C) 4
   (D) 6
   (E) 10

2. If n and s are integers, and $n + 5 < 7$, and
   $s - 6 < -4$, which of the following could be a
   value of $n + s$?

   (A) 2
   (B) 3
   (C) 4
   (D) 6
   (E) 9

3. A, B, C, and D lie on a line. The distance between A and
   B is 12. Point B is the midpoint of AD, and point C is the
   midpoint of AB. What is the distance between C and D ?

   (A) 6
   (B) 12
   (C) 18
   (D) 24
   (E) 36

Medium

4. Which of the following lines is perpendicular to
   $y = 2x + 7$?

   (A) $y = 3x + \dfrac{1}{7}$

   (B) $y = 3x - \dfrac{1}{7}$

   (C) $y = -\dfrac{1}{2}x + 3$

   (D) $y = \dfrac{1}{2}x + 3$

   (E) $y = \dfrac{1}{2}x + 7$

5. If S is the set of the prime factors of n, and R is the set of
   the prime factors of $2n$, how many more numbers does
   set R contain than set S ?

   (A) $2n$
   (B) n
   (C) 2
   (D) 1
   (E) 0

6. In a recent marathon, 70 percent of those who entered
   the race reached the finish line. If 7,200 did not reach the
   finish line, how many people entered the race?

   (A) 9,360
   (B) 12,240
   (C) 16,800
   (D) 21,000
   (E) 24,000

Hard

7. What is the area of an equilateral triangle with a side length of 10 ?

   (A) 25
   (B) $25\sqrt{2}$
   (C) $25\sqrt{3}$
   (D) 50
   (E) $50\sqrt{3}$

8. Point A (x, y), where x and y are negative numbers, is reflected about the x-axis to Point B, and Point B is then reflected about the x-axis to Point C. In terms of x and y, what is the sum of the coordinates about the y-axis to Point C ?

   (A) $x + y$
   (B) $x - y$
   (C) $-x + y$
   (D) $-x - y$
   (E) $2x + 2y$

9. When positive integer a is divided by 5, the remainder is 3. When positive integer b is divided by 5, the remainder is 4. What is the remainder when the product ab is divided by 5 ?

   (A) 0
   (B) 1
   (C) 2
   (D) 3
   (E) 4

10. A four-digit number is formed such that the units digit is 3, the thousands digit is 5, and the tens and hundreds digits are different from each (but may be the same as either the units or thousands digit). How many different numbers can be created?

   (A) 56
   (B) 90
   (C) 100
   (D) 1,350
   (E) 9,000

Answers and Explanations: Problem Set 14

Easy

1. **B** *BC* has a length of 6. *AB* has a length of 4. So *BC* − *AB* = 2.

> On number line problems, sometimes you want the distance between 2 points, as in the problem above. And sometimes you want the number of a point on the line—for instance, using this number line, $A + B = -4$, because $A = -4$ and $B = 0$. You can have a negative value for a point on the line, but not a negative distance. Read the problem carefully and mark up your diagram so you don't confuse the two.

2. **A** First fix the ranges. You can see $n < 2$ and $s < 2$. Since they both must be integers, the greatest either n or s could be is 1. 1 + 1 is 2, so that is the only answer that works.

3. **C** The easiest way to solve this problem is to draw a number line. Say that point *A* is at 0 on the number line and that *B* is at 12. Since 6 is the midpoint of *AB*, this puts *C* at 6. Therefore, the distance between *C* and *D* is 24 − 6, or 18.

Medium

4. **C** In the form $y = mx + b$, m is the slope, which means that the line given by the equation $y = 2x + 7$ has a slope of 2. A line perpendicular to $y = 2x + 7$ will have a slope that is the negative reciprocal to 2. (C) has a slope of $-\dfrac{1}{2}$.

5. **D** Plug in. Try $n = 10$. The prime factors of 10 are 2 and 5. It has 2 prime factors. $2n = 20$. The prime factors of 20 are 2, 2, and 5. It has 3 prime factors. 20 has 1 more prime factor than 10. Plug $n = 10$ into the answers to find 1. Only (D) works.

These questions are a bummer because sometimes it's hard to know where to begin. If you don't see any starting point, just try some numbers and see what happens. If you try a couple of different things and nothing seems to work, skip the question and come back to it later. These questions appear most often in the easy and medium sections. Depending on how the question is asked, you may be able to plug in.

6. **E** You can plug in the answers, starting with (C). If 16,800 entered the race and 70% crossed the finish line, then 11,760 would have crossed the finish line. This leaves 5,040 who did not cross the finish line, which is too low. (E) works.

Hard

7. **C** In order to find the area, you need to find the height first. It's important to draw a picture. When you draw in the height, notice that it makes a 30-60-90 triangle, with the hypotenuse as 10, and the short side as 5. This must mean that the other side (the height) is $5\sqrt{3}$. Just remember that the area formula is: $\frac{1}{2}b \times h$, so it is $\frac{1}{2} \times 10 \times 5\sqrt{3} = 25\sqrt{3}$.

8. **D** Draw the graph and plug in. You know that x and y must both be negative, so make $x = -2$ and $y = -3$. Draw point A at $(-2, -3)$. A reflection creates a mirror image across the axis. So, when Point A reflects across the x axis to Point B in the second quadrant, the coordinates will be $(-2, 3)$. Next, we reflect that point across the y axis to Point C. Here, the mirror image will be $(2, 3)$. The question asks for the sum of these points, so our target answer is 5. Be very careful with your negative signs as you test the answers. (A) = –5. (B) = 1. (C) = –1. (D) = 5. (E) = –10. Thus, (D) is your answer.

9. **C** You can plug in. Pick a number that, when divided by 5, gives a remainder of 3. The first (and easiest) such number is 8. Now pick a number that, when divided by 5, gives a remainder of 4. How about 9? Now find the product, which is 72. When 72 is divided by 5, the remainder is 2.

10. **B** In an arrangements question, first create placeholders. As there are four digits, create four placeholders:

— — — —

Consider the thousands digit. Because the number for that digit is given, we have only 1 possible choice for that digit. So, put a 1 in the placeholder, and do the same for the units digit, which is also restricted to one choice:

1 — — 1

It is important not to put the actual numbers—just the quantity of available choices—in the slots, as we will multiply soon. Now, let's take one of the other digits; it doesn't matter which one, so let's use the tens. As the tens digit may repeat numbers already used in the ones and thousands digit, we have 10 options (0, 1, 2, 3, 4, 5, 6, 7, 8, and 9) to choose from. So, put 10 in the placeholder.

1 — 10 1

For the hundreds digit, we are told that it may repeat numbers from the ones and thousands digits but not from the tens digit, so we have only 9 numbers to choose from. So, our complete placeholder row looks like this:

1 9 10 1

Last step: multiply. That's it!

PROBLEM SET 15: GRID-INS

Easy

1. If $x - y = -6$, then y is how much greater than x?

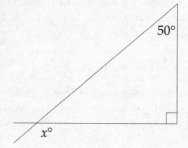

2. In the figure above, what is the value of x?

3. A certain solution requires $3\frac{1}{2}$ grams of additive for each 7 liters of water. At this rate, how many grams of additive should be used with 11 liters of water?

Medium

4. On a number line, the number q is the midpoint between 4 and 7. What is the value of $|2 - q|$?

5. If $\left(\dfrac{x+2}{y+2} \right) = \dfrac{3}{4}$, then what is the value of $\left(\dfrac{2+y}{2+x} \right)^2$?

6. The speed, in miles per hour, of a particular experimental spacecraft t minutes after it is launched is modeled by the function M, which is defined as $M(t) = 200(3)^{\frac{t}{3}}$. According to this model, what is the speed, in miles per hour, 9 minutes after the spacecraft is launched?

Hard

CLIMATE PREFERENCES

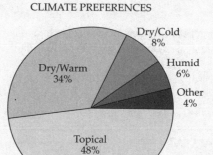

7. The graph above shows the results of a survey in which adults were asked to name their first preference among various types of climates. Of the adults surveyed, a total of 280 answered "Humid" or "Other." How many answered "Other" in the survey?

$$- 4, 0, 2, 3$$

8. A sequence of numbers is formed by repeating the set of numbers until 80 numbers have been listed. What is the sum of the first 31 terms of the sequence?

9. In the figure below, rectangle *LMNO* has dimensions of 18 by 8. Segments *PQ* and *RS* are diagonals of the squares shown. What is the area of the shaded region?

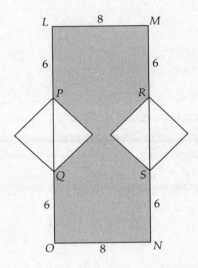

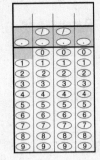

10. The integer *a* is the product of three consecutive positive integers less than 12. The integer *b* is the product of three consecutive positive integers less than 8. What is the greatest possible value of $\frac{b}{a}$?

Answers and Explanations: Problem Set 15

Easy

1. **6**

   Set the equation equal to y, since that's what the question asks for. You get $-y = -6 - x$. Multiply through by -1 and you get $y = 6 + x$, so the answer is 6. For an easier solution, you could also plug in here: Say $x = 2$ and $y = 8$, which satisfies the equation. Then y is equal to x plus 6.

2. **140**

   The unmarked angle in the triangle is $40°$, since triangles have $180°$ and the other angles are $50°$ and $90°$. The $40°$ angle and x lie on a straight line, so $40 + x = 180$, and $x = 140$.

3. **5.5**

   You can set up the proportions as follows and cross-multiply:

   $$\frac{3.5g}{7l} = \frac{x}{11l}$$

   However, if you noticed that the number of grams is one-half the number of liters (not accounting for units), then all you need to do is divide 11 by 2.

Medium

4. **3.5**

   Draw the number line and identify that midpoint is 5.5. You can also find the midpoint by calculating the average of 4 and 7. The absolute value of $2 - 5.5$ is 3.5.

5. $\dfrac{16}{9}$

   This is a good example of plugging in on a grid-in question. If you make $x = 1$ and $y = 2$, the equation will work:

   $$\left(\frac{1+2}{2+2}\right) = \frac{3}{4}$$

   Now it is easy to solve the problem. By the way, if you noticed that $\left(\dfrac{2+y}{2+x}\right)$ is the reciprocal of $\left(\dfrac{x+2}{y+2}\right)$, you didn't need to plug in. Just square $\dfrac{4}{3}$!

6.   1800

This question asks you to plug $t = 9$ into the given formula:

$$M(t) = 200(3)^{\frac{9}{3}} = 200(3)^3 = 200(9) = 1800.$$

Hard

7.   112

Make sure you understand the information you are given and the information you need to find before trying to answer the question. There are 280 people who answered "Humid" or "Other," not 280 total people, so don't take 10 percent of 280. Also, there is no need to calculate the total number of people surveyed. Of the people who answered "Humid" and "Other," 4 out of 10 answered "Other." Thus, the number of people who answer "Other" is $\frac{4}{10}$ of 280, or 112.

8.   5

If you are stumped here, you can always type the pattern into your calculator and find the answer. However, on pattern questions, once you understand how the pattern operates, you can arrive at the answer faster. Here, add up the first four numbers of the repeating sequence. They add up to 1. Thus, every time you add another set of the sequence, the total sum will increase by 1. Because you are interested in the first 31 terms of the sequence, there will be 7 complete sets (the first 28 terms) added together and then part of a set (the remaining 3 terms). Those 7 complete sets will add up to 7. So now add in − 4, 0, and 2.

9. **126**

Without answer choices, it's tough to ballpark, so you need to slog through! The area of the entire rectangle is 144 (18 × 8). Now you need to find the area of the triangles inside of the rectangle. You can see that the measurements on either side of the squares are all 6 and the entire length of the rectangle is 18, so the portion of the rectangle inside each square is also 6. When a square is cut in half along its diagonal, two 45-45-90 triangles are created. If you don't know how 45-45-90 triangles work, you can look up the ratio in the formula box at the beginning of the section. If each side of the triangle (here the sides of the square) is x, the hypotenuse (here, the diagonal) is $x\sqrt{2}$. Thus, here $6 = x\sqrt{2}$, so $x = \dfrac{6}{\sqrt{2}}$. Now that you have the sides of the squares, you can find the areas of the squares: $\dfrac{6}{\sqrt{2}} \times \dfrac{6}{\sqrt{2}} = \dfrac{36}{2} = 18$. Because the two triangles inside the rectangle add up to one square, you can subtract 18 from 144 to find the area of the shaded region.

10. **35**

Before you engage in a lot of trial by error, think about what will make $\dfrac{b}{a}$ as large as possible. If you have the largest possible b and the smallest possible a, you will have the largest possible $\dfrac{b}{a}$. As b is the product of three consecutive positive integers less than 8, calculate b as 5 × 6 × 7. As a is the product of three consecutive positive integers less than 12, calculate a as 1 × 2 × 3 = 6. Thus, $\dfrac{b}{a} = \dfrac{5 \times 6 \times 7}{6} = 35$.

PROBLEM SET 16: MORE GRID-INS

Easy

1. If $2x - 3y = 7$ and $y = 3$, then what is the value of x ?

2. In the figure above, if $a = 170$, what is the value of b ?

3. At a certain beach, the cost of renting a beach umbrella is $4.25 per day or $28.00 per week. If Kelly and Brandon rent a beach umbrella for 2 weeks instead of renting one each day for 14 days, how much money, in dollars, will they save? (Leave off the dollar sign when gridding in your answer.)

Medium

4. The average (arithmetic mean) of 8 numbers is 65. If one of the numbers, 65, is removed, what is the average of the remaining 7 numbers?

5. The face of a wall measures 30 yards by 24 yards. If the wall is to be completely covered with square bricks measuring 3 yards on each side, how many bricks will be needed to cover the wall?

All even integers that are not multiples of 4 must be multiples of 6.

6. What is one possible number between 24 and 42 that proves that the statement above is FALSE?

Hard

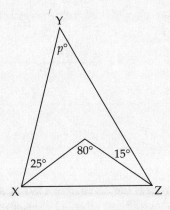

Note: Figure not drawn to scale.

7. In Triangle *XYZ* above, what is the value of *p* ?

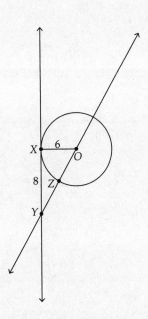

8. In the figure above, *O* is the center of the circle, the length of segment *XY* is 8, and the line passing through points *X* and *Y* is tangent to the circle at point *X*. What is the length of segment *ZY* ?

9. Let the function g be defined as $g(x) = -3x + 6$. If $g(6) = r$, what is the value of $g(r)$?

10. When a number is subtracted from 8 less than three times the number, the result is 142. What is the number?

Answers and Explanations: Problem Set 16

Easy

1. **8**

    The problem tells you that $y = 3$, so plug that into the equation and you get $2x - 9 = 7$. So $2x = 16$ and $x = 8$.

2. **10**

    Write 170° ° next to a. There are 180 degrees in a line, so $b = 10$.

3. **3.50**

    Kelly and Brandon spent $28 per week for 2 weeks for a total of $56. If they had rented the umbrella by the day, they would've spent $14 \times \$4.25$ for a total of $59.50. That means they saved $59.50 - 56 = 3.50$.

Medium

4. **65**

    You can use the average pie. 8 (the number of items) times 65 (the average) gives you a sum of 520. If you subtract 65, the new sum is 455. Divide 455 by 7 (the new number of items) to get the new average: 65. You can also think about this logically: if all 8 numbers were 65, and we removed one of the numbers, the remaining 7 numbers would still average 65.

5. **80**

    To find out how many bricks will fit on the wall, you need to divide the dimensions of the wall by the dimensions of the bricks:

    $$\frac{30 \times 24}{3 \times 3}$$

6.   **26, 34, or 38**

Make sure you understand exactly what the question is asking. First, you need to find a number in the range that is *not* a multiple of 4. Thus, to prove that the statement is false, you need to make sure that the number is also not a multiple of 6. It may be useful to list out all of the numbers—just the even ones, as that is part of the statement, and not 24 or 32, as the question did not say "inclusive":

26, 28, 30, 32, 34, 36, 38, 40

Now, eliminate all those that are multiples of 4:

26, ~~28~~, 30, ~~32~~, 34, ~~36~~, 38, ~~40~~

Next, you need to eliminate any remaining numbers that are divisible by 6:

26, ~~30~~, 34, 38

Any of the three numbers that remain prove the statement false and will be an acceptable answer.

Hard

7.   **40**

This figure is not drawn to scale, so be careful as you fill in the information you need. In order to find the value of p, you need to find the sum of angles *YXZ* and *YZX*. You are given some information about those angles: the measurements 25 and 15 above the smaller triangle. However, because the figure is not drawn to scale, there is no way to determine the missing measurements—but that does not matter. We don't care what angles *YXZ* and *YZX* actually are. We just care about their sum. So, let's look at the smaller triangle. The top vertex is 80, which means that the sum of the bottom vertices is 100. So, plug in, such as 50 and 50. Now we have measures for *YXZ* and *YZX*: 75 and 65, for a sum of 140. Subtract that from 180 to find angle p.

8.   **4**

To get this question right, you need to know that a line tangent to a circle forms a right angle with the radius at the point of tangency. Thus, triangle *XOY* is a right triangle. You can use the Pythagorean Theorem or recognize the 6-8-10 triangle to find that the hypotenuse is 10. You're not done yet, though. To find *YZ*, you need to subtract the length of *OZ* from 10. *OZ* is a radius, just as is *OX*. As *OX* is 6, so is *OZ*, leaving 4 for *YZ*.

9. **42**

When you are given a function, always take the number inside the parentheses and plug it into the function. Here, you must plug 6 into the function:

$$g(6) = -3(6) + 6 = -18 + 16 = -12$$

Thus $r = -12$. Are you worried that there is no way to grid in a negative number? Actually, you are not done. The question asks for $g(r)$, not $g(6)$. Now that we know $r = -12$, you can plug that number into the function:

$$g(-12) = -3(-12) + 6 = 36 + 6 = 42$$

10. **125**

You need to translate English into Math. Let's call "a number" x. You need to subtract x from 8 less than 3 times x. Three times x is $3x$. To find the number 8 less than $3x$, you need to subtract 8. Thus, putting it all together, you get:

$$(3x - 8) - x$$

You are told that the result of this operation is 142, so:

$$(3x - 8) - x = 142$$

Now, you can solve for x:

$$2x - 8 = 142$$
$$2x = 150$$
$$x = 125$$

PROBLEM SET 17: MORE MIXED BAG

Easy

1. If $x = 14 - y$, what is $3x$ when $y = 11$?

   (A) -9
   (B) -3
   (C) 3
   (D) 6
   (E) 9

2. At Rose's Flower Shop, the cost of purchasing a bundle of 8 ferns is $57. The cost of each fern, when purchased separately, is $9. How much money would be saved by purchasing a bundle of 8 ferns, rather than purchasing 8 ferns separately?

   (A) 12
   (B) 13
   (C) 14
   (D) 15
   (E) 16

3. In isosceles triangle ABC, one angle measures 55 degrees and another angle measures 70 degrees? Which one of the following is the measure of the third angle?

   (A) 40
   (B) 55
   (C) 65
   (D) 70
   (E) It cannot be determined from the information given.

Medium

4. If $24b^2 - 4x = 32$, what is the value of $6b^2 - x$?

   (A) 4
   (B) 6
   (C) 8
   (D) 12
   (E) 16

5. Sasha has a collection of 60 vinyl records, some of which are classic jazz and the rest of which are hip hop. If Sasha has $\frac{1}{4}$ as many classic jazz records as she has hip hop records, how many classic jazz records does she have?

   (A) 12
   (B) 15
   (C) 30
   (D) 45
   (E) 48

6. If p is an integer such that $-5 < p < 5$ and $q = 3p - p^3$, what is the least possible value of q ?

   (A) −76
   (B) −52
   (C) −28
   (D) −4
   (E) 0

Hard

7. In terms of x, what is the difference between $6x + 9$ and $2x - 4$, if $x > 2$?

   (A) $3x + 5$
   (B) $4x - 5$
   (C) $4x + 5$
   (D) $4x + 13$
   (E) $5x - 13$

8. In triangle ABC, the measures of angles a, b, and c, respectively, are in the ratio 2:3:4. What is the value of angle b ?

   (A) 20
   (B) 40
   (C) 60
   (D) 80
   (E) 100

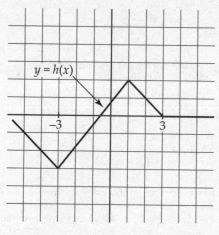

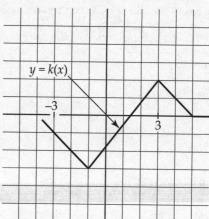

9. The graphs above show the complete functions h and k. Which one of the following expresses $k(x)$ in terms of $h(x)$?

(A) $k(x) = h(x) + 2$
(B) $k(x) = h(x) - 2$
(C) $k(x) = h(x + 2)$
(D) $k(x) = h(x - 2)$
(E) $k(x) = 2h(x)$

10. If $h^{\frac{2}{3}} = k^2$, then in terms of k, what is the value of h^2 ?

(A) $k^{\frac{2}{3}}$

(B) $k^{\frac{4}{9}}$

(C) k^3

(D) k^4

(E) k^6

Answers and Explanations: Problem Set 17

Easy

1. **E** Plug $y = 11$ into the equation to find that $x = 3$. Therefore, $3x = 9$.

2. **D** Calculate the cost of buying 8 ferns separately: $8 \times 9 = 72$. Now, subtract the package price of 57 from 72.

3. **B** In an isosceles triangle, two of three angles are the same. Thus, the only two possible numerical answers here are (B) and (D). Before you decide that it cannot be determined between the two answers, try them out. If the third angle is 55, then the sum of all three angles is 180. That works. But if the third angle is 70, then the sum of all three angles is 195, which is not possible in a triangle.

Medium

4. **D** Before you start performing complex manipulations and calculations, ask yourself "Of all the questions in the world, why ask for $6b^2 - x$?" The answer is: $6b^2 - x$ is just $24b^2 - 4x$ divided by 4!

5. **A** Plug in the answers here, starting with (C). If she has 30 classic jazz albums and this represents $\frac{1}{4}$ of the number of hip hop albums she has, she would have 120 hip hop albums. This is way too big. (B) will be too big, as well. For (A), she would have 48 hip hop albums—for a total of 60.

6. **B** To obtain the least possible value of q, you need to use the greatest possible value of p. If you are not sure about this, try out several values of p. When $p = 4$, $q = -52$. Take care not to select a negative p, as the cube p will also be negative and when you subtract that negative from $3p$, you will be adding.

Hard

7. **D** Plug in. If $x = 3$, then $6x + 9 = 27$, and $2x - 4 = 2$. The difference is 25. Plug 3 into the answer choices, and you get (D).

8. **C** Create a ratio box. For the actual total, use 180, as there are 180 degrees in a triangle. Your completed ratio box will look like this:

a	b	c	Total
2	3	4	9
20	20	20	20
40	60	80	180

9. **D** The easiest way to answer this question is to understand transformation of graphs. Just count how many units the graph moved. It moved 2 units to the right but did not move up or down. When a graph moves to the right, you need to subtract the number of units from x *inside* the parentheses.

10. **E** If you are comfortable manipulating equations with exponents, first isolate h by raising $h^{\frac{2}{3}}$ to the power of $\frac{3}{2}$. Having done so on the left side of the equation, you must do the same on the right side. Thus, we get: $h = k^3$. The question, however, asks for h^2, not x, so square both sides. As an alternative, you can plug in. To plug in here, it is useful to understand that $h^{\frac{2}{3}} = \sqrt[3]{h^2}$, as you will then pick an easy number, such as $h = 8$. In that case, the left side of the equation is 4, so $k^2 = 4$, and $k = 2$. As the question asks for h^2, our target answer is 16.

NOTES

NOTES

NOTES

NOTES

NOTES

Score Your Best on Both of the Tests

Get proven prep for the SAT and ACT at **PrincetonReviewBooks.com**

Beat the SAT:

Essential SAT Vocabulary (Flashcards)
978-0-375-42964-4
$16.99/$21.99 Can.

11 Practice Tests for the SAT and PSAT, 2014 Edition
978-0-307-94616-4
$24.99/$27.95 Can.

Cracking the SAT, 2014 Edition
978-0-307-94561-7
$21.99/$24.95 Can.
eBook: 978-0-307-94588-4

Cracking the SAT with DVD, 2014 Edition
978-0-307-94562-4
$34.99/$39.95 Can.

Crash Course for the SAT, 4th Edition
978-0-375-42831-9
$9.99/$10.99 Can.

Math Workout for the SAT, 3rd Edition
978-0-375-42833-3
$17.99/$20.99 Can.

Reading and Writing Workout for the SAT, 2nd Edition
978-0-375-42832-6
$16.99/$18.99 Can.

SAT Power Vocab
978-0-8041-2456-0
$14.99/$16.95 Can.
eBook: 978-0-8041-2457-7

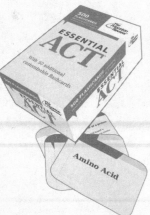

Crack the ACT, Too!

Cracking the ACT, 2013 Edition
978-0-307-94535-8
$19.99/$23.99 Can.
eBook: 978-0-307-94540-2

Cracking the ACT with DVD, 2013 Edition
978-0-307-94536-5
$31.99/$37.99 Can.

Crash Course for the ACT, 4th Edition
978-0-375-42762-6
$9.99/$11.99 Can.
eBook: 978-0-307-94471-9

Essential ACT (Flashcards)
978-0-375-42806-7
$17.99/$19.99 Can.

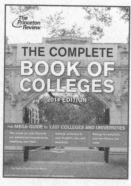

Admissions Advice from the Experts:

The Best 378 Colleges, 2014 Edition
978-0-307-94605-8
$23.99/$26.99 Can.

Paying for College Without Going Broke, 2014 Edition
978-0-8041-2436-2
$20.00/$23.00 Can.
eBook: 978-0-8041-2437-9

The Best Value Colleges, 2013 Edition
978-0-307-94598-3
$21.99/$25.99 Can.

The Complete Book of Colleges, 2014 Edition
978-0-307-94628-7
$26.99/$31.00 Can.

NOTES

NOTES